ROUND IRELAND
IN LOW GEAR

ERIC NEWBY

Round
IRELAND
in Low Gear

VIKING

VIKING
Published by the Penguin Group
Viking Penguin Inc., 40 West 23rd Street,
New York, New York 10010, U.S.A.
Penguin Books Ltd, 27 Wrights Lane,
London W8 5TZ England
Penguin Books Australia Ltd, Ringwood,
Victoria, Australia
Penguin Books Canada Ltd, 2801 John Street,
Markham, Ontario, Canada L3R 1B4
Penguin Books (N. Z.) Ltd, 182–190 Wairau Road,
Auckland 10, New Zealand

Penguin Books Ltd, Registered Offices:
Harmondsworth, Middlesex, England

First American Edition
Published in 1988 by Viking Penguin Inc.

Copyright © Eric Newby, 1987
Illustrations copyright © Jonathan Newby, 1987
All rights reserved

LIBRARY OF CONGRESS CATALOGING IN PUBLICATION DATA
Newby, Eric.
Round Ireland in low gear.
Bibliography: p.
Includes index.
1. Ireland—Description and travel—1981–   .
2. Cycling—Ireland. 3. Newby, Eric—Journeys—Ireland.
I. Title.
DA978.2.N48   1988   914.17′04824   87-40441
ISBN 0-670-82244-2

Printed in the United States of America by
Haddon Craftsmen, Scranton, Pennsylvania
Set in Sabon

For the Irish,
the Eighth Walking (and Talking)
Wonders of the World

CONTENTS

ACKNOWLEDGEMENTS

I would like to take the opportunity to express my gratitude to Terry Sheehy, who many years ago first kindled my enthusiasm for travelling in Ireland and, by presenting me with *Rambles in Eirinn* by William Bulfin, first drew my attention to the charms of cycling round it. I am particularly indebted to John Lahiffe of Bord Failte (the Irish Tourist Board) in London for the tremendous patience he displayed in searching out the most difficult information; and also for their help to Tom Magennis in Dublin and the following members of the regional tourism organizations under the auspices of Bord Failte: Frank Donaldson in Cork; Michael Manning in Skibbereen and Joe Palmer in Sligo along with their staffs; and Vincent Tobin, Joe Vaughan and Mary Watson of Shannon Development. I am grateful, too, to the director and managers of Sealink UK who facilitated our various passages to and from Ireland, often at very short notice.

I would also like to express my thanks to Peter Yapp, editor of *The Traveller's Dictionary of Quotation*, for providing such a rich selection of quotes on Ireland and the Irish; and to Ariane Goodman, Ron Clark and Vera Brice of Collins for their indefatigable assistance in bringing the book to fruition.

INTRODUCTION

The roads are very variable, some being grand, others very bad. Intercourse with the peasantry will be found interesting and amusing. Nothing can exceed their civility and courtesy; and for those who are not too particular it will be found an excellent plan to lunch in their cottages, excellent tea, home-made bread, butter and eggs being procurable for 1s. [5p] a head.

The Cyclists' Touring Club Irish Road Book, c. 1899

In the autumn of 1985, more or less on the spur of the moment, we decided to go back to Ireland and travel through as much of it as we could in the space of three months or so, starting in the South. The North could wait. If things improved there, so much the better. If they got worse we would simply not go there. We were not going to travel in the guise of sociologists, journalists or contemporary historians. I was unlikely to write a book called *Whither Ireland?* or *Ireland Now*. We were not going there, we hoped, to be shot at. We remembered it as it had been some twenty years previously, when it had been idiosyncratic and fun. (Romantic Ireland was long since dead and gone, as Yeats wrote, 'with O'Leary in the grave' – that is, if it had ever existed.) We were going there, in short, to enjoy ourselves, an unfashionable aspiration in the 1980s.

It was now mid-November. All Souls' Day was already past. The dead season, as far as weather went, was in full sway all over the northern hemisphere and would last until Easter, and probably longer. We had no illusions about the dead season. Anywhere in the British Isles and in most parts of the Mediterranean it conjured up vistas of matchstick figures bent double by the wind, silhouetted against a colourless sea without a vessel in sight to break the monotony; sun lounges in hotels and guest houses filled with rolled-up carpet, those still open soldiering on with a skeleton staff, their proprietors in the Canaries, those left in charge in their absence never quite sober.

But it will be better in Ireland, we said, putting our faith in the Gulf Stream, and in the Irish themselves with their humour, and trying to forget, while adding up their other virtues, their cooking, though even that was said to have improved.

The reason we chose to begin our journey in this dead season was simply that at home in Dorset in the not-so-dead seasons we are engaged in extensive gardening operations without any sort of outside help. We have a large kitchen garden in which we grow all our own vegetables; large expanses of grass to be cut, a lot of it in a steep-sided orchard which, no sooner than one turns one's back on it, becomes infested with moles whose excavations knock hell out of a mower; not to speak of a long, tapering field and quite an extensive beech wood to try and keep under control.

Having decided to explore as much of Ireland as we could between December and March and the rest of it when we could afford the time, we then had to decide what means of transportation to employ. My first impulse, one not shared by my wife Wanda, was to walk it; but what makes Ireland such a meal from the walker's point of view is its coastline, which is 3500 miles long, more than a thousand miles longer than that of England and Wales and exactly a thousand miles longer than that of Scotland, and a lot of it on the Atlantic coasts very indented. Peninsulas such as the Iveragh, the Beara, the Dingle and Mizen Head Peninsulas are between thirty and forty miles long. To skirt the perimeter of these four adjacent peninsulas would involve a journey of at least

255 miles – the Ring of Kerry on the Iveragh Peninsula alone is over a hundred miles – and at the end of it one would only be about sixty miles further on one's way. Similar vast detours would also have to be made, if one was serious about it, all the way up the West coast.

According to the excellent *Ireland Guide*, published by the Irish Tourist Board (otherwise Bord Failte, the Welcome Board), it is possible to visit the country 'in its entirety in a couple of weeks' by car or motorcycle; they then go on to say, however, rather like a band of roguish leprechauns, that 'you cannot see everything, of course'. But we both rejected the idea of using a car on the grounds that whoever is driving sees hardly anything except the road ahead – if not they shouldn't be driving – and the one who isn't is either permanently map-reading or looking things up in guide books to entertain the driver, and getting ticked off if he fails to do so, which leads to what my wife calls 'rowls'. In this way no one sees anything. Motorcycles we regarded, and still do, as just plain dangerous.

Buses sounded a little more promising but a closer look at the *Amchlar Bus do na Cuigi agus Expressway*, otherwise the *Provincial and Expressway Timetable* (not surprisingly there is no equivalent for 'Bus' and 'Expressway' in the Irish language) showed that some of the services were pretty skeletal in the winter months. The *Amchlar Traenach*, or *Train Timetable* (trains, presumably because of their more ancient lineage, having somehow contrived to get themselves incorporated into the language) offered even less hope. However carefree the image the Irish Railways tried to project, it was obvious that the system had suffered the attentions of some Irish equivalent, if such can be imagined, of Beeching, the destroyer of the British railway system. To understand what had been lost as a result it was only necessary to look at the railway map in the 1912, and last, edition of that splendid work, *Murray's Handbook to Ireland*.

We also ruled out horses, as we are both terrified of them. Anyway, we would have had the problem of feeding them. I could foresee us buying them dozens of packets of All Bran in supermarkets and getting soundly kicked for our pains. Remembering what happened to Mr Toad we were less than enthusiastic about hiring a caravan. What we really needed was a balloon, but that would have meant employing a balloonist, and most likely ending up beyond the Urals.

The only other practical method of making the journey, although I was not sanguine about persuading Wanda to agree, was by bicycle.

PART 1

DECEMBER

Chapter 1

STATE-OF-THE-ART

STATE-OF-THE-ART *adj. (prenominal)* (of hi-fi equipment, recordings, etc.) the most recent and therefore considered the best; up-to-the-minute: *a state-of-the-art amplifier*.
                                      Collins English Dictionary

A bike is a very personal thing and the only person who can really judge it is the rider.

                        The Bicycle Buyer's Bible, 1985/6

When I was seven or eight I used to have an awful recurrent nightmare about Germans invading England on bicycles.

It was inspired by a story in a germ-laden, pre-First World War magazine which I rescued from a dustbin behind the block of flats we lived in by Hammersmith Bridge in south-west London. In this tale, the Germans were landed on the shores of the Wash under cover of fog – a difficult feat, but Germans were up to it. Instead of horsed cavalry, however, which would have had a pretty glutinous time of it out in the marshes, battalions of them squelched ashore with folding bicycles strapped on their backs.

Once on *terra firma* these *pickelhaubed* hordes split up into flying columns and, led by expert local navigators, traitors to a man, of whom there were inexhaustible supplies even before 1914, swept through the fog-bound low country at a terrific rate. In the course of the following night they seized all the principal cities of the Midlands, including Birmingham ('Only ninety kilometres as the crow flies, Herr Hauptmann,' said some unspeakable turncoat, clicking his heels.) Cambridge fell without a shot being fired, which was not surprising considering its subsequent record – or was it the long vacation? Other columns were directed towards the metropolis. At this point the narrative ended. It was a serial and by the time I went back to have another dig in the dustbin to find the sequel it had been emptied.

They must have been foiled in the end because we later won the Great War, but for years I had this terrifying vision of Germans with spiked helmets pedalling swiftly and silently over Hammersmith Bridge in the night, finding my bedroom and spitting me on their bayonets like a *knackwurst*.

4

It was therefore to some extent paradoxical that the swiftness and silence of the bicycles about which I had dreamt with such horror, as irrational as the horror of whiteness described in *Moby Dick*, but equally real, were the very qualities which subsequently attracted me to this form of transport, and turned me into a keen cyclist and owner of many bicycles of varying degrees of splendour.

My first really good bicycle was a second-hand Selbach which I bought from a boy at school for £3 – it would have cost about £12 new. I was heartbroken when it was stolen from the school bicycle shed. Selbachs were the Bugattis of the cycle world. The frames were made from tapered tubes which, although almost paper thin, were immensely strong, and they were fitted with Timken roller bearings instead of conventional ball-bearings. The lightest machine Selbach built is in the Science Museum in London. He flourished between the wars, and was far ahead of his time. He was killed when the front wheel of his bicycle got stuck in a tramline in South London; he didn't even rate an obituary in *The Times*. Ever since the 1890s, when for a time it was fashionable, though never as a competitive sport, cycling had been and still is hopelessly *déclassé*. Even today the only socially acceptable bike for a member of the British upper crust is one that looks as if it has been retrieved from a municipal rubbish dump, and probably has.

The finest bicycle I ever had was a Holdsworth which my father allowed me to order when I was sixteen. He had arranged with a Swiss business acquaintance of his called Mr Guggenheim that I should work in his silk firm in Zurich in order to learn the business and the German language, and no doubt he thought that cycling up and down the Alps would keep my thoughts in wholesome channels. It was a model called Stelvio, and was specially designed for cycling in the Alps.

It was hand-built in a small shed at the back of Holdsworth's shop in Putney by a thin, energetic, chain-smoking genius with wispy hair and a terrible cough. He had lined the walls of the shed with a really wonderful collection of pin-ups all of which displayed enormous tits, presumably to stimulate him to even greater activity. They certainly stimulated me. It was the finest bicycle procurable at that time and it cost a colossal £20. The day I took delivery of it I remember him bouncing it up and down on its over-size hand-made tyres as if it was a ping-pong ball.

'Luvly job,' he said, with a cigarette stuck to his lower lip. 'A real iron. Go out and give them Alps a bashing. Funny to think I'll never see 'em.'

I never saw the Alps either, let alone gave them a bashing. The arrangement with Mr Guggenheim was shelved when my father found out that the kind of *Schweitzerdeutsch* they spoke in Zurich was so extraordinarily funny that if real German speakers heard it they fell about. I never dared tell the creator of the 'iron' that the furthest I got was the Black Mountains on the Welsh border.

In the war I rode huge bicycles with 28″ wheels that weighed 60 lbs or more, of the sort still popular in parts of India and Africa. At the Royal Military College, Sandhurst, which I attended in 1940, a special drill had been invented for riding these monsters:

'Number One Platoon!' (or whatever it was) ''Arf Sections Left! *Prepare to Meount*! . . . *Meount*!' And we would wobble off into the asylum country round Broadmoor.

Wanda's affair with the bicycle was very different from mine. For her there was, and still is, a Platonic, archetypal bicycle, the first one she ever had. It was the sort of bicycle on which droves of girls used to cycle past the prison camp in which I was incarcerated in the Po Valley, near Parma, during the war. Similar droves were to be seen riding through the equally flat countryside around pre-war Ferrara in Visconti's film *The Garden of the Finzi-Continis*.

It was a single-speed lightweight roadster with an open frame, raised handlebars fitted with a wicker basket and a back pedalling brake on the rear wheel, the upper part of which was covered with thin cords to prevent the wearer's skirt becoming entangled in it, which made the whole thing look like some archaic stringed instrument on wheels.

It was a present to her from her godmother on her sixteenth birthday. Originally she had given her a wristwatch but Wanda displayed such obvious disappointment on receiving it that her godmother eventually wrung from her the confession that what she really longed for was a bicycle. Unfortunately Wanda's

6

godmother had no idea how much a bicycle cost, and the money she gave Wanda in lieu of the wristwatch was totally insufficient to buy even a good secondhand one, which was why Wanda's bicycle came to be made up of salvaged parts, re-assembled by the village bicycle repairer. In spite of this it was a good bicycle, with a frame made by the still excellent firm of Bianchi.

Because of all this Wanda had the fierce affection for her bicycle that most people reserve for the living. So when the Germans occupied Italy in September 1943, and her father was arrested by the Gestapo as an anti-Fascist, her bicycle was impounded as an additional punishment, to which she took strong exception. Eventually she succeeded in tracking it down to a German military headquarters at Salsomaggiore, a spa miles away from where she lived in the foothills of the Apennines, to which literally thousands of confiscated bicycles had been taken.

'You have stolen my bicycle,' she said without preamble to the first German officer she encountered there, who happened to be a colonel taking a turn in the open air.

'What, me?' he said in genuine astonishment, saluting. 'Why should I take your bicycle? I have no need of a bicycle.'

'Well, if you didn't take it your soldiers did. My father was in the Austrian Imperial Army. *He* never stole ladies' bicycles.'

'Where is your bicycle?' he asked.

'In there,' she said, indicating through open doors in a hangar what appeared to be the biggest second-hand bicycle shop in the world.

'*Signorina,*' he said gallantly, anxious to be rid of this Slovenian fury he had somehow unwittingly fielded, 'if we have taken your bicycle I can only apologize on behalf of the Wehrmacht. We are not here to make war on young ladies. We will restore you a bicycle. Please take *any* bicycle. I will personally authorize it. Take a *good* bicycle.'

'I don't want *any* bicycle,' she said. 'I want *my* bicycle.'

Eventually the colonel was constrained to send for a couple of soldiers and order them to force their way through the masses of bicycles, many of them superb machines, any of which she could have had for the asking, until they reached the enclave in which Wanda's humble machine was finally located. For with Teutonic

7

efficiency they were grouped according to whichever town or village they had been impounded in.

Knowing all this, and that a facsimile of her old bicycle was the only thing that would really make her content, I felt myself in the same sort of spot as the German colonel at Salsomaggiore in 1943. In one of my wilder, more fanciful moments I imagined trying to sell her the idea that dropped handlebars are nothing more than raised handlebars installed upside down. And in my mind's eye I could see her wrestling with them, like an Amazon with the antlers of a stag at bay, trying to return them to what she regarded as their proper position.

The heart of rural Dorset is not the easiest place to find out about the latest developments in the world of bicycles, but by good fortune our local newsagent in Wareham had a copy of a magazine called *The Bicycle Buyer's Bible, 1985/6* on its shelves. By this time the question of what sort of bikes we were going to take with us if we were going to get moving before Christmas was becoming extremely urgent. *The Bible* gave detailed specifications of about three hundred machines with prices ranging from £105 to £1147, and £1418 for a tandem.

The machines that interested me most were the mountain bicycles, otherwise ATBs, All Terrain Bicycles. Everything about a mountain bike is big, except for the frame, which is usually smaller than that of normal lightweight touring bicycles. They are built of over-size tubing and have big pedals, ideal for someone like me with huge feet; wheels with big knobbly tyres which can be inflated with four times as much air as an ordinary high-pressure tyre; very wide flat handlebars, like motorcycle handlebars, fitted with thumb-operated gear change levers; and motorcycle-type brake levers connected to cantilever brakes of the sort originally designed for tandems, which have enormous stopping power.

Most of them are fitted with 15- or 18-speed derailleur gears made up by fitting a five- or six-sprocket freewheel block on the rear hub and three chainwheels of different sizes on the main axle in the bottom bracket where the cranks are situated; a sophistication so conspicuously unnecessary that it would have had Thorstein Veblen ecstatically adding another chapter to his great work, *The Theory of the Leisure Class*, had he lived to see it. This equipment produces gears ranging from 20″ or even lower (which can be a godsend when climbing mountains) to 90″ or even higher for racing downhill, or with a following wind on the flat.[*] Not all these gears are practicable or even usable, however, for technical reasons.

These mountain bikes looked very ugly, very old-fashioned and very American, which was not surprising as they were the lineal descendants of the fat-tyred newspaper delivery bikes first produced by a man called Ignaz Schwinn in the United States in 1933. To me they looked even older. They made me think of Mack Sennett and Fatty Arbuckle and Jackie Coogan. If I got round to buying one I knew that I would have to wear a big flat peaked cap like Coogan's. Eighteen gears apart – perhaps she would settle for fifteen – and providing we could find one with an open rather than a man's diamond frame model, this seemed exactly the sort of bike, in the absence of her beloved Bianchi, that Wanda needed to carry her the length and breadth of Ireland and even up and down a holy mountain or two.

'"To buy a mountain bike now",' I read, '"is to win yourself a place in the first of the few rather than the last of the many."'

It was a wet Sunday evening in Dorset. We were in bed surrounded by the avalanche of catalogues and lists I had brought down on us by clipping out the coupons in *The Bicycle Buyer's Bible*. One dealer, in what seemed to me an excess of optimism, had also sent order forms which read:

PLEASE SEND ... MOUNTAIN BICYCLES(S), MODEL(S) ... FRAME SIZE(S) ... COLOUR(S) ... PLEASE GIVE ALTERNATE COLOUR(S). I ENCLOSE A CHEQUE/BANKER'S ORDER, VALUE. ...

[*]The gear ratio (as a single figure) in inches is calculated by dividing the number of teeth on the chainwheel by the number of teeth on the rear sprocket and multiplying the result by the wheel diameter, in the case of most mountain bikes, 26″.

'I don't want to be one of the first of the few,' Wanda said.

'Shall I go on?' I said. 'There's worse to follow.'

'Okay, go on.'

'"From prototype to production model they have been around for less than a decade. In that short time they have been blasted across the Sahara, up Kilimanjaro, down the Rockies and along the Great Wall of China."'

'Isn't it true that the Great Wall of China's got so many holes in it that you can't even walk along it, let alone cycle along it?'

'Yes, I know,' I said, 'but there is a picture here of two men sitting on their bikes on the top of Kilimanjaro. And anyway, just listen to this: "With each off-the-wall off- the-road adventure, with each unlikely test-to-destruction, the off-road-state-of-knowledge has rolled the off-road-state-of-the-art further forward."'

'Read it again,' she said. 'More slowly. It sounds like bloddy nonsense to me.'

'There's no need to be foul-mouthed,' I said.

'It was you who taught me,' she replied.

I read it again. It still sounded like bloody nonsense and it came as no surprise when I later discovered that some of the early practitioners of this off-the-road-state-of-the-art mountain bike business hailed from Marin, that deceptively normal-looking county out beyond the Golden Gate Bridge on the way up to the big redwoods, which gives shelter to more well-heeled loonies to the square mile within its confines, all of them into everything from free association in Zen to biodegradable chain cleaning fluid, than any other comparable suburban area in the entire United States.

'Read on,' Wanda said.

'"You don't have to be some gung-ho lunatic to get your kicks",' I read on. '"Take a mountain bike along the next time the family or a group of friends head off for a picnic in the woods. There'll be plenty of places to put the bike through its paces and it sure beats playing Frisbee after lunch [interval while I explained the nature of this, I thought outmoded, pastime to Wanda]. Or take the bike on a trip to the seaside – rock-hopping along the beach is a blast."'

'That's enough,' she said in the Balkan version of her voice. 'I can just see you on your mountain bike, a gong-ho (what is gong-ho?), Frisbee-playing, rock-hopping lunatic.'

'I say,' I said, some time later when the lights were out, 'I hope all this isn't going to make you lose your enthusiasm.'

'Enthusiasm for what?'

'For these bikes, and Ireland and everything,' I said, lamely.

'Not for these bikes, I haven't,' she said. 'I've never had any. Nor for Ireland in winter. If I come it will only be to make sure you don't get into trobble.'

'What sort of trouble?'

'In Ireland all sorts of trobble,' she said, darkly.

We went to London to make the rounds of shops selling mountain bicycles, and if possible purchase some. Under the arches off the Strand, in the substructure which was all that remained of the Adelphi, the Adam brothers' great riverside composition, we saw and rode our first mountain bikes. Wanda tried something called a Muddy Fox Seeker Mixte, which had an open frame constructed from Japanese fully lugged chrome molybdenum tubing with Mangaloy manganese alloy forks; I tried a Muddy Fox Pathfinder which had a lugless frame of the same material, put together by the TIG (Tungsten Inert Gas) welding process. Wanda quite liked her Mixte which reminded her a bit of the old Bianchi open-framed bike on which she had ridden out to bring me and my friends food and clothing in the autumn of 1943.

What the staff of most of the bicycle shops we visited had in common, we discovered, was almost complete indifference as to whether we bought one of their bikes or not. This was surprising, considering how much money was involved and the fact that the industry was going through one of its periodic slumps. In mountain bikes there was nothing worth buying under £200. From £200 to £300 the choice was very limited and it was only in the £300 to £500 range that one started to find high quality bikes. From £500 to around £1000 or more, one was in a world of prototypes and purely competitive machines in which everything, as the *Buyer's Bible* put it in a way that I was beginning to find insidiously corrupting, was 'silly money'. One thing we had learned was that whatever make we bought, our bikes should come from a firm that actually built, or at least assembled them, on the premises. But time was now running out and if we did not leave for Ireland within ten days we would have to wait until after Christmas. One of the firms we had not yet visited was called Overbury's, in Bristol, who designed and built their own racing, touring and mountain bikes. And Bristol had the added attraction that our daughter, son-in-law and grandchildren lived there.

Overbury's premises, in Ashley Road, can scarcely be described as being at 'the better end' of Bristol; in fact Bristol has no better end. The more enviable parts are perched high above the city at the top of impossibly steep hills or on huge cliffs above the Avon Gorge, from both of which eyries the inhabitants look down with Olympian detachment on those less fortunate mortals below. Overbury's, which is run by Andy Powell and his mother, Enid, is about the size of an average newsagent's and is crammed with bikes that are either beautiful or sophisticated, or both, and all the complex bits and pieces that go to make them up. What space remains is taken up by machines in various states of malfunction or collapse awaiting attention. In fact on the Monday morning we visited, it was rather like being in a National Health doctor's waiting room during surgery hours. One of the more spectacular accidents had befallen an *ATB* - riding log-hopper who had failed to clear a huge pile of them in a Forestry Commission conifer wood. The resulting smash had destroyed the special welded guard bar, fitted under the bottom bracket to protect the triple chain rings from just such a mishap, doing a wealth of damage.

'You're looking at more than a hundred nicker,' the owner said with gloomy pride, when I showed an interest in it. 'That's the end of guards for me.'

We were lent a couple of test bikes on deposit and we set off with them in the back of our van for an attractive open expanse called Ashton Court Park, to try them out. Wanda's was the most expensive and the most unconventional in appearance. It was called the Wild Cat and was going to take a bit of living up to.

Mine was a Crossfell, at that time the most expensive of Overbury's diamond frame mountain bikes.

By the end of this outing Wanda was very depressed. It was not surprising: the last bicycle she had ridden had been a borrowed ladies' Marston Golden Sunbeam which she had used while house-hunting in South London in the 1970s, perhaps the finest conventional bicycle ever made. This was the bicycle on male versions of which deceptively fragile-looking curates used to zoom past me, as I frantically pedalled my Selbach back in the 1930s. She liked the semi-open frame of the Wild Cat, but found it difficult to live up to the image conjured up by its name. She couldn't cope with the complexity of the twin-change shift mechanisms on the handlebars which controlled the eighteen gears: the right-hand one which shifted the chain from any one of the six sprockets to another on the Shimano Extra Duty Freewheel Block; the left-hand one which shifted the chain on the costly oval Shimano Biopace triple ring chainset. 'Biopace delivers power when you need it most,' the blurb said. 'Computer analysis shows round rings force unnatural leg dynamics that interfere with smooth cadence and can lead to knee strain.'

In comparison with a traditional lightweight bicycle fitted with narrow, high-pressure tyres I found the knobbly mountain tyres sluggish uphill, but very good downhill at speed on a track full of pot-holes. The saddles, amalgams of leather and plastic, we both agreed were hell. By the time our trial run through the wilds of the Ashton Court Park was over I had resigned myself to giving up the idea of mountain biking, or any other sort of biking, in Ireland; but when we got back to the shop and redeemed our deposits Wanda, to my surprise, told me to go ahead and order. 'If I have it I will *have* to use it,' she said.

There was no problem in producing my Crossfell in time, as there was a frame in stock of the right size that only needed stove enamelling. Wanda's Wild Cat, as its name suggested, was more difficult. It would have to be built from scratch in seven days. But first her inside leg had to be measured for the frame — a feat difficult to accomplish in a crowded bike shop when the subject is wearing a skirt – and all work ceased while I performed it.

In a state of shock at the realization of the enormity of what I was doing I allowed Andy Powell to persuade me that I should also have eighteen gears. I forget the reason he gave. Perhaps he had run out of five-sprocket freewheel blocks, the last shipment from Osaka having gone down with all hands in the South China Sea to become a source of wonder to marine archaeologists around 3000 AD, who would eventually identify them as amulets against the evil eye.

In the course of the next hour or so I spent vast amounts of money – we paid for everything ourselves – on what bicycle builders laughingly refer to as 'optional extras': pumps, front and rear reflectors, guards to protect the derailleur mechanisms, frame pads to make it easier to lift my diamond-framed Crossfell over gates and fences, over-sized mud guards for the over-sized tyres, two sets of front and rear panniers, front and rear pannier frames to hook them on, 'stuff sacs', rudely named bags to keep our waterproof clothing in, front and rear lights, drinking bottles, Sam Browne belts and trouser clips made of reflective material that might improve our chance of not being knocked down and squashed flat at night. Foolishly, having donned them and then looked at one another, we decided against crash helmets – 'head protection for the thinking cyclist', as one catalogue put it.

We also needed a whole lot of tools and spares: a three-way spanner, a ten-in-one dumbbell spanner, two brake spanners, a pair of cone spanners, a Shimano crank bolt spanner and freewheel remover, a 4" adjustable wrench, three Allen keys, a spoke key, a cable cutter, a pair of pointed pliers, a tyre pressure gauge, an adaptor so that a garage air-line or a car foot pump could be used with Presta bicycle valves, a set of tyre levers, spare spokes, two spare inner tubes, spare gear change and brake cables, spare brake blocks (at a colossal £3.90 a pair), and valve caps.

My next purchase was something called a Citadel Lock which had a half-inch metal shackle said to be proof against a pair of 42" bolt cutters and big enough to lock both bikes to a parking meter or a set of railings at the same time. However it was so heavy that we left it at home and took with us instead a couple of pre-coiled 5ft steel cable locks which would last about ten seconds against bolt cutters.

By this time I began to feel myself in a state of euphoria, like a character in a Fitzgerald novel going shopping – Gatsby stocking up on shirts, or Nicole Diver buying an army of toy soldiers in Paris in 1925: 'It was fun spending money in the sunlight of the foreign city, with healthy bodies . . . that sent streams of colour up to their faces; with arms and hands, legs and ankles that stretched out confidently, reaching or stepping with the confidence of women lovely to men.' Although it was a bit different in Bristol in deep December for a senior citizen with all the confidence of a man unlovely to women – well, most women.

Then we shopped for clothes. The most difficult to find on the spur of the moment, because they were very expensive, were the long zip jackets with baggy trousers to match made from Gore-Tex, a wind and waterproof material which allows perspiration to evaporate. Shoes were another problem. Cycling shoes designed for riding lightweight bikes on the road would be hopeless anywhere off it in waterlogged old Ireland. In the end we both took climbing boots and short, wool-lined wellingtons which were warm and could be accommodated on the big mountain bike pedals but soon lost their linings. And we bought long wool and nylon stockings with elasticated tops that came up over the knee and waterproof over-mitts with warm inner linings.

We also spent a gruesome hour in company with other senior citizens stocking up for the winter, buying thermal underwear, which everyone said we must have: long johns to sleep in and underwear to ride in. Some of it looked terrible, especially a particular brand of men's underpants which came down to the knees and gave the wearer, in this case myself, an air of geriatric instability. It also, when it warmed up, gave off an awful pong. 'I wonder,' Wanda said, emerging from the fitting room in which she had given the thumbs-down to the underpants, and surveying the milling throng, 'if they are all going to Ireland, too, on bicycles. If they are we shall look pretty silly.'

As I had promised myself, I took with me a huge cap that had belonged to my father – almost a dead ringer of that worn by the now dead and gone Jackie Coogan, which Wanda from now on referred to as my 'Jackie Hooghly'.

The bikes were delivered to us by van from Bristol the following Tuesday at what was literally the eleventh hour. Together with the optional and non-optional extras, all done up in protective wadding, they made an impressive pair of packages, and the bikes themselves, which had been wrapped like Egyptian mummies in the equivalent of cerements, were so scintillating when finally exposed to the light of day that it seemed a pity to foul them up by riding them. If there really was such a concept as state-of-the-art, this was it.

'We can put it all down to expenses,' I said to Wanda.

'I wouldn't count on it,' she said. 'I can just see the expression on the Inspector of Taxes' face. He'll laugh all the way to your funeral.'

'Well, why did you let me buy all this stuff if that's what you think?' I asked.

'I was going to stop you,' she said, 'but when I saw how much you were enjoying yourself, somehow I couldn't. You looked like a small boy in a sweet shop.'

We set off to negotiate some of the network of lanes in the Isle of Purbeck, the majority of which involve ascents of unnatural steepness. The first part included a fairly hard climb along the flanks of Smedmore Hill. This time I rode behind Wanda in order to be able to tell her when to operate the front and rear gear shift mechanisms. This worked all right until she suddenly pulled the left hand lever back and at the same time pushed the right hand one forward, while still riding on the flat, which transferred her instantly to the lowest gear available to her, 23.6″, leaving her with her legs whirring round until she fell off.

In spite of this setback, she did succeed in climbing the hill, from the top of which we roared down hill towards the hamlet of Steeple, which consists of a manor, a vicarage, a very old church which houses a giant eighteenth-century version of a pianola and a plaque displaying the stars and stripes of the Lawrences, a family who were collateral ancestors of George Washington.

From here a hill climbs to the summit of West Creech Hill, a rise of about 295 feet in 1000 yards, which may not seem much, and certainly doesn't look much, but is in fact excruciating. If any of the Alpine passes I rode over on my way to Italy in 1971 had been as difficult as parts of this hill, I would never have ridden a bike over the Alps at all.

'You go on,' said Wanda, when the time came to tackle it. 'Don't watch me.'

From the top, completely breathless, I watched the little figure gallantly toiling up, very slowly, very wobbly at times, but she made it.

'I did it,' she said. 'Not bad for a grandmother, am I?'

I felt so proud of her I wanted to cry; but privately I prayed that there wouldn't be many similar hills in Ireland.

When we got back to the house Wanda allowed me a fleeting glimpse of what her hand-finished, calf leather, high-density, memory-retentive foam Desmoplan base saddle had done to her in the course of about six miles and I knew that unless a better alternative could be found she would be a non-starter in the Irish Cycling Stakes, 1985. So I got on the telephone to Enid in Bristol and the following morning a large carton full of saddles arrived by special delivery.

I had solved the saddle problem on my mountain bike by ordering a Brooks B66 leather saddle which had big springs at the back. Most mountain bike saddles seem to have been designed by men who don't realize that on a mountain bike the rider sits more or less upright, as on a roadster, so that the whole weight of the body, divided on a bicycle with dropped handlebars between the saddle and the bars, falls on the saddle. It is even worse for women. Women have wider hips and, as the *Buyer's Bible* delicately put it, having presumably taken female advice, 'the pubic arch between the legs is shallower, making the genital area very vulnerable to pressure'.

The saddles we now received were mostly similar in construction to the one that had originally come with Wanda's bike. Some had been injected with silicon fluid, to make them more bouncy beneath the layer of 'high-density memory-retentive foam' already referred to. With all these lying around in the hall, it resembled a saddle fetishist's den. Eventually, Wanda chose a Brooks B72 leather touring saddle, 'specially designed for women cyclists and those wanting a broader support'.

I now spent the time, when not engaged in packing my pannier bags (we were leaving the next day), in bashing her saddle with a lump of wood, and rubbing it with Brooks Proofhide and something called Neatsfoot Oil in order to take some of the sting out of it for Wanda's inaugural Irish ride, which I was planning with my customary inefficiency.

Chapter 2

TO THE EMERALD ISLE

'There lay the green shore of Ireland, like some coast of plenty. We could see towns, towers, churches, harvests; but the curse of eight hundred years we could not discern.'

RALPH WALDO EMERSON. *English Traits*, 1856

'Ireland is not Paradise.'

JONATHAN SWIFT, in a letter to Alexander Pope.
30 August 1716

I spent our last evening in England in the basement bedroom of our daughter and son-in-law's house up on the highest heights of Bristol, where those who are chronic worriers wear oxygen masks, making final adjustments to the Crossfell and the Wild Cat.

There were no other contenders for this utterly boring task. Somewhere upstairs, above ground, my eleven-year-old grandson, using his father's computer, was extracting information in a matter of seconds from what appeared to be thin air. Elsewhere in the building my granddaughter was dancing the sort of dances that little girls of six habitually execute, dreaming of being Flossie Footlights or Fonteyn. In the kitchen my daughter was about to start roasting a duck, happy, one hoped, at the thought of going back to work in the outside world from which bringing up her children had largely excluded her. Half a mile up the road, immured somewhere in a wing of the University, her husband, a mathematician turned biologist, was locked in what looked like becoming a lifelong struggle to extract the secret of what makes eyes and ears function.

And somewhere in the house was Wanda. She was about as interested in the finer points of her Wild Cat as I imagine Queen Boadicea would have been in the alignment of scythes on the axles of her chariot wheels. Both assumed, rightly, that some member of the *lumpenproletariat* would be keeping their equipment up to scratch. For Shimano Deore XT hubs, Biopace computer-designed drive system chainwheels, 600 EX headsets with O ring seals, and such – all items I had been forced to take an interest in, simply to know what to try and do if they went wrong – she cared not a hoot.

One of the best reasons for owning an ordinary bicycle with no expensive trimmings is that everything about it, apart from mending punctures, which is a bore whatever sort of bike you have, is comparatively simple. With expensive, thoroughbred bicycles it is another matter altogether.

If I had ever forgotten this I re-discovered it when I tried to fit Wanda's final selection, the Brooks B72 leather saddle, the one 'for those wanting a broader support', to a highly sophisticated, space age Sr Laprade XL forged alloy fluted seatpin with micro-adjustment and a replacement value of around £20. A lot of money, you may say. But worth every penny of it since, according to those who know, anything nameless in the field of seatpins may snap off with rough off-the-road usage, leaving the rider either impaled on what is left of it or, at the very least, pedalling away without any visible means of support, rather like a fakir using a bicycle to perform a variation of the Indian rope trick. I had asked Overbury's for a seatpin which gave the maximum amount of adjustment and this was it.

By now it was seven o'clock. 'It won't take long,' I said, talking to myself in the absence of an audience.

The saddle was mounted on a frame which consisted of two sets of parallel wire tracks and each of these tracks had to be attached to the Laprade pin by means of a clamp with two parallel grooves on it. The principal difficulty I experienced in performing this ostensibly easy task was that the track wires were not only too far apart to fit into the grooves but were extraordinarily resistant to being drawn together. However I finally succeeded in doing this making use of a form of Spanish windlass made with a lace from a climbing boot and a skewer.

I was so pleased with myself at having accomplished this feat that I failed to notice that when I inserted the tracks into the grooves I did so with the saddle the wrong way up.

This was the moment when my daughter, fearing for her dinner and my sanity, set off in the rain and darkness to enlist the help of Charlie Quinn, who lived a few doors away. Apparently Charlie Quinn was a schoolboy who was completely dotty about bikes and when not engaged in doing his homework spent most of his spare time either riding them or working on them in a part-time capacity at Clifton Cycles, a rival bike shop to Overbury's.

Charlie arrived with a comprehensive tool kit which included a pair of clamps, with the help of which he drew the wire tracks together with shameful ease, and inserted them in the grooves. It was therefore not without a certain despicable satisfaction that I noted that when he tightened the bolt the tracks were still loose in the grooves and the saddle wobbled.

By this time I would have been in despair, but not Charlie. 'That's all right,' he said, 'I'll get some scrim. That'll hold it.' It did indeed hold it. By now the duck was nearly ready.

'Is there anything else?' he asked.

'Well, if you wouldn't mind terribly I've got to fit some pannier adaptor plates. It's quite a simple job. But what about your dinner?'

'I've already eaten it,' he said. 'I call it supper.'

All those bored by the horrendous complexities of bicycle mechanics should skip the rest of this section and resurface on page 23. For those who are not, I should explain that pannier adaptor plates are flat pieces of alloy with holes cut in them and drilled to take a single nut and bolt. These plates had to be fitted because the hooks on the elastic cords supplied with the Karrimor rear panniers to keep them in place were not a proper fit on the American-designed Blackburn alloy carriers. Although they will work at a pinch the hooks cannot be guaranteed to remain hooked on, especially when the bicycle is being used on rough ground.

It was soon obvious that we were in trouble. In order to fit the plates, the bolts used to attach them to the carriers had to be inserted through the brazed-on carrier eyes at the lower end of the chain stays, and then through eyes in the triangulated struts at the bottom of the carriers. The devilish thing was that it was not possible to insert one of these bolts from the outside in, and secure it with a nut on the inside of the carrier eye, because any nut on the inside would become enmeshed with the teeth of the outermost low-gear sprocket on the freewheel block.

This meant that both rear wheels had to be taken out so that the bolts could be inserted from the inside. At the same time the rear axles had to be packed with sufficient washers between the cone locking nuts on the hub axles and the wheel drop-outs to spread the chainstays sufficiently to give the necessary clearance to keep the bolt heads out of range of the teeth of the outermost sprocket.

But this was not the end of it. The addition of these washers had the effect of throwing the rear derailleur shift mechanism out of its pre-set alignment and this in turn affected the alignment of the front derailleur which shifted the chain on the triple chainwheels. And it was not only the shift mechanisms that went on the bum. The springing of the seat stays with the washers on the axles caused subtle alterations to the settings of the Aztec brake blocks fitted to the XT cantilever brakes operating on the rear rims and also to the amount of travel on the brake levers.

Almost literally enmeshed in all this Charlie was in his element, rushing backwards and forwards between our house and his in pouring rain, for nuts, bolts, washers, more tools and so forth. Meanwhile, I wondered if it would be all right to desert him and go off and eat the duck. When I did, feeling a pig for doing so, I don't think he even noticed I'd gone.

It was not until we got back to England that I discovered that there had not been any need to fit these plates at all, as Blackburn marketed special shock cords to attach Karrimor panniers to Blackburn carriers.

The morning after Quinn the bicycle wizard had performed his magic and we had eaten the duck and gone to bed, we set off in torrential rain that turned day into night to drive our van with the bikes in it to Fishguard.

Here, on the coast of Dyfed, otherwise Pembroke, in what is known as England beyond Wales, in windswept, watery Fish-guard with rainbows overhead, with its brightly painted houses glittering in the sunlight and its harbour built in the 1900s, itself a period piece, there was already a feeling of Ireland. Perhaps the French thought they were in Ireland when they undertook the last invasion of Britain here in 1797, commanded by an American, Colonel William Tate, and laid down their arms before a bevy of Welsh ladies dressed in traditional cloaks, under the impression, it is said, that they were soldiers.

We spent most of the voyage re-packing our pannier bags.

Sitting surrounded by them in the ferry saloon we looked like beleaguered settlers on the old Oregon Trail. It was remarkable how much room two sets of front and rear panniers, not to speak of the stuff sacs, took up when removed from the bicycles. All the contents had to be put in plastic liners as the panniers were not guaranteed waterproof against torrential rain, and since these liners were opaque, once they were packed it was difficult to remember what was in them. We had started off very efficiently at home before leaving, sticking on little labels bearing the legends 'spare thermal underwear', 'boots and spare inner tubes', and so on, but now Wanda decided on a complete and more logical redistribution, while other passengers looked on with fascination.

It was seven-thirty before we finally disembarked at Rosslare; and a cold, dark evening with the wind driving great clouds of spray over the jetty. We had planned to stay the night there in a bed and breakfast and take a train to Limerick, where we proposed to start our cycling, the following morning, but we now discovered that in winter there was only one train a day to Limerick, and this was due to leave in seven minutes. We had to buy tickets and somehow find something to eat and drink as we had eaten nothing except a cold sausage each and a rather nasty 'individual rabbit pie' in a pub since leaving Bristol.

A porter told us to put our bikes in a van at the end of the train. When I had finished locking them up he changed his mind and told me to put them in an identical van at the other end of the train, so I unlocked them and did so. Another man said that was wrong too, so I unlocked them again and took them back to the original one. Meanwhile Wanda was buying the tickets at a reduced rate using our international old age pensioners' cards. By now, in theory, the train should have left.

The station buffet was warm and friendly, but served no hot food, only ham sandwiches which had to be made-to-measure. Wanda boarded the train while I waited for the sandwiches, but after a minute she got down and rushed into the buffet crying, 'The train, the train is leaving!'

'It isn't leaving, whatever your good lady says,' remarked a rather quiet man in railway uniform whom I hadn't noticed before, who was only about a quarter of the way through a pint of

Guinness. 'Not without me, it isn't. I'm the guard,' and he took another long draw at his drink. Emboldened by this I ordered a second one myself. Eventually we left more or less on time: the station clock turned out to be about ten minutes fast.

There ensued an interminable journey through parts of Counties Wexford, Kilkenny, a large segment of Tipperary and Limerick, in a hearselike, black upholstered carriage with doors to the lavatories that looked as if they had been gnawed by famine-stricken rats. Outside it was still as black as your hat with a howling wind and torrential rain, and the dimly-lit, battered stations at which the train stopped reminded me of our travels in Siberia. At Wexford our kindly guard, who was in his early sixties, and very old-fashioned-looking in his peaked cap and blue overcoat – infinitely preferable to the ludicrous Swiss-type uniforms affected by British Rail – brought us a jug of hot tea which, after two pints of Guinness in something like five minutes, I was unready for. Meanwhile we spent an hour or so continuing with our re-packing, forgetting which container was which and starting all over again, but this time without an audience.

At Limerick Junction a man with wild hair, a huge protruding lower jaw, wearing a crumpled check suit and looking like a *Punch* 1850s cartoon of an Irishman joined us in our carriage and began producing unidentifiable items of food from plastic bags.

His meal was interrupted by the arrival of the guard to inspect his ticket, and he spent the next twenty minutes slowly and laboriously going through his pockets and his plastic bags, time after time, without ever finding it. Eventually he produced a 50p piece which he offered to the guard who, by this time bored with the whole business, rejected it. The train – could it be called the *Limerick Express* I wondered? – arrived at Limerick thirty minutes late, at 11.45 p.m. The weather was still appalling but the area round the station at least still seemed lively and the pubs were still taking orders.

Pushing our bikes through the rain we arrived on the threshold of the Station Hotel, from which the last revellers were being ejected, to find that a double room was £22 a night and the night was half over.

So instead we went round the corner to Boylan's, part gift shop, part B and B, where we were warmly welcomed and our bikes put in the shop to see the rest of the night through in company with a consignment of nylon pandas. A kindly girl, Miss Boylan, brought tea and cakes – 'Try and eat them,' she begged, as if we were convalescing from an illness – and we went to bed after a nice hot shower, whacked and surrounded by our mounds of kit.

'What a fucking day,' Wanda said before she dropped off. It was difficult not to agree with her.

Chapter 3

BIRTHDAY ON A BICYCLE

'Nothing in Ireland lasts long except the miles.'

GEORGE MOORE. *Ave*, 1911
(An Irish mile is 2240 yards – an English one 1760 yards.)

'As there is more rain in this country than in any other,
and as therefore, naturally, the inhabitants should be
inured to the weather, and made to despise an
inconvenience which they cannot avoid, the travelling
conveyances are arranged so that you may get as much
practice in being as wet as possible.'

W. M. THACKERAY. *The Irish Sketch Book of 1842*

The next morning I opened a window and was confronted by a painting of a double-headed eagle glaring at me from a wall across what had once been an alley three feet wide, presumably the sign of some former mediaeval hostelry. Rain was falling in torrents and I was in a state of despair and indecision as to what we should do. I could see ourselves sitting in tea shops for days on end waiting for it to abate, playing with nylon pandas and sleeping for endless nights in Boylan's B and B.

I became even more depressed when I suddenly remembered that it was my birthday. Wanda had forgotten it, and this made her depressed, too. Anyway, she gave me a kiss. Then, after a huge breakfast, we sallied out with our bicycles into the terrifying early morning rush hour traffic of Limerick, among drivers many of whom appeared to have only recently arrived in the machine age or were still on the way to it, with Miss Boylan's warning still echoing in our ears. 'Be careful, now, on the Sarsfield Bridge, for there are a whole lot of people blown off their cycles on it every year by the wind of the lorries, and *kilt!*'*

We were heading for County Clare, via the dread Sarsfield Bridge, passing on the way the establishments of purveyors of bacon (bacon is to Limerick what caviar is to Astrakhan) and tall, often beautifully proportioned eighteenth-century brick houses, many of them decrepit to the point of collapse.

It was somewhere in O'Connell Street that Wanda contrived to

---

*For those who find my attempts at reproducing fragments of Irish English as spoken by the inhabitants unacceptable, I can only plead that this is what they sounded like to me. What my own fruity accent sounded like to them can only be a matter of conjecture.

get in the wrong lane and was borne away on a tidal wave of traffic, crying 'Hurruck, help me!' at the top of her voice, although what I was supposed to do to help her was not clear. The last I saw of her for some time to come was disappearing round the corner into that part of the city where stood or used to stand some of the relics of British Imperial rule, such as the County Gaol, the Lunatic Asylum and the Court House of 1810. She finally fetched up back at the station, after which she took a right into Parnell Street and started all over again.

'You've chosen a grand day for it,' an old geezer about the same age as me said as, reunited at last, we were crossing the Sarsfield Bridge. He let out an insane kind of 'Heh, heh, heh!' cackle as an afterthought.

He was wearing a white beard with lovely yellow stains in it that looked like the principal ingredient in a prescription for birds' nest soup; an ankle-length oilskin coat to match the stains in his beard and a sou'wester ditto, an ensemble that made him resemble the fisherman on a tin of Norwegian-type sardines. I would have hated to live next door to him, in Limerick or anywhere else. 'Wise guy, eh?' I shouted after him, but he didn't get it, probably because his sou'wester was fitted with flaps.

We were pushing our bikes along the footpath, not even riding them, but still being deluged with un-recycled Irish rainwater that was being thrown up by the west-bound trucks whose drivers, deprived of the pleasure of actually 'kilting' us, were now doing their best to drown us, and were damn nearly succeeding – the very same men who, reunited with their wives and eight children all under the age of fifteen at weekends, wear subfusc suits and take the collection bags round on the ends of long sticks at Mass, eventually leaving a bundle, and generous bequests to the Society of the Holy Name.

Meanwhile, huge and pale and speckled in the rain, the Shannon flowed on, under the bridge towards the mighty sea, past what looked like a disused Indian chutney factory in Bengal with a tall chimney, and past quays built in the 1870s for what was to be another Liverpool, though it never became one in spite of there being nineteen feet of water off them at high water springs.

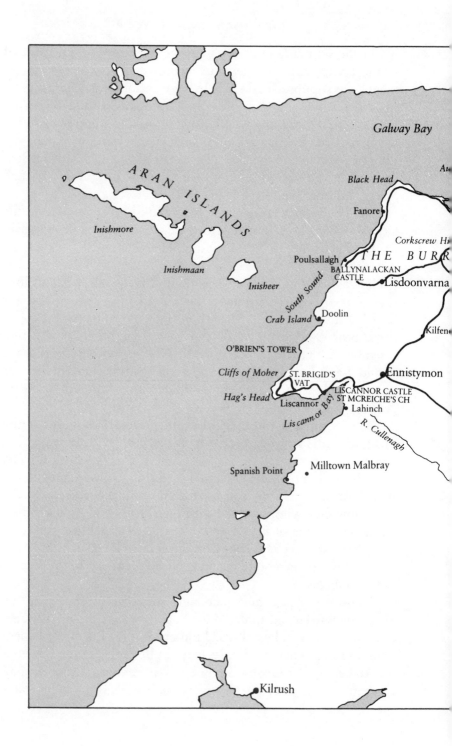

Galway Bay

Black Head

Au

Fanore

Corkscrew H

ARAN ISLANDS

Poulsallagh

THE BURR

Inishmore

BALLYNALACKAN
CASTLE

Lisdoonvarna

Inishmaan

Inisheer

South Sound

Kilfen

Crab Island Doolin

O'BRIEN'S TOWER

Cliffs of Moher

Ennistymon

ST. BRIGID'S
VAT

LISCANNOR CASTLE
ST MCREICHE'S CH

Hag's Head

Liscannor

Lis cann or Bay

Lahinch

R. Cullenagh

Spanish Point

Milltown Malbray

Kilrush

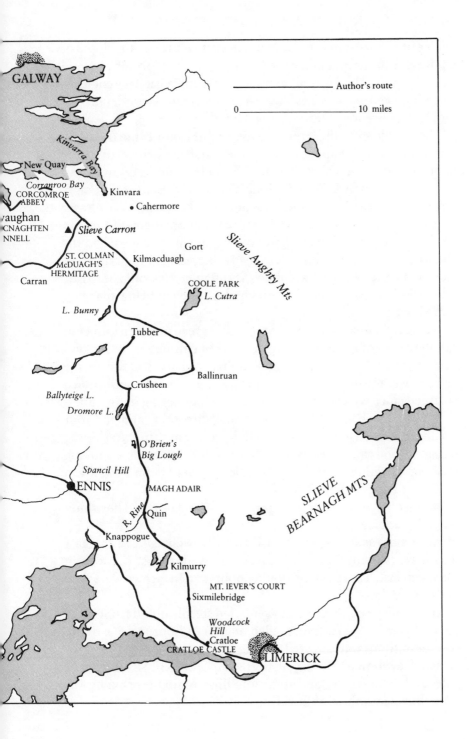

GALWAY

Kinvarra Bay

New Quay

Corranroo Bay
CORCOMROE
ABBEY

Kinvara

Cahermore

vaughan
CNAGHTEN
NNELL

▲ Slieve Carron

ST. COLMAN
McDUAGH'S
HERMITAGE

Kilmacduagh

Gort

Slieve Aughty Mts

Carran

COOLE PARK
L. Cutra

L. Bunny

Tubber

Ballyteige L.

Crusheen

Ballinruan

Dromore L.

O'Brien's
Big Lough

Spancil Hill

ENNIS

MAGH ADAIR

R. Rine

Quin

SLIEVE
BEARNAGH MTS

Knappogue

Kilmurry

MT. IEVER'S COURT
Sixmilebridge

Woodcock
Hill
Cratloe
CRATLOE CASTLE

LIMERICK

Author's route

0 _____ 10 miles

Here, the Shannon was 154 miles from its source on the slopes of Cuilcagh Mountain in County Cavan, near the Northern Ireland Border, a place I had promised myself we would visit if we could do so without getting our nuts blown off. At this rate, I wondered if we would ever live long enough to reach it.

Then, suddenly, the rain stopped and the sun came out. Too unnerved by the happenings on the Sarsfield Bridge to really appreciate the fact, we pushed our bikes a few hundred yards or so through suburban Limerick along the N18 to Ennis and points north, then turned off it and rode out into the country on a lesser road between thin ribbons of bungalows, some of them offering yet more beds and breakfasts. And now for the first time we had the chance to appreciate what it was really like riding mountain bikes laden with gear. To me it was much as I imagined it would be to ride a heavily loaded camel, the principal difference being that you don't have to pedal a camel.

To the right now was Woodcock Hill, a green, western outlier of the Slieve Bearnagh hills; to the left were fields in which donkeys bemoaned their loneliness and battered old trees stood in the hedgerows, and beyond all this to the south was the Shannon, much enlarged since we had last set eyes on it, shimmering in the sun.

A car passed, going in the opposite direction, and the four occupants waved to us cheerily, as did a young man in shirt sleeves, waistcoat and cap who was in a ditch, wielding a fearsome-looking slashing instrument on a long handle that made him look like a survivor of the Peasants' Revolt.

'It must be your Jackie Hooghly hat,' Wanda said. 'They think we're Americans.'

The wind was strong and cool, if not downright cold, but at least the sun was shining and the road was flat – well, almost. We were in Ireland at last. There was no doubt about that. In fact we were now in County Clare.

At the village of Cratloe, an avenue led steeply uphill from silver painted gates to a grotto modelled on that of Lourdes, one of the countless thousands erected during 1954, the Marian Year of Special Devotion to the Virgin, decreed by Pius XII. Silver painted gates and railings in Ireland are an infallible sign of the proximity of something Catholic and therefore holy.

To the south of the road was Cratloe Wood. Inside it was wet and dim and mysterious, with long, diagonal shafts of sunlight reaching down into it through the trees. Some of the oaks were descendants of those that had provided timber for the hammer-beam roof of London's Westminster Hall, when it was built in 1399; and for the roof of the Amsterdam Town Hall, later the Royal Palace, built in 1648 on a foundation of more than 13,000 wooden piles. And long before all this, in the ninth century, men had come here all the way from Ulster to cut down oaks and carry them away northwards to make a roof for the Grianan of Aileach, the summer palace of the O'Neills, Kings of Ulster, on Greenan Mountain, near Londonderry. At some very far-off period the wood had been cut in two by what is now the N18, and another beautiful part of it is still to be found south of this road in a walled enclosure, which forms part of the demesne* of Cratloe Castle. It belonged to the Macnamaras who, together with the O'Briens, seem to have had more castles in these parts alone – the remains of more than fifty have been identified – than most other families had in the whole of Ireland. At Cratloe itself there are three castles within half a mile of one another, which could constitute some kind of record.

After paddling around in these woods for a bit, wishing we had brought our waterwings, we resumed our journey; but not before Wanda, one of whose foibles is to have no faith in maps, however good, or map readers, however accomplished, had knocked on a cottage door to inquire the way to Sixmilebridge, for which we were bound and to which I already knew the route.

The misinformation she was given by an innocuous-looking old body – 'Sure, it's just away down the hill' – sent her zooming off by herself under a railway line in the direction of Bunratty Castle, the largest of all the Irish tower houses. Had she actually reached it, she would have received no more than her deserts if the directors had put her to work as a serving wench at the mediaeval-type banquets for which they are internationally renowned.

The village of Sixmilebridge bestrode the deep, dark, narrow Owenogarney river. It was really two villages, Old Sixmilebridge on the west bank and New Sixmilebridge on the east bank, built in

---

Demesne: a word not much used in Britain but in Ireland signifying the land surrounding a house, or castle, retained by the owner for his or her own use.

the early eighteenth century, when an iron works was opened. It had brightly painted houses – a bit like Fishguard – streets with royal names such as Orange, George, Frederick and Hanover, which sounded a bit odd in the depths of republican Ireland, and seven pubs, only one of which served any kind of food, something which seemed extraordinary at the time but which, as we proceeded on our way through Ireland, we came to regard as commonplace. This pub was huge, considering the size of the village. It had three bars, decorated with imitation half-timbering, wallpaper of a sultry tropical design and hue and glass cases containing stuffed, predatory animals. I asked the landlord whether he thought a place the size of Sixmilebridge could really support seven pubs, since I know many villages of a similar size in England that can scarcely support one.

'Why, yes,' he said, apparently genuinely surprised by what he obviously regarded as a daft question in a place which in 1931 had a population of 325, and probably had even less now. 'There's a living for all of us.'

'There was no need at all to be chaining your bikes up in Sixmilebridge,' said a small girl of about seven with a hint of reproof, as we were unchaining them, preparatory to continuing on our way.

We were still only nine miles from Limerick. If we went on like this and I continued to record what I saw in such superfluous detail it would take us five years to travel round Ireland, and the rest of my life to write about it. I put this to Wanda and she said perhaps it didn't matter, and what other plans had I got for spending the evening of my days; but I knew she wasn't serious about it. Nevertheless, emboldened by her hardening attitude I talked her into a detour of a mile or two to see Mount Ievers Court, a country house at the foot of the Slieve Bearnagh hills.

As it was not open to the public, we hid our bicycles near the entrance and approached the house on foot across the park, in which it stood half hidden among trees, some of them enormous beeches, and invisible from the three roads that hemmed the property in.

It was a tall house in every way: three storeys high, with a steeply pitched, tiled roof, tall chimneys, tall doorways and tall windows with white glazing bars. Both its fronts had seven bays and each upper storey was slightly narrower than the one below.

The garden front was faced with bricks of a beautiful pale pink colour and the quoins, the cornerstones, the string courses and the window surrounds were cut from a silvery limestone. A flight of steps led up to a simple doorway on the first floor. The entrance front was entirely faced with this silvery stone, and with what was to be the last of a pale, wintry afternoon sun illuminating the windows the house was an enchanting sight. It could have been the abode of some sleeping princess, waiting to be awakened after a sleep of centuries.

There was no sign of life but we skulked among the trees, anxious not to be detected, certain that if there were any occupants they would not want to be bothered with trespassers in Gore-Tex suits. Neither of us was keen to see the inside in case it failed to equal the exterior of what has been described by Mark Bence-Jones, the author of *Burke's Guide to Irish Country Houses*, as 'the most perfect and also probably the earliest of the tall Irish houses', but apparently it is well worth seeing.

The house was built by John Rothery and his son Isaac for Colonel Henry Ievers[*] sometime between 1730 and 1737, and is thought to have been based on the design of Chevening, in Kent. The beautiful pink bricks used in its construction were brought back as ballast in a vessel that had carried rape-seed oil to Holland, oil that was milled at Oil Mill Bridge, which we had cycled over on our way from Cratloe.

After this detour we set off northwards under what was now a grey sky, bound for Kilmurry and Quin, through a wide expanse of flat, rural Clare with the Slieve Bearnagh hills running away to the north-east on our right.

The road was the site of intensive ribbon development. Along it on either side stood bungalows in an astonishing medley of styles – Spanish hacienda, Dallas ranch house, American Colonial, Teutonic love-nests with stained glass in their front doors, and others in styles difficult to put a name to. Some were already occupied and their windswept, treeless gardens and patios were

---

[*]A descendant of another Henry Ievers, a quit-rent collector to the King's Commissioners, who acquired 12,000 acres in Clare, and who died in 1691.

enclosed with breeze-block walls or with balustrades made from reconstituted stone. Some still had the builders on the premises – their vans and battered cars stood outside and you could hear their owners whistling and their radios on the go. Some were empty shells, abandoned by both the builders and those whom they were building them for, until the present dire state of the Irish economy improved.

If it did, it would only be a matter of time before every secondary road in Ireland would suffer in the same way; many, we subsequently found, already had. These bungalows were alien in the Irish countryside: most of them for instance had no porch in which to hang coats and keep gumboots, an absolute necessity in a place like Ireland. But obviously the Irish love them and they are infinitely better to live in than the damp-courseless, thatched, whitewashed cottages in which their forebears crouched in a single smoke-filled room, stirring some mess suspended over the fire in a blackened pot and fulfilling their destiny by satisfying visitors in search of the picturesque such as ourselves.

Kilmurry, when we finally reached it, having emerged from this Irish subtopia, was a very small place indeed. Of the six roads which met there, five meandered to it across country from points on the map which had no names at all. There were the pictureque ruins of a church and an equally picturesque abandoned church-yard and the sort of picturesque house the Irish were abandoning in droves, with blackbirds in residence in its grass-grown thatch. In the distance the little loughs with which the region abounded sprang to life when from time to time sunbeams forced their way through the clouds that had now gathered overhead.

After this we rode past Knappogue, a Macnamara castle. It was open (morning and afternoon teas were served), and providing a quorum could be found ready to participate, med-iaeval banquets could be served at the drop of a hat. But according to the *Blue Guide*, although built in 1467 it had since been over-restored, not by some Victorian nutcase, as might be expected, but in 1966. So we gave it a miss and pressed on to Quin, a pretty, rural village, with two long, picturesque barns; across the road from Malachy's Bar.

It was three-thirty, and mad for a pot of tea we entered the bar, in which two locals were drinking Guinness and playing darts. They immediately offered to play a foursome, but we were too thirsty to do anything but drink tea and eat a bit of cake, brought by a young girl, for which we paid an Irish *punt* (or pound). While doing so I tried to imagine a couple of foreigners entering one of our local pubs in Dorset at three-thirty on a winter's afternoon and finding customers inside, drinking and offering to play darts, and then being provided with tea and cakes; but I failed. Malachy's Bar may not have been all that much to look at – inside it resembled a 1935 Wardour Street half-timbered film set – but its occupants were kind and welcoming and I realized that if we were going to attempt to equate aesthetics with happiness while travelling through Ireland we might just as well give up and go and be miserable in the comfort of our own, lovely home.

Outside, on a bank of the little River Rine were the impressive ruins of the Franciscan Abbey founded and built in the fifteenth century by Sioda Cam Macnamara within the perimeter of a Norman castle which had been destroyed, presumably by the Macnamaras around 1286. Other members of this clan were also buried here, among them the Macnamara of Knappogue castle who, had his precise location been known to its restorers, would probably have been dug up and restored too.

Those Franciscans were extremely tenacious. In 1541 they were expelled from their premises, as were other religious communities in Ireland, by Henry VIII in his new guise as King of Ireland and Head of the newly established Protestant Church of Ireland,* but after the death of Elizabeth I in 1603 the monks returned. In 1649–50 Cromwell initiated his ghastly campaigns in Leinster and in Munster, of which County Clare formed a part, together with what are now Cork, Kerry, Limerick, Tipperary and Waterford. The following year, 1651, they were again driven out and in 1652 eleven years of rebellion by the Irish came to an end.

*The kingdom Henry established in Ireland endured until 1800, governed from England through English viceroys. In that year the Irish Parliament passed the Act of Union with England – but the State Church, the Church of Ireland, continued until 1869, when Gladstone disestablished and disendowed it. Always the Church of a minority, in its last few years it claimed only 10 per cent of the entire Irish community as worshippers.

In the course of them one third of the Catholic Irish population had been killed; uncounted thousands were shipped to the West Indies, to all intents and purposes to work as slaves; Irish towns were re-populated with English men or English sympathizers; and twenty million acres of land were expropriated and handed over to Protestant settlers.

In spite of these horrors the Franciscans of Quin appear to have been more or less ineradicable. Although driven out of their Friary they contrived to remain in the neighbourhood for the next 150 years. The last surviving member of the order at Quin, Father John Hogan, died in 1820 and his tomb is in the north-east cloister.

Up to now Wanda had been doing very well with her cycling, but after tea at Malachy's Bar some of the fight appeared to go out of her and when I suggested that we should go and look at Danganbrack, perhaps the most extraordinary of all the fortress houses of the Macnamaras, which the *Shell Guide* said was three quarters of a mile east-north-east, and which I said, having been there twenty years previously, was only half a mile north-north-east, she said, 'All right, providing you're sure it isn't five miles,' but without much enthusiasm. But then she hadn't seen it, as I had twenty years ago.

Then, I had reached it by a tree trunk bridge over a deeply sunken stream at the end of a very muddy track which ran eastwards from a road that led due north from Quin to nowhere. There, in a field, I saw what was known as the 'ill-fated tower of Mahon Maechuin', in which the Cromwellian troops, after taking it, spent some time refreshing themselves before moving on that night in 1651 to sack the Abbey. One woman escaped from the tower to bring news of what was happening to Hugh O'Neill, the beleaguered defender of Limerick, which at that time was invested by a Cromwellian army commanded by Henry Ireton until, after six months, he died of the plague.

I remembered Danganbrack as a miniature skyscraper over-grown with ivy as thick as a ship's hawsers, with machicolations[*] and tall gables crowned with chimneys. The ground floor was

---

[*] *Machicolation*: a projecting gallery or parapet with openings through which missiles, boiling oil and suchlike could be hurled on an enemy below.

used as a byre and the lower courses supporting it looked dangerously eroded. The doorway was whitewashed, presumably to discourage the cattle from butting the doorposts and bringing some thousands of tons of masonry down about their ears. I wondered if it was still standing. By the time I thought of asking someone, as is usual in such moments, there was no one to ask.

The first track we now took was certainly muddy enough to be the right one, and it led more or less due east, but after a few hundred yards it made a ninety-degree turn to the north and eventually delivered us into a farmyard filled with liquid mud and policed by a pair of ferocious amphibious sheep dogs. 'And what are you thinking of doing now?' my helpmeet and companion in life's race asked me when we were back on the road.

I looked at the Irish half-inch map – the one-inch map had not been on offer when I was stocking up with them – and heartily wished that it had been the latter. Those half inches make all the difference between locating a fortress house of the Macnamaras and being eaten alive by sheep dogs in a pool of slime.

'Give up,' I said. 'There's only one castle marked on this map that fulfils anyone's description of where it really is, dammit. I've even got a six-figure map reference. We must have been within feet of it at that farm. But why didn't we see it? It's almost as tall as the Woolworth Building. It *must* have fallen down.'

So we gave up. And as to whether Danganbrack is still standing, we didn't meet anyone to ask in the succeeding ten miles or so, and when we did meet someone he didn't know and thought we were enquiring about some new brand of breakfast cereal.

By now both of us were consumed by the unspoken fear that the short December day might give out and leave us blundering about on our bikes in Irish darkness, far from our destination. This was a farm near Crusheen, where we had stayed some eighteen years before, but it was still miles away to the north, and its occupants were still blissfully unaware that we were proposing to stay with them. En route we made one rapid detour down a lane to see Magh Adhair, the Inauguration Place of the Kings of Thomond (now County Clare), one of whom was Brian Boru, High King of Ireland – a grassy mound surrounded by a deep ditch by the banks of the Hell River. On the far side of the river there was a tall, slender standing stone which probably had some ceremonial significance, though the actual inauguration is thought to have taken place under a great oak tree nearby.

This mound has a violent history. In 877 Lorcan, King of Thomond, whose crowning place it was, fought a battle there against Flan, High King of Ireland, which sounds as if it had more of the quality of *opera bouffe*. In the course of it Flan, to denigrate his adversary and to decrease the sanctity of the place, started to play a game of chess on the mound – a present-day equivalent from the point of view of sacrilege would be to play Bingo in Westminster Abbey – but was driven from it by Lorcan, whose fury can only be imagined. Forced to take refuge among the thorn thickets in which the area still abounds Flan promptly got lost and after three days blundering about in them had to surrender. Two other kings, Malachy, High King of Ireland in 982, and Aedh O'Conor, King of Connacht in 1051, committed even greater sacrilege by cutting down the sacred tree, which must have been pretty small the second time round. The last Coronation took place there in the reign of Elizabeth I.

Standing on this mound, looking out over what is partly a natural amphitheatre at the beginning of a long-drawn-out and sulphurous sunset, the feeling of mystery that this place would otherwise have had about it was destroyed by a ribbon of brightly lit bungalows along a nearby lane. It was only going to be a matter of getting a few more building permissions before Magh Adhair would be completely hemmed in by them, a triumph for the developers who will have succeeded in destroying what more than a thousand years, three kings and innumerable wars have failed to do.

Then we set off on what proved to be an interminable ride past O'Brien's Big Lough and Knocknemucky Hill, at 239 feet the highest point in a plain that extended all the way north from the Shannon estuary to Galway Bay. By the time we reached Crusheen, at a crossroads on the fearful N18, it was quite dark. The only human beings we had seen on our journey from Quin, a distance of some seven or eight miles, were two small boys playing outside the lodge gate of a demesne. There were three pubs at Crusheen, and parked outside them were a number of huge heavy goods vehicles, drop-outs from what was currently taking place on the N18 which looked like an HGV version of the Mille Miglia. Inside, one hoped, their drivers were taking it nice and steady and not mixing the J. Arthur Guinness Extra Stout with the Paddy, or vice versa. Of the three, we chose O'Hagerty's, the inside of which was even more attractive than the outside, small and snug and a sort of amber colour, a compound of varnish and smoke applied liberally to what was perhaps, half a century ago, white lincrusta. Mr O'Hagerty had been a horse breeder and dealer until one bad day he was kicked in the neck by one of his stallions. This had left his neck and left hand partially paralysed but had by no means destroyed his animation; in fact he was such a great conversationalist and raconteur that, listening to him, we wondered what he must have been like before his mishap. He talked about Irish tinkers or, as they themselves like to be called, 'travelling people', with whom he had an affinity because of a shared passion for horses; and about the great horse fairs, the best of which he said was and still is the one held at Spancil Hill in June each year. Mr O'Hagerty remembered the horses being brought in to Spancil Hill, nose to tail, from as far away as Cork, by drovers who slept rough in the open and kept going on tobacco and booze.

While he was telling us all this we drank strong, orange-coloured, very sweet tea brewed by Mrs O'Hagerty and ate slices of a delicious cake, one of a number she had made for Halloween, which was remarkably fresh considering that she had baked it thirty-seven days previously. The only other visitor while we were there – he could scarcely be described as a customer – was a rather grim-looking elderly priest who had come to empty a collecting box for some overseas mission and who didn't seem exactly overjoyed at what he found in it.

All Crusheen's other booze customers were next door on Clark's premises, where, some said, the best Guinness in Ireland was served. Apparently, Clark got so worried about Mr O'Hagerty's Guinness that he very kindly let Mr O'Hagerty have a set of his own pipes to connect up to his barrels, clean pipes being of crucial importance to the quality of any beer; but in spite of this poor Mr O'Hagerty's Guinness was still not thought to be as good. Personally, having sunk a couple of pints of both Mr Clark's Guinness and Mr O'Hagerty's, I couldn't detect any significant difference between them, and I rather fancy myself when it comes to appraising beer.

Then I went to telephone the farm, which eventually turned out to be so close that if I'd brought a megaphone with me I could have communicated with it direct. I wished I had. Telephoning from a call box in Ireland is a hazardous and expensive business. You place a number of silver-coloured coins on an inclined plane and watch them disappear into the machine, rather like a landslide. Once this has happened there is no possibility of getting any of them back even if, by no fault of your own, you are disconnected, unless you take a sledgehammer to it. This may explain why the IRA spend so much time robbing banks at gunpoint: to reimburse themselves, at least partially, for all the money they have lost in Irish call boxes.

Mrs Griffey, the owner, was getting dressed up to attend an end-of-the-year do organized by Pan Am in Limerick, but whoever answered said it would be fine for us to stay. There was no food in the house, however, so we should find a place to eat either in Crusheen or in Ennis (ignoring the fact that we were on our bikes and it was fourteen miles to Ennis and back).

The third pub in Crusheen, we were told, did evening meals; but when I went to ask it was closed, it looked as if for ever. So we went to the supermarket and Wanda bought the ingredients of a dinner which, if necessary and providing the stove was still going at the farm, she could cook herself.

Then, in the teeth of the gale, we set off on our bikes for the farm down the N18 in the direction of Ennis, as we had been told to do. It was not marked on the map, but no one I asked could read one anyway. 'It's only half a mile,' said someone, a bloody know-all if ever there was one. 'Sure, and you can't miss it, you take a roight after the railway bridge. There's a great soign.' And more in the same vein, which in Ireland usually means that you will never find what you are looking for and you yourself will probably never be seen again.

In London and Paris, the Elephant and Castle and the Place de la Concorde on a bicycle are for me the equivalent of St Lawrence's red hot griddle. In Rome the one-way sections of the Lungotevere are exactly as I imagine they would be for an early Christian mounted on a bicycle and taking part in a chariot race with charioteers, all of whom have received instructions to squash him flat. I have also been scared stiff in New York, pedalling flat-out on Seventh and St Nicholas' Avenue, Harlem, where everyone else is doing 50 m.p.h. with the windows wound up to escape being mugged. But nowhere have I been anywhere like as frightened as I was that night of my birthday on the four hundred yards or so of the N18 (it may have been shorter but it seemed much longer) leading down from Crusheen to the bridge.

'I don't like this,' Wanda said as we pedalled off in line ahead, echoing my own thoughts on the subject with uncanny fidelity. 'I'm frightened, *really* frightened.' And she was right to be. This particular section of the N18 was single carriageway; it was unilluminated, either due to a power failure or because someone had forgotten to switch on the street lights, or because there weren't any to switch on; and big container trucks, a lot of them with trailers that doubled their length, were hurtling down it at between 60 and 70 m.p.h. in. both directions, with about fifty feet between them. Cars didn't constitute a problem: there were so few of them and their drivers were probably as scared as we were – if they weren't they needed their heads examined.

The trucks travelling towards us gave us the full treatment with their headlamps so that we could see nothing else. Our feeble little Everready battery lamps that had been barely strong enough to allow us steerage way in the lanes on the way from Quin to Crusheen were a joke. (Anyway, it was our own fault: we had promised ourselves that we would never ride at night and here we were on the first one doing just that.) All that we could see of the road ahead was illuminated by what was overtaking us.

When whatever it was actually did pass us I had the eerie impression of something huge and black looming up on my offside, rather as if a contractor was moving a section of the Berlin Wall to Ennis by road. This took place to the accompaniment of a terrible roaring sound and a blast of air, more like a shock wave really, the sort of thing one might expect to occur when one's neighbourhood munitions dump goes up.

It was only too obvious that the majority of the drivers didn't even see us despite the fact that our machines and ourselves were bristling with almost every procurable electric and fluorescent retro-reflective safety aid, in brilliant shades of red, yellow or orange: glittering Sam Browne belts with shoulder straps, reflective trouser clips and pedals, and pannier bags with panels of the same material, as well as front and rear reflectors, wheel reflectors and the Everready front and rear battery lamps.

The bridge spanned the road downhill from the village at one of those sharp bends that were the pride and joy of the more perverse Victorian and Edwardian railway bridge builders, a bend which continued to curve away to the left for a considerable distance on the other side of the bridge before straightening out again. This meant that anyone or anything, in this case our two selves and our bikes, would be invisible to any following traffic until it was literally on top of us.

It was at this moment, as we emerged from beneath the arch, that I heard Wanda cry out – her actual words were, 'They've killed us, the bastards!' – and the next thing I remember was being literally lifted off the road by what seemed like a giant hand and deposited, lying on my side but still on my bicycle, in something cold and nasty, which turned out to be a mud-filled expanse that had been churned up by vehicles such as this one taking the corner so fine that they had completely destroyed the hard shoulder. The same thing had happened to Wanda. By screwing my head round I could see the light from her bicycle's headlamp, but I could see and hear nothing else because of the pandemonium on the road and I had a terrible feeling of panic, afraid that she might be either dead or badly injured.

'Are you all right?' I shouted and heard her shout back 'Yes' and something else extremely rude and knew that she was. Like me, she was still on her bicycle, lying on her left side in the ditch, half buried in mud, but miraculously alive and uninjured. If there had been any trees on the roadside for us to be hurled against we would have been goners.

The question was, how long could we continue to stay where

we were and still remain alive? The trucks and trailers were still coming, their drivers changing down before the bridge on the downhill stretch, then screaming round the corner under it, hugging it close and blinding us with their headlights.

I had a job to get the bikes out. Both the front nearside panniers had jumped off the carriers and were sinking in the slime but with the rest of the gear on them both machines were still very heavy. As far as I could make out, they were undamaged, as they had fallen on us and, most important of all at this moment, the rear lights were still working.

When I finally succeeded in getting them out I left Wanda cowering with her bicycle as far from the road as possible and, during a momentary lull in the traffic, I sprinted twenty or thirty yards down the road with my own bike to the point where the road straightened out, and parked it against a tree. Then I went back to fetch Wanda's bike and we both ran for our lives. In doing all this we failed to see the entrance to the lane which led to the farm, or the 'great soign' which was supposed to draw attention to it. Even if we had seen the lane it would have been impossible to turn into it on such a night, as it would have meant crossing both streams of traffic.

The next half-mile was slightly less unpleasant than what had gone before. The road was without any dangerous bends and ran, so far as I could see, through fairly open country, although the trucks kept on coming and there was no footpath to push our bikes along. We were much too unnerved to cycle. We were also covered in mud from head to foot. We passed two small roads which led off to the right, neither of which, although we did not understand the reason at the time, was marked by any sort of 'soign', let alone a great one.

It now began to pour with rain, which was a blessing in that it washed away the worst of the mud from our boots and our Gore-Tex suits, and just as we were beginning to despair of ever finding the right road, we came abreast of a couple of workmen's cottages which stood above the road on the left, one of which had a light in its front room and a front door without a knocker. After battering on it with my fists for some time – the roar of the traffic must have made it almost impossible to hear anything within – it opened to reveal the outline of a tall figure standing against the blacked-out entrance. 'Ah, it's Dilly Griffey you're wanting,' the figure said in the voice of a youngish man. 'You should have turned away at the bridge. You will have to go back to the bridge, now, and you'll see the soign and a road running away up along the railway to the left. It's no distance, with your boikes.'

I wondered if this man, who presumably had been brought up in the automobile age in Ireland, had the slightest idea of what travelling along the N18 at night on a bicycle was like. Or perhaps he had. Perhaps he was one of those cyclists one encounters in rural Ireland on wet nights who wear black suits, long black overcoats and black caps with buttons on and who wobble down the middle of the road on machines without any sort of lights or reflectors, yet are somehow never touched, let alone blown off them, knocked down and 'kilt'. Whatever he was, I told him that nothing would persuade us to go back to the bridge. Was there no other way of getting to it?

'Well, there is,' he said. 'You can take the next right down past Ballyline House – you'll be knowing Ballyline House, no doubt – then you don't take the road to Dromore or Ruan, but the one up the hill and you'll be there. There's a soign for it.'

So we did another half mile on the road, then scuttled across it into a lane which led past an expensive-looking illuminated blur to the left which was presumably Ballyline House, in which I imagined Anglo-Irish ladies with high voices and men wearing waistcoats and watch chains downing Beefeater's gin and Glenlivet. Then we turned sharp right up a nasty hill (anything not dead flat was nasty by this time) past a conifer plantation. Half way up it we met a man with an electric torch who had the impertinence (or perhaps he was feeble-minded), since it had only stopped pouring with rain a few seconds previously, to say that it was a grand noight – grand noight for what? Murder? He also said that the farm was down the hill on the other side, a bit, and that there was a crossroads and a 'soign', and we couldn't miss it.

At the crossroads, using my bicycle lamp and promising to buy myself a pocket torch for map reading at noight on future events such as this, I eventually discovered the soign, which was not at all that great, coyly hidden in a hedgerow, half-covered by vegetation and pointing uphill in the general direction of Ballyline House, the way by which we had come.

I felt my reason going. Perhaps it had, already. Was I already one with the great Gaels of Ireland, the men that God made mad, as most of the other Gaels I had met on this, my first day in Ireland, appeared to be?

I told Wanda to stay where she was at the crossroads and guard herself, the soign and her boike, and let no one take any of them away, or otherwise interfere with them. Then I engaged the lowest gear at my disposal and pedalled away uphill in pursuit of the man with the torch who had so foully misused us. By the time I had climbed it and gone down the other side and caught up with him he was practically at Ballyline House. Perhaps he was on his way there to tell the assembled house party what a trick he had played on two foreigners. 'Ah,' he said courteously, 'I should have told you about the soign. It should point left at the cross but then the wind catches and turns it back on itself. It often happens with it. It's a strange thing.'

I went back up the hill, past the conifers, and down the other side to the crossroads where Wanda, like the Roman soldier faithful unto death at Pompeii, kept her vigil, and told her that it was left at the crossroads we had to turn, to which she replied that it all depended whether he meant left going towards Ballyline House or left going away from it.

We plumped for the latter, and tackled another steep hill, from the top of which, to our inexpressible relief, we could see the lights of the farm shining in a hollow below.

We were welcomed by Mrs Griffey's small grandson, Gary, an enthusiastic cyclist who was so enamoured of Wanda's pint-sized mountain bike that he wanted immediately to ride away into the boondocks on it, and by Mrs Griffey's grown-up son, Tom, who had been lying on a sofa watching telly with his shoes off and who said it was a funny thing about the soign that the wind always twisted it. Present also was Mrs Griffey's daughter-in-law, the girl to whom I had spoken on the telephone, who said she would cook the food Wanda had brought at the supermarket.

After all this, and a couple of very hot baths (hot baths, as we subsequently discovered, being something of a rarity in Irish B and Bs, especially in winter) we went to bed, whacked, although altogether we had only covered about thirty-five miles. By now it was a fine night and a moon in its last quarter shone down from a sky filled with stars in the last hours of my birthday, which I shared with Henry VI, born 1421, and Warren Hastings, born 1732. If the next ten days in Ireland produced cycling anywhere near as exciting as this evening's we would probably be dead before Christmas.

Chapter 4

ROUND THE BURREN

The Burren, 'of which it is said that it is a country where there is not water enough to drown a man, wood enough to hang one, nor earth enough to bury him, which last is so scarce that the inhabitants steal it from each other, and yet their cattle are very fat, for the grass growing in tufts of earth of two or three foot square that lie between the rocks which are of limestone, is very sweet and nourishing.'

Memoirs of EDMUND LUDLOW, one of Cromwell's generals

The following morning we woke around seven-thirty to find brilliant sunshine pouring in through the bedroom windows. Anxious to make the most of the day, we got dressed and went downstairs to find no one about, except Gary, the grandson of the house, a fount of energy and of information about everything connected with the property and its occupants.

'It'll be a good bit yet before you get a sniff of your breakfast,' he put it, picturesquely; and indeed it was ten o'clock before it finally appeared, or indeed there were any signs of life at all. It had certainly been a working farm when we had stayed on it last, but now showed signs, in spite of a tractor parked outside, of being an erstwhile one.

Inside, the house was still much as we remembered it, almost twenty years previously, enlarged but still homely and welcoming. The most recent acquisition appeared to be a set of large armchairs, upholstered in delicate green velvet, which would make a happy stamping ground for dogs whose owners had forgotten to bring their dog baskets and for children equipped with bubble gum and muddy rubber boots. Mrs Griffey now appeared, after her late night out with Pan Am, and gave us a warm welcome. Her husband, whom we remembered well, had been dead for some years.

How did we come to stay in this remote, pleasant spot in the first place? Back in 1964 the Irish Tourist Board began to compile a list of farmhouses and other houses in rural situations whose owners were prepared to take in visitors, and at the same time provide a certain modicum of comfort for them, which might or might not be forthcoming if anyone knocked on a door at random and unannounced.

To encourage the farmers' wives and others on whom the brunt of the work would fall, and to give them confidence in their abilities and the opportunity to exchange ideas, courses were arranged in a large country house near Drogheda in County Louth, with the cooperation of the Irish Countrywomen's Association. The courses lasted a week, which was reckoned to be about as long as the average Irish farmer could survive with his family but without his wife. They were a great success: among other subjects they dealt with cookery, interior decoration and household management. The culmination was the answering of an impossibly difficult letter from an apprehensive potential guest. As a result of all this a tremendous esprit de corps was built up among the ladies who had been on what they proudly referred to as 'The Course'.

As a result, the number of recommended farmhouses rose rapidly. The only trouble was that the guests failed to materialize. Understandably, after the expenditure of so much effort and money by all concerned, depression reigned. Alarmed at their lack of success the Irish Tourist Board asked me, in my then capacity as Travel Editor of the *Observer*, if I would like to visit some of these houses and see for myself what I thought of them. They produced a complete list, helped me to whittle it down to about thirty, and then left Wanda and myself to get on with it in our own way.

It was an extraordinarily interesting experience. Some were working farms with eighteenth- or nineteenth-century buildings, such as the one we were now staying in. Some were not farms at all but quite large country houses, standing in their own parklands, and with or without farms and rambling outbuildings. Some were neat and modern bungalows, rather early prototypes of those we had passed the previous day on the way from Sixmilebridge to Quin, some with plastic gnomes in their front gardens, which were fashionable then. Indistinguishable from ordinary B and Bs, we gave them a miss.

All had one thing in common: they were very clean. Many had washbasins in the bedrooms; others had vast bathrooms with washbasins like fonts, and baths commodious enough to hold a baby whale. In one of them the lavatory was on a dais in a long, narrow chamber so far from the door that, installed on it, I was in a perpetual state of uncertainty as to whether or not I had locked myself in. Students of early plumbing, I noted, would find a visit to such houses worthwhile for these features alone.

Some of the most modest-looking houses concealed within them beautiful fireplaces and remarkable furniture, some of it very fine, some very eccentric, such as bog oak bookcases and extraordinary what-nots. The interior decorations were unpredictable. Some of the ladies, after being visited by a representative of the Tourist Board, panicked and replaced their nice old floral wallpaper with contemporary stuff covered with designs of Dubonnet bottles and skyscrapers, and coated the slender glazing bars of their eighteenth-century windows with a thick coating of bilious yellow paint.

In the course of our journey we played croquet and tennis, got stung by bees, struck up friendships with various donkeys, one of which was called Noël, and innumerable tame rabbits, puppies and dogs. Often there was riding, which we were no good at, and fishing, at which we were not much better but which we enjoyed.

And there was the food, which was always abundant, too abundant. I was anxious to do my best by the ladies but it was not always possible to be kind and at the same time truthful. When it came to bacon, ham, eggs and sausages, soda bread and butter, home-made cakes, jam and cream, everything was fine. Let them loose on a steak, a piece of meat to roast, or even on a cut of freshly landed salmon, and they would turn it into something that resembled an old tobacco pouch, which is, I am sorry to say, in my own judgment, the story of Irish cooking. In spite of this they did me the honour of referring to me very kindly in their brochure, by which time the scheme had become a resounding success.

What followed was what lawyers call a *dies non*, a day on which no legal business may be transacted (a prohibition which has the effect of making them bad-tempered), and what I call a no-day. In some mysterious way, although some parts of it were pleasant, altogether it added up to a day with something wrong with it, and it made us bad-tempered too.

After breakfast that almost qualified as lunch we set off in the brilliant sunshine on a circular tour of the middle part of the nameless plain which extends from the Shannon to the Bay of Galway, or as much of it as we could manage. No sooner had we got to the 'soign' at the cross-roads than a downpour of tropical intensity began to fall on us, but by the time we had both struggled into our rainproof suits (the trousers, although made ample on purpose, are particularly difficult to get into when wearing climbing boots) it had stopped and Wanda insisted on taking her trousers off. Within a couple of minutes it began to rain all over again, so she put them back on. The trouble was it was unseasonably warm with it, and in the sort of conifer woods which should only be allowed in Scandinavia, Russia, Siberia, the Yukon and Canada the insects were beginning to tune up for what they apparently thought was the onset of summer. At this point I took my waterproof trousers off. All this effort to see Dromore, a castle of the O'Briens, in a region where castles, except as appendages to the landscape, or notably eccentric, can easily become a bit of a drug on the market.

We pedalled on through these endless woods and past Bally-teige Lough and fissured beds of grey, karstic limestone, du-plicates of similar beds in the Kras, in Wanda's native Slovenia, to which so many times in the course of our life together she had threatened to return, leaving me for ever. Then on past a couple more castles and across a snipe bog on a narrow causeway, with Ballylogan Lough beyond it, golden in the sun, and ahead the mountains of the Burren, stretching across the horizon as far as the eye could see like a fossilized tidal wave. Overhead, clouds with liver-covered undersides, pink on the upper parts where the sun caught them, drifted majestically eastwards. Here it was colder. I put on my trousers again.

In the middle of this bog, we met three young men gathered round a tractor who stopped talking when we passed them and didn't reply when we said it was a lovely day, something so unusual in our admittedly still limited experience of talking to the natives that it gave us both the creeps – another nail in the coffin of the no-day. Dogs to match them emerged from a farm on the far side of the bog and tried to take chunks out of our costly Gore-Tex trousers.

Beyond the bog was Coolbaun, a hamlet in which most of the houses were in ruins. In it the minute Coolbaun National School, built in 1895 and abandoned probably some time in the 1950s, still had a roof, and its front door was ajar. Inside there was a bedstead, a table with two unopened tins of soup on it, a raincoat hanging on a nail and a pair of rubber boots. It was like finding a footprint on a desert island. Hastily, we beat a retreat.

The first real village we came to was Tubber, a place a mile long with a pub at either end (neither of which had any food on offer), in fact so long that on my already battered half-inch map one part of it appeared to be in Clare, the other in Galway. The pub nearest to Galway was terribly dark, as if the proprietor catered only for spiritualists; the other had three customers all glued to the telly watching a steeplechase, none of whom spoke to us even between races. Meanwhile we drank, and ate soda bread and butter and spam bought in the village shop. 'Is this what they call "Ireland of the Welcomes?"' Wanda asked with her mouth full. Another coffin nail.

The nicest looking places in Tubber were the post office and Derryvowen Cottage, which was painted pink and which we passed on the way to look for something marked on the map as O'Donohue's Chair. What is or was O'Donohue's Chair? No guide book that I have ever subsequently been able to lay my hands on refers to it. Is it, or was it, some kind of mediaeval hot seat stoked with peat? Or a throne over an oubliette that precipitates anyone who sits on it into the bottomless rivers of the limestone karst? Whatever it is, if it isn't the product of some Irish Ordnance Surveyor's imagination, further inflamed by a spam lunch in Tubber, it is situated in a thicket impenetrable to persons wearing Gore-Tex suits, and hemmed in by an equally impenetrable hedge reinforced with old cast iron bedsteads, worth a bomb to any tinker with a pair of hedging gloves.

After this, misled by two of the innocent-looking children in which Ireland abounds – leprechauns in disguise – we made an equally futile attempt to see at close quarters Fiddaun Castle, another spectacular tower house more or less in the same class as the unfindable Danganbrack. 'Sure and you can't miss it. It's up there and away down,' one of these little dumplings said, while the other sucked her thumb, directing us along a track that eventually became so deep in mire that it almost engulfed us. From the top of the hill they indicated, however, we did have a momentary view of the Castle and of Lough Fiddaun to the north, with three swans floating on it, before the whole scene was obliterated by a hellish hailstorm.

The next part of our tour was supposed to take in the monastic ruins of Kilmacduagh, over the frontier from Clare in Galway. However, one more December day was beginning to show signs of drawing to a close, and so we set off back in the direction of Crusheen. It really had been a no-day. Not only had we not seen the Kilmacduagh Monastery, but we had not seen, as we had planned to do, the early nineteenth-century castle built by John Nash for the first Viscount Gort on the shores of Lough Cutra, similar to the one he built at East Cowes on the Isle of Wight, now scandalously demolished; or the Punchbowl, a series of green, cup-shaped depressions in a wood of chestnut and beech trees where the River Beagh runs through a gorge 80 feet deep and disappears underground, perhaps to flow beneath O'Donohue's Chair; or Coole Park, the site of the great house which was the home of Augusta, Lady Gregory, whose distinguished guests, among them Shaw, O'Casey, W. B. and J. B. Yeats, AE (George) Russell and Katherine Tynan – a bit much to have all of them together, one would have thought – used a giant copper beech in the grounds as a visitors' book. To see all these would have taken days at the speed we were travelling. Well, we would never see them now.

So home to dinner, after which Tom took us to Saturday evening Mass in Crusheen. His mother was going the following morning, but if you attended Mass on Saturday evening you didn't have to do so again on Sunday. If asked, he said, we were to say that he too had been present. Meanwhile, he headed for Clark's, to which most of my own impulses were, I admit, to accompany him.

The church was almost full; and the subject of the sermon was Temperance, an obligatory one in Ireland for the First Sunday in Advent. This being Saturday, perhaps the priest was giving it a trial run. He certainly had a large enough audience for it. He was a formidable figure, this priest. Was he, I wondered, the same one we encountered in O'Hagerty's taking a dim view of the contents of a collection box? To me priests in mufti look entirely different when robed. Ireland, he said, was as boozy as Russia – a bit much, I thought, to accuse any country of being, with the possible exception of Finland. He then went on to castigate the licensed trade as spreaders of evil, something I have always fervently believed myself. If any Guinnesses had been present they would have been writhing with embarrassment. 'Just too awful,' I could imagine them saying, but then one imagines that any Catholic Guinnesses, if such there be, give the First Sunday in Advent and the Saturday preceding it a miss. And there were prayers for the wives of drunks, but none for the drunks themselves, or the husbands of drunks, all of whom I would have thought were equally in need of them.

We were in bed by nine-thirty, slept nine hours and woke to another brilliant day, this time completely cloudless. After another good breakfast, we set off on what, for Wanda, proved to be a really awful four-mile uphill climb to Ballinruan, a lonely hamlet high on the slopes of the Slieve Aughty Mountains, where a Sunday meet of the County Clare Foxhounds was to take place. Its cottages were rendered in bright, primary colours, or finished in grey pebbledash – one house was the ghostly silver-grey of an old photographic plate. The church sparkled like icing sugar in the sunshine, and across the road from it, in Walsh's Lounge Bar and Food Store, four old men, all wearing caps, were drinking whiskey and stout and sharing a newspaper between them.

The view from the village was an amazing one. Behind it gentle slopes led up to a long, treeless ridge; immediately below it, and on either side, the ground was rougher, with outcrops of rock – a wilderness of gorse and heather interspersed with stunted, windswept trees. Out beyond this a vast landscape opened up: the level plain, part of which we had travelled through with so many setbacks the previous day. Its innumerable loughs, now a brilliant Mediterranean blue, blazed among green fields of irregular shape, bogs, woodlands and tracts of limestone, with here and there a white cottage or the tower of a castle rising among them.

And beyond all this, the far more immense bare limestone expanses of the Burren rose golden in the morning sunlight; Galway Bay could just be seen to the north-west; while to the south, beyond the Shannon, were the hills and mountains of County Limerick, their feet shrouded in a mist which gave an impression of almost tropical heat.

At twelve-thirty the hounds arrived in a big van, very well behaved, and soon more vans and horse boxes trundled up the hill, some drawn by Mercedes. Here, the hunt was more or less on the extreme limits of its territory. It normally hunted over stone walls on the west side of the County, and over banks and fly fences on the east and south. The rough country round us, on the other hand, might give shelter to hordes of hill foxes. Anyway, they were safe today. This was a drag hunt in which the hounds would follow an artificial scent.

By one o'clock those horses still in their boxes were becoming impatient, kicking the sides of them, and catching the air of excitement that was gradually gathering in the street outside. People were beginning to saddle up and mount now, especially the children, of whom there were quite a number. A big van with four horses in it arrived and one of their owners said to the driver, 'It's a lovely day! Let's go and have a jar now in Walsh's.' By now the bar was splitting at the seams.

This was not a smart hunt such as the County Galway, otherwise known as the Blazers, the County Limerick, the Kildare, or the Scarteen, otherwise the Black and Tans. It was not the sort of hunt that Empress Elizabeth of Austria, who loved hunting in Ireland more than anything else on earth and was so proud of her figure that she had herself sewn into her habit every hunting day, would have patronized. Most were in black jackets and velvet caps, some were in tweeds, others wore crash helmets, and one man with a craggy, early nineteenth-century face wore a bowler. One man in a tweed coat sounded suspiciously like a Frenchman, there was an elegant American girl in a tweed coat, and what looked like several members of the scrap metal business. A cosmopolitan lot.

The hounds were released; there were eight and a half couple of them, which is a hunter's way of saying seventeen. After a brief period in which they were allowed to savour delicious smells, one of the Joint Masters, who was wearing a green coat with red facings and black boots with brown tops, took them up the road to cries of what sounded like, 'Ged in! Ged in!' and 'Ollin! Ollin!' Then they were suddenly turned, and ran back down the street through a press of people and out through the village, down and over the flanks of Derryvoagh Hill and into the eye of the now declining sun. Soon they were lost to view to us and other followers, watching their progress from one of the rocks below the village.

'By God,' someone said, 'the next thing we'll be hearing of them they'll be in America.'

I left Wanda to take the long downhill back to Crusheen and the farm, where Tom was very kindly waiting to take her to Ballyvaughan, on the shores of Galway Bay, where we were going to stay for a few days. Then I, too, zoomed downhill bound for the Monastery of Kilmacduagh, which we had failed to see the previous day. I was so exhilarated by the fast cooling air that I almost felt I was flying.

Six miles out as the crow flies from Ballinruan, I zoomed past the site of a ruined castle on the shores of Lough Bunny, then right, past a field in which a small boy was trying to catch a wild-looking horse and bridle it, the Burren blue-black against the setting sun, the plain close under it already in shadow, and on, having missed the road to Kilmacduagh, through the bare, limestone karst from which black and white cattle were somehow scratching a living, spotting an occasional small white farmhouse in what was effectively a limestone desert. Suddenly, there was the monastery, far off to the right across a wide expanse of limestone pavement riven with deep, parallel crevices that looked like an ice floe breaking up: a collection of silver-grey buildings with the last of the sunlight illuminating the conical cap of its enormously tall round tower – 112 feet high and two feet out of the perpendicular. This was the monastery founded in the sixth century by Guaire

Aidhneach, King of Connacht (I was now just in Galway and therefore in the old County of Connacht) for his kinsman St Colman Macduagh, on the very spot where the saint's girdle fell to the ground. The girdle was preserved in the monastery until the seventeenth century.

I pedalled on for another four or five miles through the bare limestone plain, the only visible living things in it now blackbirds and rooks. The last of the sun on this beautiful day was shining on the high, treeless tops of the Burren mountains, so convincingly sculpted by nature into the forms of prehistoric camps and forts that it was difficult to know whether I was looking at the work of nature or of man.

At the intersection of this loneliest of lonely roads with the main road, I nearly ran into the car in which Tom was taking Wanda and her bicycle to Ballyvaughan, together with Gary, the infant prodigy. A signpost still showed thirteen miles to Ballyvaughan and I cycled on, a bit tired, through a landscape by now an improbable shade of purple. I passed a wild-looking girl on a bicycle, and saw two young men in an enclosure full of rocks pushing them to one side with a bulldozer, the only way in the Burren, which is Ireland's largest rockery, in which you can ever create a field. Until the invention of the bulldozer the inhabitants of the Burren removed all the rocks by hand, either using them for building walls or forming great mounds with them, which are still to be seen. In those days it would have required the help of many people, possibly an entire community, to make a field; now most of those people are either dead or emigrated or both.

The road ran close under the Burren mountains now and along the side of Abbey Hill, which conceals within its folds the beautiful, pale, lichen-encrusted ruins of Corcomroe, a Cistercian abbey built by a king of Munster. High above it, on a saddle, are the three ruined twelfth-century churches of Oughtmama, all that remain of yet another monastery of St Colman Macduagh. To the right, fields of an almost impossible greenness ran down to the shores of Aughinish and Corranroo Bays, long, beautiful, secretive inlets from Galway Bay. Then a delicious descent to a little hamlet called Burren, beside a reedy pond. Then up and down again to Bell Harbour on Poulnaclough Bay; the water in it like steel, with the mountains black above it and above that cobalt clouds against an otherwise pale sky in which Venus was suspended. When it comes to thoroughly unnatural effects it is possible to equal Ireland, difficult to surpass it.* By the time I got to Ballyvaughan I had covered forty-five miles and it was dark.

*I wondered what Evelyn Waugh would have thought of it. He had a nasty experience of an aesthetic sort, watching a sunset over Mount Etna. 'Nothing I have ever seen in Art or Nature was quite so revolting,' he wrote.

Chapter 5

LAND OF SAINTS AND HERMITS

Stony seaboard, far and foreign,
Stony hills poured over space,
Stony outcrop of the Burren,
Stones in every fertile place,
Little fields with boulders dotted,
Grey-stone shoulders saffron-spotted,
Stone-walled cabins thatched with reeds,
Where a Stone Age people breeds
The last of Europe's stone age race.

JOHN BETJEMAN. 'Sunday in Ireland', *Selected Poems*, 1948

The whitewashed cottage we were to stay in (looking at it no one would have guessed that it was built with breeze blocks), at which Wanda had already arrived in Tom's car, with her bike strapped precariously on top, had a thatched roof and a green front door with a top and bottom part that could be opened separately so that if you opened the bottom and kept the top closed, or vice versa, you looked from the outside as if you had been sawn in half.

The ceiling of the principal living room went right up to the roof and was lined with pine. The floor was of big, olive-coloured grit flagstones from the Cliffs of Moher, and there was an open fireplace with a merry fire burning in it, fuelled by blocks of compressed peat. There was a large table which would have been ideal if I had actually been going to write a book instead of thinking about doing so, which I could do better in bed, and traditional chairs with corded backs and seats. To be authentic they should have been upholstered with plaited straw, but straw had apparently played hell with the guests' nylons.

The rugs on the floor, all made locally in County Cork, were of plaited cotton which produced a patchwork effect, and there were oil lamps on the walls with metal reflectors behind the glass shades, but wired for electricity. A wooden staircase led to a room above with two beds in it, the equivalent of a mediaeval solar. Leading off the living room was a very well-fitted kitchen, and there were two more bedrooms on the ground floor: altogether, counting a sofa bed and a secret bed that emerged from a cupboard, there were eight, a lot of beds for the two of us. The rooms, primarily intended for the visiting Americans, could be made fantastically hot: they had under-floor heating, convectors, a portable fan heater upstairs, infra-red heating in the bathroom, plus the open fire. Gary was bowled over by all this. He was even more pleased with it than we were. 'Never,' he said, 'in all my born days' had he seen anything like it.

'When I get married,' he confided, 'I'm going to bring my wife here for our honeymoon.'

'How old did you say you are?'

'Eight.'

'Tell me,' I said, 'is there any girl you really like?'

'There's one in First Grade. I like her.'

'How old is she?'

'About six.'

'But would you marry her?'

'I would not.'

'Why wouldn't you?'

'Because she's an O'Hanrahan. You can't marry an O'Hanrahan in the parts we come from.'

Later, after he had eaten three apples, a banana and a large plate of salted nuts and drunk three large bottles of Coke, left as a welcoming present by the proprietors (together with a bottle of gin for us), Wanda asked him if he spoke Gaelic.

'No way!' he said firmly.

'But I thought they taught you Gaelic in school.'

'No, they only teach us Irish,' he said.

After this we went to a pub where he ate all the nuts on sale there and drank three large orange juices.

Ballyvaughan is a small village and one-time fishing port. Until well into the twentieth century it imported Galway turf for fuel in sailing vessels called hookers – something which makes Americans when they read about them or see a rare survivor go off into peals of laughter – exporting in return grain, bacon and vegetables. Until the First World War and for some time after it there was a regular steamship service to and from Galway in the summer months.

There was not much of Ballyvaughan but what there was we liked: two streets of cottages and shops, one of them running along the shore with a pub restaurant at the western end, open most of the year, which served fish. In the other street there was the post office, Claire's Place, a restaurant now closed for the winter, a couple of miniature supermarkets and two of the four pubs. Of the pubs, O'Lochlan's was of the sort that in Ireland was already a rarity: dark in the daytime behind the engraved glass panel in its front door; at night still dark but glittering with light reflected off a hundred bottles and off the glasses and the brass handles of the black wooden drawers stacked one above the other like those in an old-fashioned apothecary's shop. Behind the bar was a turf-burning stove which kept whoever was serving warm.

The equivalent of Piccadilly Circus in Ballyvaughan was where the roads from Galway and Ennis met; the equivalent of Eros was a monument-cum-fountain equipped with faucets in the shape of lions' heads erected in 1874 by Colonel the Hon. Charles Wynn, son of the Baron Newborough, who at that time was Lieutenant of Clare. Behind the village the steep, terrace limestone slopes of a mountain called Cappanawalla, which means 'the stony tillage lands', rose 1200 feet above it.

Our cottage stood in a meadow in which cows grazed and overlooked one of the two jetties in the harbour which, apart from one fishing boat, was empty. Beyond it was the expanse of Galway Bay and beyond that again, the best part of forty miles away and barely visible, the Twelve Bens of Connemara, at the feet of which, completely invisible, was the Lough of Ballynahinch. This still held the record for having more rainy days in a year than anywhere else in the United Kingdom and Ireland – 309 in 1923 – and was somewhere that I felt we should do our best to avoid.

The next morning was cold, cloudless and brilliant with an east wind, and with what looked like a vaporous wig of mist on the mountains above. While we were eating rashers and eggs we received a visit from an elderly man wearing a long black overcoat and cap to match who offered to sell me a walking stick he had made – one of the last things I really needed, travelling on a bicycle. 'I'll bring you a pail of mussels this evening, if you like,' he said, negotiations having fallen flat on the blackthorn. The whole coast was one vast mussel bed where it wasn't knee-deep in oysters, but as the tide was going to be in for most of the morning and it was also very cold, it seemed sensible to let him gather them for us.

Our destination that day was Lisdoonvarna: ' "Ireland's Premier Spa," ' I read to Wanda in excerpts from Murray's *Guide* (1912) over breakfast. ' "Known since the middle of the 18th century . . . situated at a height of about 600 feet above the sea . . . its climate excellent . . . the rainfall never rests long upon the limestone surface. The air, heated by contact with the bare sun-scorched rock of the surrounding district, is tempered by the moisture-laden breezes from the Atlantic three or four miles distant, and is singularly bracing and refreshing owing to the elevation." ' It also spoke of spring water conveyed to the Spa House in glass-lined pipes, thus ensuring its absolute purity. More modern authorities spoke of a rock which discharged both sulphurous and chalybeate (iron) waters, rich in iodine and with radioactive properties, within a few inches of one another, the former to the accompaniment of disgusting smells.

The town was equally famous as a centre of match-making. Farmers in search of a wife were in the habit of coming to stay in the hotels in Lisdoonvarna in September after the harvest; there they found unmarried girls intent on finding themselves a husband. The arrangements were conducted by professional match-makers, in much the same way as sales of cattle and horses are still concluded by professional go-betweens at Irish fairs. This marriage market is still said to thrive, although to a lesser extent than previously. Professional match-makers, masseurs and masseuses, sauna baths, sun lounges, springs, bath and pump houses, cafés, dances and pitch-and-putt competitions, all taking place on a bed of warm limestone – it all sounded a bit like Firbank's *Valmouth*. With the addition of a black masseuse it could have been.

'Did you know,' I said to Wanda, 'that according to the *Illustrated Ireland Guide* "its sulphur water contains more than *three times as much hydrogen sulphide gas as the spring at Harrogate*"?' To which she uttered an exclamation, the equivalent to 'Cor!' in Slovene, which I knew from a lifetime of experience meant that she wasn't in the slightest bit interested.

We set off in the sunshine in the general direction of Lisdoonvarna, this being the nearest thing attainable in this part of the world to going from A to B by the shortest route. All was well at first. The road ran through meadowy country interspersed with hazel thickets, 'fairly level but with a strong upward tendency' as the Cyclists' Touring Club *Irish Road Book* of 1899 rather charmingly put it, en route passing close to the Ailwee Cave, closed for two million years until its discovery in 1976, and now closed again because it was winter.

At this point the 'strong upward tendency' began in earnest – a succession of steep hairpin bends up Corkscrew Hill. At the same moment the sun vanished and we found ourselves in what seemed another world, enveloped in dense, freezing cloud which whirled across our path borne on the wings of the east wind and reduced visibility to not more than twenty yards. In spite of all this, once she had stopped changing up instead of down, and falling off when her Wild Cat subsequently ground to a halt, Wanda very nearly succeeded in winding her way to the top, and only had to get off and push the last fifty yards or so.

From the top, if it really was the top, there was nothing to be seen of the famous view over the Burren to Galway extolled by every guide book. Indeed it was difficult to imagine that on every side now, enveloped in what resembled cold gruel, were a host of natural wonders, some of them so extraordinary as to be positive freaks of nature: what are known – how uncouth the terms used by geologists sometimes sound – as clints, grykes, glacial erratics, and potholes and turloughs (what Wanda knew in her own country as *doline* and *polje*).* Here, the last glaciation took place only about fifteen thousand years ago, making this one of the most recently created landscapes in the whole of Europe. What we were riding over now was hollow; beneath us rivers ran, quite literally, through caverns measureless to man down to a sunless sea.

It was equally difficult to imagine that hidden among these arid rocks, nurtured by often infinitesimal quantities of soil, something like a thousand different species of flowering plants and ferns were

---

Clints are the blocks of limestone paving. *Grykes* are the open crevices in the clints. *Glacial erratics* are rounded blocks of limestone, some of them very large, deposited in the wake of an ice-cap. *Turloughs* are grassy hollows, sometimes created by the collapse of the roof of an underground cavern and often filled with water from below (*doline* being the smaller ones and *polje* the larger ones, the biggest of which is the Carran Depression in the eastern Burren).

waiting for spring and summer to appear, at this meeting place of the northern (Hibernian) flora, brought here in the form of seeds during the last glaciation, and the southern (Lusitanian) flora, which had previously flourished there and continued to do so. Among them were creamy white mountain avens, spring gentians, hoary rockroses, fairy foxgloves, limestone bugles, various violas, greater butterwort, ladies' bedstraw, bloody cranesbill, seven types of orchid and broomrape.

About the only thing currently visible on the High Burren and able to continue growing there throughout the winter was grass. The limestone retains the heat of the summer sun, turning it into a species of giant storage heater and making the hilltops and the higher valleys much warmer than the low-lying country below. For this reason the cattle are left high up to forage for themselves from November to late April and are then taken down to the lowlands for the summer months, the reverse of what happens in most other places. Herds of wild goats perform an invaluable function in keeping down the hazel scrub which rampages in summer.

At this moment, as if wanting to prove to us that they really were living up there, a herd of Burren cattle came sweeping round a corner towards us in close formation, steaming and smoking and completely filling the road, and looking to me very much as the Sixth Iniskilling Dragoons must have done to the French infantry when they were being charged by them on the afternoon of Waterloo. We did what the French would probably have done had it been available: took refuge in the entrance to the Corkscrew Hill National School, built in 1885 and now abandoned, while they thundered past it and on down the hill, apparently unaccompanied, in the direction of Ballyvaughan. Where did they think they were going? To the seaside for a dip?

For the next seven miles the only living soul we met with was a young Australian girl, sopping wet, padding gamely through the muck in her training shoes with a big, rectangular pack on her back the size of a large suitcase. She was a bit pissed off, she said, having been given a lift from Ballyvaughan post office by this old guy who said he was bound for Lisdoonvarna, but then changed his mind and dumped her at a fork in the road, with a six mile hike to go. Unfortunately, there was nothing we could do to help her. 'You should have brought a tandem,' Wanda said to me. 'Then you could have given people lifts.'

Lisdoonvarna, when we reached it after a gratifying downhill run, came as a bit of a shock after all the build-up it had been given by the various guide books I had consulted. In fact I wondered if some of the authors could have been there at all. Admittedly, no resort looks its best in the depths of winter – that is, unless it is a winter resort – and Lisdoonvarna, with the east wind hurrying clouds of freezing vapour through its streets, was no exception. I tried to imagine excited farmers with straw in their hair, accompanied by their match-makers, pursuing unmarried ladies through its streets and down the corridors of the Spa Hotel, which had broken windows and looked as if it would never open again, but failed.

Now, in December, it seemed a decrepit and terribly melancholy place, like the film set of a shanty town. Its hotels, souvenir and fast-food shops had closed down in October and would not re-open until March, some of the hotels not until June. But would what the Irish call the crack – what others call the action – start even then? Rough-looking youths stood on the pavement outside a betting shop, one of the few places open at this hour. The wind struck deep into the marrow of one's bones; in spite of being dressed in almost everything we possessed we were frozen, and took refuge in a pub, the Roadside Tavern, run by two nice ladies, the walls of which were covered with picture postcards. They stoked up the fire for us and we gradually thawed out in front of it while we ate ham and soda bread and I drank the health of the priest at Crusheen in Guinness, while Wanda drank port.

Too fed up with Lisdoonvarna to seek out the various sources of its waters, smelly or otherwise, and the various pleasure domes in which customers were given the treatment, we quitted Ireland's premier spa, and set off westwards up yet another cloud-bound road. Suddenly, as suddenly as we had left it at the foot of Corkscrew Hill, we emerged into dazzling sunshine on the western escarpment of the Burren. Below us it dropped away to a rocky coast on which, in spite of the wind being offshore, heavy seas were breaking, throwing up clouds of glittering spray. Just to look at the shimmering sea after the miseries that had gone before gave us a new lease of life – and we roared down towards it via a series of marvellous bends with the Aztec Super brake blocks on our Shimano Deore XT cantilever brakes screaming (a malfunction) on the Rigida 25/32 rims (for the benefit of those who like a bit of technical detail from time to time), past the ivy-clad tower of Ballynalackan Castle, a fifteenth-century seaside house of the O'Briens perched on a steep-sided rock high above the road, with a magical-looking wood at the foot of it, and on down to the limestone shore.

We were at Poulsallagh, nothing more than a name on the map. Somewhere out to sea to the west, hidden from view in their own mantle of cloud, were the Aran Islands. To the right dense yellow vapour flooded out over the Burren escarpment as if in some First World War gas attack, over a wilderness of stone, interspersed with walled fields and extravagantly painted cottages, their windows ablaze in the light of the declining sun, while high above, squadrons of clouds like pink Zeppelins were moving out over the Atlantic. Here, the haystacks were mound-shaped and covered with nets against the wind, or shaped like upturned boats, hidden behind the drystone walls. To the left, between the road and the sea, were endless expanses of limestone on which the glacial erratics rested, like huge marbles, rolled down from the screes above. Here and there a walled field gave shelter to giant sheep solidly munching the green grass. At Fanore, six miles north of Poulsallagh, we spoke with the first human being we had set eyes on since leaving Lisdoonvarna. He was a small man of about fifty, who was working in a plot beside the road. He had a large head, abundant flaxen hair with a touch of red in it, of the kind that always looks as if it has just been combed, a high forehead and very clear blue eyes like T. E. Lawrence. And he had a voice of indescribable sadness, like the wind keening about a house. After exchanging remarks about the grandness of the day I asked him about the absence of people.

'Ah,' he said, 'there are more than meet the eye; but most of them are old, and are by their fires, out of the wind. You can see the smoke of them.'

'But what about the school? It's quite new. There must be some children,' Wanda said.

'There are children,' he said, 'but when those children leave the school, their parents will leave Fanore, and the school will be closed. They are the last ones.'

'But what will happen to their houses? Surely they won't be allowed to fall into ruin?'

'The old ones will be allowed to fall into ruin. The newer ones will be holiday houses. Many of them are already.'

'And what will you yourself do when the old people are dead, and the children and the younger people have all gone away?'

'I will give an eye to the holiday houses,' he said.

As if to prove his words, a few miles beyond the lighthouse at Black Head we came to a ruined village. Close under the mountain the cottages, or what remained of them, were hidden under trees, moss-grown and covered with ivy, some of it as thick as a man's arm. It was difficult to believe that people had lived in it during our own lifetime. The ruins might have been prehistoric. Down by the water below the road there was a slip, and smooth rocks with numbers and a white cross painted on them. A little further on was a ruined tower with a spiral staircase leading to the upper part, turrets and machicolations. Nearby was an over-grown, roofless church with gravestones in the churchyard that were simply unworked limestone rocks from the Burren; and Tobar Cornan, a holy well with a little Gothic well house, where a human cranium used to serve as a drinking cup until a priest put a stop to the practice.

By the time we got back to Ballyvaughan, having covered a modest thirty-six miles, the wind had dropped completely and in the afterglow the still waters of the bay were the colour of the lees of wine. Thirty thousand feet or so overhead jets bound for the New World drew dead straight orange crayon lines across a sky still blue and filled with sunshine. There was a tremendous silence, broken only by the whistling of the oystercatchers and the gulls foraging in the shallows. The inhabitants of Ballyvaughan were eating their evening meals and watching telly. If we hadn't seen them going about their business we might have thought they were dead. Looking at what they presumably subsisted on lining the shelves of the supermarkets, it was surprising that they weren't. Did they really eat prepacked mashed potato and tins of meat and fish that could easily have doubled as pet food with a change of labels, on which the additives listed by law read like the formula for something nasty?

Famished, we took the edge off our appetites with scones and raspberry jam – the mussels had arrived and stood outside the door in a sack, a huge quantity for £2, enough for two copious meals. Then we went to O'Lochlan's and sat in its magical interior, a bit like an Aladdin's Cave with newspapers on sale. Mr O'Lochlan, it transpired, was a member of one of the historically most powerful septs in this part of the Burren. They had owned the great hazel thickets which still grow at the foot of Cappanawalla, and the great stone fort of Cahermore up among the limestone pavements, and the Ballylaban Ringfort, down near sea level, which contained a single homestead and which, with its earth walls crowned with trees and its moat filled with water, is as romantic as the limestone forts are austere.[*]

Mr O'Lochlan spoke of the past: Ballyvaughan was not a particularly old village, he said; it really dated from the early nineteenth century when a quay was built for the fishing boats. In 1829 or thereabouts this collapsed and a new one had to be built by the Fishery Board. Gleninagh ('Glen of the Ivy'), the deserted village that looked old enough to be a candidate for carbon dating, apparently still had eighty-five men fishing from it in the mid-1930s, using *currachs*, rowing boats consisting of a light framework of laths covered with tarred canvas. In the summer they fished for mackerel, three men to a boat using long lines; in winter, two men to a boat to fish for lobsters, while others dug for worm bait.

I told him what the man at Fanore had said about the school and he had more to add. 'From Loop Head,' he said (which is the extreme south-westerly point of County Clare at the mouth of the

[*]According to Bord Failte's *Ireland Guide*, 1982, there are between 30,000 and 40,000 of these ringforts in Ireland North and South. No one can be sure who lived in most of them, or when: the hundred or more sites excavated in Ireland shows evidence of occupation as early as the Bronze Age and as late as the Middle Ages, the most populous period being the early Christian one.

Shannon), 'very soon you will be able to draw a line five miles inland from the sea, to the west of which, apart from people involved with holidaymakers, there will be no local inhabitants at all.' In the fifteen years from 1963 to 1978 it was thought that two-thirds of the population of marriageable age had emigrated. This tale of woe even extended to the holiday cottage in which we were staying, and its neighbours. They had been built to encourage tourists to visit the area, with money put up by the local inhabitants (who held 60 per cent of the shares), the Irish and regional tourist boards and the local councils; even some local schoolchildren held shares by proxy. But so far none of the locals had had any return on the money they had invested some sixteen years ago, and this had created a great deal of ill-feeling.

After this we went home to a delicious dinner: mussels, very good sausages, runner beans and soda bread, then walked in the rain to the end of the jetty, where the steamers from Galway used to be met by horse cars to convey their passengers to Lisdoonvarna. They had to walk up Corkscrew Hill en route.

That night our dream lives were preoccupied with the Royal Family. I dreamt of King George VI. Both of us were in naval uniform, the King like a brother. As we walked together up Old Bond Street I asked him to have dinner with me, but he said, 'Come and eat with us,' which turned out to be a group of about a dozen at a table under a sort of *porte-cochère*, rather draughty and with no view. At the same time Wanda was dreaming of walking in a garden with the Queen Mum, who was very friendly. Wanda's father featured too, having trouble with a member of the SS. He hit on the idea of having a Mass said, and that, as Wanda said, speaking of the SS man, 'put an end to him!'

It was in fact fortunate that in my dream encounter with King George VI he had not accepted my invitation to lunch. We were now in dire straits for money and I would have looked pretty silly having to borrow from him, especially as English kings and queens never have a bean on them. There was no bank in Ballyvaughan, and my Coutts cheques and various credit cards were treated with extreme suspicion. Finally, Mr O'Lochlan offered to help, provided we could work out what the exchange rate was.

We had intended to seek out together a very esoteric remain

known as St Colman Macduagh's Hermitage which was hidden away at the foot of a mountain called Slieve Carron, but by the time we had negotiated this deal and arranged for a local farmer to give us a lift to Ennistymon the following morning, it was nearly midday. The weather was beautiful, so we decided to go to a place called New Quay on the south side of Galway Bay where we could buy oysters.

New Quay was nice. There was a pub, a house or two, the sheds of the oyster company, and a jetty which the tide was doing its best to sweep away as it came ripping into Aughinish Bay at a terrific rate, covering the dark, whale-like rocks and penetrating into other bays within, Corranroo and Cloosh. On the promontory beyond it was a Martello tower, built to discourage Napoleon from landing an army there. The sea and sky were bright blue and everything else bright green, except for the grey stone walls and buildings, and the rocks along the foreshore.

Three men were working outside one of the sheds, selecting oysters and putting them in sacks. At their destination they would sell for £1 a piece, one of them said. 'Not for the likes of us,' said another. But here Wanda bought a dozen for £3.50 and they threw in two more for luck. Even here, almost at the source, lobsters were £6.50 a pound. Leaving Wanda to ride back to Ballyvaughan, where she had an appointment with a fisherman who might be able to sell her a lobster on more advantageous terms, I set off on my bike for the Hermitage, which was some eight miles off on the east side of the Burren in a wilderness called Keelhilla approached by the first section of a hellish hill, six miles long.

The Hermitage was hidden from view in the hazel thickets at the foot of the cliffs of Slieve Carron, across about three quarters of a mile of limestone pavements full of parallel and apparently bottomless grykes, so I hid my bike in one of the thickets that bordered the road and set off on foot. Some of these grykes had had slender pillars of limestone inserted in them at intervals, as if to mark the way to the Hermitage, but after a bit they came to an abrupt end in the middle of one of the pavements.

I passed a small cairn and came to a drystone wall, beyond which was the wood. Like so many other old walls in the Burren, this one was a work of art. It had been built with an infinite expenditure of effort, using thin flakes of stone set vertically instead of being laid horizontally. I climbed over the wall and went into the hazel wood. It was a magical place. Everything in it – the boles and branches of the trees and the boulders among which they had forced themselves up – was covered in a thick growth of moss, dappled by the last of the sun. The only sounds were those of the wind sighing in the trees and of running water.

By absolute chance I had arrived at the Hermitage. It was in a clearing, among the trees and the boulders. There were the remains of a minute church with a white cross in front of it, and two stone platforms one above the other. The water I had heard came from a spring in the cliff and ran down into a sort of box-shaped stone cistern in a hollow. Above the church in the face of the cliff was a cave, big enough for two people to take shelter in, though in considerable discomfort.

It was in this remote place that St Colman spent seven years of his life with only one companion, sleeping in the cave. Before retiring to his hermitage he founded churches on Inishmore, one of the Aran Islands, and the monastery at Oughtmama. It was for the saint and his companion, slowly dying of starvation in Keelhilla, that angels spirited away the Easter banquet of King Guaire Aidhneach, founder of the Monastery of Kilmacduagh. And it was across the water-eroded beds of karstic limestone known thereafter as Bothar na Mias (the Road of the Dishes) that the King and his followers pursued their banquet, all the way from his castle on the shores of Kinvarra Bay. Here, a *patron*, or parish celebration, is still held on the last Sunday in July.

It was now three-thirty and the sun had left the Hermitage. I retraced my steps across the Road of Dishes, found my bike and continued to climb the awful hill, to a ridge between the Doomore and Gortaclare mountains, where the road, to my horror, began an endless descent into the great, verdant Carran Depression through the whole of which I was pursued by a really savage dog. From it I climbed onto a great, grass-grown plateau that looked like a golden sea in the light of the setting sun, then down again and up again, the map giving no inkling of these awful un-dulations. On the way I passed a wonder called the Caherconnell Ringfort, but was dissuaded from visiting it by yet more wretched dogs which came streaming out of the neighbouring farmyard to attack me at a time when any reasonable dog would have been watching television. By now the sun had gone from the Burren and its expanses were, apart from the dogs, silent and mysterious. By now I was fed up with hills and was grateful for what followed, a wonderful, five-mile descent from the escarpment all the way to Ballyvaughan in the dusk, to find that Wanda's lobster catch had failed to appear. It didn't matter — we still had half a sack of mussels to get through.

The following morning, with fully laden bikes, we embarked in the farmer's Volkswagen van, bound for the town of Ennistymon. The sky was overcast, the wind now westerly and it looked like rain. In other words it was a grand, Irish day.

There was another passenger — a friend of the farmer's who was, he alleged, 'just going up the road a bit to take a look at his sheep'. In fact his 'up the road a bit' comprehended almost the entire journey. He settled himself firmly in front next to the driver, so that I found myself, having paid for the van hire, crouching in the back holding up the bikes and trying to avoid being stabbed to death by brake levers. As a result, I saw nothing and he got an additional eyeful of the scenery he saw every day of his life.

The driver, who was short on conversation, was in a hurry to return to his fields, so I failed to get him to stop at Cahermacnaghten, yet another ringfort with immensely thick, high walls which stands high up in the Burren, five miles from anywhere. All I saw of it as we roared past was a gateway, a white farmhouse and a grove of windswept trees. Just as with Caherconnel, I had never had any luck with Cahermacnaghten. The last time I had tried to visit it I had been beset by a tribe of tinkers and their flaxen-haired children who were camped with their carts close by, and had literally had to run for it.

It was a pity. Cahermacnaghten was more than just another Irish fort. From mediaeval times until late in the seventeenth century it housed within its walls a law school run by the O'Davorens, known as O'Davoren's Town, as unlikely a situation for a law school as the middle of Dartmoor. It was here that Dubhaltach MacFirbhisigh studied, the distinguished compiler of *Craobha Coibhneasa Agas Geuga Geneluigh Gacha Gabhala dar*

75

Ghabh Ere, otherwise *The Branches of Kindred and Genealogical Boughs of Every Plantation in Ireland*, which he completed in 1650. His family were the hereditary historians of the O'Dubha chieftains in what is now County Sligo; it was they who performed their initiation ceremonies by raising a wand above their heads and pronouncing their names. They were also responsible for an extensive collection of historical, genealogical and ecclesiastical writings in both prose and verse. After the dispossession of the O'Dubha in 1643, soon after the commencement of the Eleven Years War, Duald MacFirbis (as he was known) continued to work in Galway and later in Dublin. At the age of eighty-five he was stabbed to death in Doonflin, County Sligo, by a drunken Englishman who had been attempting to kiss a shop assistant and regarded MacFirbis as a witness to this shameful act who would be better dead.

At Kilfenora, a village about five miles short of Ennistymon, the driver stopped to fill up with petrol and we made a desperate dash for liberty, taking refuge in the Cathedral of St Fachtna, or what was left of it. In the chancel was a pair of tomb effigies: one of a bishop, said to be the saint, who founded a monastery and what became a famous theological school at Rosscarbery in County Cork, in the act of blessing all and sundry; another of a weird figure with an immensely elongated neck and head, apparently wearing a kilt. 'You know who the Bishop of Kilfenora is?' the man at the pump said when we got back to the van (the whole visit had taken just over two and a half minutes – see Ireland and die of heart failure). 'The Pope.' I'm still pondering this gnomic utterance. There was also a Burren Museum which I would have liked to have seen, but it was shut for the winter. All the shops were shut, too, and apart from the pump attendant there was not a living soul in sight.

By the time we got to Ennistymon and had been deposited at the top of its main street by a large Gothic Protestant church with an octagonal tower and a handless clock face, it was eleven o'clock and the first shops up at this end of the town were beginning to show tentative signs of opening, like early daffs. We put up at Mrs

Mary MacMahon's B and B which was situated in Church Street above a pub of the same name, of which her husband was the proprietor.

We were given a room next door to the TV Room on one of the upper floors. The TV Room was unlike any other TV Room I had ever seen. It was full of religious images executed in plaster-of-Paris, all balanced on a rather precarious-looking what-not, and on a facing wall was a large oleograph of Jesus with his heart exposed and flames coming out of it, surrounded by a circle of thorns with a cross on top. There was a lot of blood about. Religion was everywhere. Even the lavatory had the Virgin and Child of Kiev balanced on top of a spare roll of paper on top of the cistern, which made use of the arrangements extremely hazardous. In fact as soon as I set eyes on it I began to rehearse how I would break the bad news to Mrs MacMahon, who was religious and nice with it, that her picture of the Virgin and Child of Kiev had just fallen down the hole, and please where could I find the nearest religious picture repository for a replacement.

Fifteen years ago Ennistymon, which at the last count had 1013 inhabitants, had forty-eight pubs. According to Mr MacMahon, when they were last counted, a few days previously, there were twenty-one – out of a total in Southern Ireland of 10,000 (in 1985 there were 11,000) and numbers were closing every day. The town is also famous for some of the best shop fronts in Ireland. On the left-hand side going down Church Street was C. O'Lochlen, Draper and Outfitter, with what was probably Mr O'Lochlen transferring some of his stock on to the pavement outside, having come to the risky conclusion that it wouldn't rain today. Down from him was Keane's, Saddler and Harnessmaker; a butcher who described himself as a victualler; Nagles, a pub that was also, conveniently, an undertakers; and on down the road, in a little square, Killybegs Fresh Fish Stall was doing a brisk trade.

On the right hand was C. Hayes, with a perfect austere pub façade, bottles of Paddy in the window and a dim interior full of drink, which never opened during our stay and now probably never would; the premises of Twoney Walsh, Outfitter and Draper, in which Wanda brought a two-yard skirt length of expensive-looking tweed for £9. Next to that, more or less in the same line of business, was T. J. Mahoney, who emerged from his premises to present her with a card on which was printed '*Very Special Value – T. J. Mahoney*'. The drapers in Ennistymon carried stocks that would have made department store buyers curl up and die from apprehension. One of them, in a town with a thousand inhabitants, stocked five sixty-yard lengths of identical material all in the same colour. Others had enormous stocks of shoes and clothing in outmoded styles and would, I felt, if asked, produce a pair of 1950s winkle-pickers at the drop of a hat.

And so on, past more pubs, open and shut, for sale and haunted, than I had physique to visit and record, among them E. Burke, with another beautiful façade. Then Considine and Sons, a pub now a gift shop;* Hyne's, mysterious dark façade, closed, use unknown; Vaughan's, black-shuttered and said by an old man with a bike to be haunted, also use unknown; Nagle's Bar, 'Traditional Musicians Welcome', closed and for sale; McGrotty's Medical Hall, open; O'Leary's Undertakers with the smallest possible window filled with artificial flowers. Here at the far end of Church Street, perched on a hill, were the remains of a church and a cemetery.

Downstream of the bridge, which spanned the falls of the Cullenagh river, was the old Falls Hotel standing among magnificent trees on the right bank, and on the left bank was a betting shop housed in a black, corrugated iron shed, and an old house with windows painted so that it looked as if people were looking out of them. The Catholic Church, built in 1953, was much more attractive than any other modern Catholic Church we had so far seen in Ireland.

Photographs taken in the 1930s showed Church Street on market day filled with horse-drawn vehicles and people. It was a bit different now.

---

*A pub in Ireland can sell anything. In Kinvarra, where King Guaire Aidhneach had his Easter Banquet spirited away by angels, there was a dark, cavernous pub that had its windows dressed with cans of weedkiller.

Chapter 6

IN THE STEPS OF ST BRIGID

The fairies, the whole pantheon of Irish demigods are retiring, one by one from the habitations of man to the distant islands where the wild waves of the Atlantic raise their foaming crests, to render their fastnesses inaccessible to the schoolmaster and the railroad engineer.

W. R. WILDE. *Irish Popular Superstitions,* 1852

After eating well for £3.50 in what had once been McNulty's pub, now a fish and chip shop and takeaway crowded with schoolchildren playing the machines with their dinner money, we started out for the Cliffs of Moher. We set off, happily, without our luggage, for which we had long since managed to cultivate the sort of loathing that human beings normally reserve for one another. I myself particularly resented having to lug round what amounted to a mobile workshop of tools and spares as well as 14 lbs or so of guide books, most of which I by now realized I could have done without.

The question was which ones could I do without. What would happen to us, for example, if I jettisoned the great, out-of-print *Shell Guide to Ireland*, whose compilers can scarcely have envisaged anyone cycling with it, weighing in as it does at just over 3 lbs? On the contrary, its authors, men such as Lord Killanin and Professor Michael Duignan, probably travelled from cromlech to cromlech in a jaunting car equipped with four-wheel drive, with weeks' of provisions on board, before taking off into the sticks in waders, in search of their quarry. In fact any quotation taken at random from the *Guide*, which covers the whole of Ireland in equal detail, will convince the reader that a bike would be the last vehicle suitable for such a purpose, as the following typical extract, which appears under *Ballyvaghan* (as they chose to spell it), will show:

' . . . 2m.S. of the Glenisheen tombs, to the E. of the road in Poulnabrone, is Cromlech, a fine portal dolmen. ¾m.S. of this, in Caherconnell, is the stone ringfort from which the townland takes its name. 1¼m.NE. of Caherconnell crossroads the side road enters Cragballyconoal; 150 yds N. of the road is Cromlech, a ruined gallery grave in a long mound; 500 yds NNE. is another cairn with a wedge-shaped gallery grave (also Cromlech), 1m.SSW. of Caherconnell crossroads, in Poulawack, is a cemetry cairn (Nat. Mon.) excavated by Harvard archaeologists in 1934: Food Vessel, Urn, and other burials (including Beaker?). 4m.SW. of the cairn, in Poulacarran, are the ruins of St Cronan's Church, a parish church of c.1500 marking an early monastic site; St Cronan's Well cures sore eyes (*see* Termon *under* Carran) . . .'

At which point, reluctantly, we must leave them, just as they are getting into their stride. How did they ever manage to complete their appointed task, one wonders, without either sinking into a bog or going round the bend?

Three miles outward bound from Ennistymon we reached Lahinch on the shores of Liscannor Bay, an old-fashioned seaside resort that became popular at the end of the last century with the opening of the West Clare Railway and of a golf course. The old part of Lahinch, if one ignored the existence of a bungalow belt and an Entertainment Centre near the beach, complete with ballroom, cinema, theatre, sea-water swimming pool, children's pool, playground, games room and tennis courts, looked a bit like a stage set designed by Osbert Lancaster in collaboration with Edward Ardizzone, but one from which the actors had departed. It was the sort of place, with its modest promenade, which might also have boasted a modest pier, had it been sited on the shores of the English Channel instead of the wild Atlantic.

At this time of year it was pretty quiet. Vaughan's Aberdeen Arms, the oldest and best hotel, was closed until April. I was sorry about that: I remembered the present proprietor, Michael Vaughan, as a jolly fellow with a wealth of curious, some of it scandalous, knowledge about the neighbourhood and its inhabitants past and present – something I could have done with at that moment with the sun now in and none of the things that writers normally count on happening, especially when travelling in Ireland, actually happening. There were several hermetically sealed pubs and not a living soul in sight. Little did I realize that somewhere within his shut-up hotel was Vaughan, hidden away for the winter, longing to entertain us.

North of the town the road ran close to the shores of Liscannor Bay, but separated from it by sand dunes held together by tussocky vegetation. It was among these dunes, on the night of 22 September 1920, that the inhabitants of Lahinch took refuge when the Royal Irish Constabulary together with what were known as the Black and Tans and the Auxiliaries* went on the rampage, partially wrecking the town and setting a number of buildings on fire. This disgraceful operation was carried out as a reprisal for the equally disgraceful ambushing and killing of four members of the RIC (only one of whom was in fact an Englishman, the other three all being Catholic Irish from County Cork, Roscommon and Sligo), a pattern of behaviour which was to become commonplace and still is more than sixty years later in the North. The constables had been killed either by the Sinn Fein, the Irish Volunteers, the Irish Republican Army, or the Irish Republican Brotherhood, the head of which was the fearful, brilliant Michael Collins.[†]

*The *Black and Tans* was the name given by the Irish to British recruits to the Royal Irish Constabulary when recruiting began in December 1919. The name was taken from a pack of Irish foxhounds, though the actual reference was to the colour of their uniforms. They were mostly recruited from the ranks of demobilized British Army soldiers, and were required to have been given an honourable discharge from their regiments. The story, so often quoted that it has become almost universally believed, that they were the criminal sweepings of the jails and gutters, is largely mythical. Altogether they numbered about 5000.

The *Auxiliary Division* of the RIC (the 'Auxiliaries') was made up of ex-British officers, known as Cadets. They were intended to operate in flying columns against the IRA (Irish Republican Army) and the Irish Volunteers.

Both the *Black and Tans* and the *Auxiliaries* had an effective life in Ireland of less than a year, in the course of which terrible atrocities were committed by both sides.

[†]*Sinn Fein* (inadequately translated as 'We Ourselves'): Irish Republican political movement, founded about 1905 by Arthur Griffith and originally linked to the revolutionary IRA, which was and still is dedicated to bringing about a united, independent Ireland by means of civil war. The IRA was originally composed of armed Fenians, Fenians being members of an Irish revolutionary organization founded in the United States in 1858.

Since 1969 *Sinn Fein* and the IRA have been divided by a split in opinion into a Provisional and an Official movement.

The *Irish Volunteers*, otherwise known as the *Sinn Fein Volunteers*: a splinter

The heady pleasures to be derived from this sort of fighting, for those on both sides, are well summed up by the following ballad commemorating the annihilation of two lorry loads of Auxiliaries in November 1920 in west Cork:

> 'Twas the twenty-eighth of November
> Outside the town of Macroom
> The Tans in their big Crossley tender
> Were hurtling to their doom.
> The lads in the column were waiting
> Their hand grenades pinned, on the spot,
> And the Irish Republican Army
> Made balls of the whole fucking lot.

Ironically, it was in a somewhat similar ambush just under two years later, in August 1922, that Michael Collins was killed by his fellow Irishmen while travelling in an open Rolls Royce with a Crossley tender and armoured car escort on the Macroom – Bandon road by anti-Treaty Republicans.[*]

During that night of terror at Lahinch, the local secretary of the Irish Transport and General Workers Union was shot and his body thrown back into the flames of his burning house, from which his wife had already been driven with her baby in her arms. Another man was shot for attempting to extinguish the fire in a neighbour's house, and most of the inhabitants of Lahinch fled to the sand dunes.

group of the *Irish National Volunteers*, the former founded in November 1913, the same year as Sir Edward Carson's Ulster Volunteers, with whom it was intended they should act in concert.

The *Irish Republican Brotherhood*, later referred to as the Fenians, was a secret society founded in 1858 which originally masqueraded under the name of the Phoenix National and Literary Society in Co. Cork. It was the Brotherhood who decided, in August 1914, that a rising should take place; who approved Sir Roger Casement's largely abortive mission to Germany in 1915; and who drafted the original plans for the Dublin Rising on Easter Monday, 1916. After the failure of the insurrection the Brotherhood was re-organized by Michael Collins, in 1916–17, and it continued to exist until his assassination in 1922.

[*]By the terms of the Anglo-Irish Treaty of 1921, the twenty-six Counties of the Irish Free State were conceded dominion status and the remaining six were to form an integral part of the United Kingdom.

'You never saw anything so sad as the sight in the sandhills that morning,' an eye-witness wrote.

> Groups of men and women, some of them over seventy years, practically naked, cold, wet, worn looking and terrified, huddled in groups on the wet grass. I met two mothers with babies not three weeks old, little boys, partly naked, leading horses that had gone mad in their stables with the heat, and then when we got near the village a group of men standing round the unrecognisable corpse of Salmon [the man who had been shot while attempting to put out a fire], distracted people running in all directions looking for their friends with the awful thought haunting them that the burned corpse might be some relative of their own. Oh, it was awful! Every evening since then there is a sorrowful procession out of the village. The people too terrified to stay in their houses sleep out in the fields.[*]

Such killings would continue for years, long after the Black and Tans and the Auxiliaries were but a memory, of Irish by British, British by Irish and, most common of all as time went by, of Irish by Irish.

We now left this area with its melancholy associations for a more agreeable and eccentric one, via a fine stone bridge built by Cornelius O'Brien MP, an eccentric if ever there was one. Beneath it, overlooked by the tower block of the ruined Dough Castle, the little river Cullenagh wound its way through lush meadows on its final stretch to Liscannor Bay and the sea.

On the seashore to our left were the low roofless ruins of the mediaeval church of St Macreiche. St Macreiche was a legendary destroyer of plagues, dragons and of a great eel, an oll-pheist, which reputedly came ashore here to feast on the corpses in the cemetery in the sixth century. Just the nave and chancel of the church remained, separated by a pointed arch. To the south-east were the dunes of unhappy memory in which there are, or were, sand holes, the abodes of Donn na Duimche (Donn of the Sand

[*]*Freeman's Journal,* 11 October 1920, quoted in Robert Kee, *The Green Flag, A History of Irish Nationalism,* London, 1972, and gratefully acknowledged.

Dune) a fairy king. There are many Donns in Irish myth. One was the Brown Bull of Cuailgne who slew the Bull of Maeve, Queen of Connacht; another a foster-brother of Mael Fhothartaig, the wondrous son of Ronan, King of Leinster, whose stepmother made advances to him. And there is oc Donn, the Irish God of the Dead, in more modern folklore associated with shipwrecks, failure of crops, death of cattle and storms at sea.

Close by the church there was a holy well, and down on the beach, lapped by the tide, were two rocks, the saint's bed or grave. At one time people took sand from one of the graves in the churchyard and threw it into the sea to calm it; emigrants are still said to do this before setting out on their journey. Offshore, somewhere in the Bay, is said to lie Cill Stuihin, a submerged city. It was difficult to imagine a place with a greater concentration of magic in and around it, but what with the cold wind and the now driving rain it simply contrived to look thoroughly depressing.

By now very wet, we took refuge in McHugh's pub in Liscannor, strongly recommended by Mrs MacMahon. 'The finest Guinness in Ireland,' was how she had described it, very loyally considering that her husband was also engaged in peddling the stuff. 'And the very best rashers.'

Inside, McHugh's was long, narrow and dark. Beside McHugh himself, a bright-eyed, friendly man, and innumerable trophies won by his dogs at coursing, a sport in which he was a folk hero, the pub housed three men of indeterminate age with dark hair and thin, creased faces, all dressed in the sort of dark suits the Irish use for working in the fields, caps and rubber boots. It was difficult to guess their age: they could have been anything from fifty to seventy – the sort of men who are impervious to bad weather of the kind that was raging outside.

'I can't drink any more of that cider,' said Wanda. 'I'll have a port, a large one.' Her teeth were literally chattering.

While I was ordering the drinks, Mrs McHugh appeared and gave one of the men a bucket, and he went out into the deluge to milk a cow. Then, after one of the two remaining men had poured a Paddy into what remained of his pint of Guinness, the conversation turned to how much drink anyone could take without coming over peculiar. 'Now there was this English truck

driver I used to know when I was over in Kilburn,' the one
drinking the mixture said, making Kilburn sound as remote as
Shangri-la. 'And he couldn't drive his truck at all until he had
twenty pints inside him. And there's another feller I know who's
ready to be locked away by the Gardai after only a couple. It's a
strange business, the drink.' At the same time he ordered another.

We were reluctant to leave this agreeable refuge, but forced
ourselves out into the wind and sheets of rain. Out beyond the
little harbour, from which the Liscannor flags that had formed the
kitchen floor of our sumptuous cottage at Ballyvaughan had been
shipped away, the sea broke white on what looked like an
offshore reef. Or could it be the remains of the lost city of Cill
Stuihin, finally breaking the surface after centuries of submer-
sion? To the west of the village on the cliffs stood Liscannor
Castle, once occupied by Sir Turlough O'Brien who, in 1588,
busied himself with the extermination of survivors of the Armada.
For it was here, in Liscannor Bay, that the Spanish galleass
Zuniga, which had just failed to weather the Blaskets on its way
back to Spain, having sailed with the rest of the Armada
westwards round the north of Scotland, anchored on 5 September
1588, driven by a westerly gale back on to the coast of Clare.
There she remained for a week until the wind went to the north-
east and she was able to get clear of the Irish coasts, eventually to
reach Spain.

Other vessels were less fortunate. On 10 September two big
ships were wrecked on the west coast of the Loop Head peninsula.
The survivors were butchered by Sir Turlough O'Brien and
Boetius Clancy, Sheriff of Clare, on the orders of Sir Richard
Bingham, English Governor of Connaught, and their bodies were
buried on what is still called Spanish Point.

Everywhere we were to go subsequently on the coasts of Ireland
we were to hear stories of the Armada ships and their crews,
related as if the events had taken place only yesterday. Altogether
twenty-five ships were lost on the Irish coast, one west of
Shetland, and one on Fair Isle, while two were blown back into
the Channel, two were lost on the west coast of Scotland, and a
number were unaccounted for. Fifty-seven vessels and some 9000
or 10,000 men got back to Spain in September and October, out

of the 129 large vessels (65 of them over 700 tons), 19,295 soldiers and 8460 sailors not including galley slaves who had set off from Lisbon at the end of May 1588.

On 2 September 1588 had come the first of a series of gales, the heaviest that summer. Most of the wrecks occurred during the north-west gale of 10 September. According to Edward Whyte, clerk of the Council of Connacht at the time, 'There blew a most extreme wind and cruel storm the like whereof hath not been seen or heard for a long time.' Numbers of Armada ships from the north-west began to fall in on the Irish coast, badly damaged; some reached Kerry, others were forced onto the coasts of Clare, Galway and Mayo, the latter sometimes literally driving onto the Mayo coast because the charts available did not show the coast extending more than forty miles west of Ballycastle as far as Eagle Island. Altogether nine ships failed to weather Eagle Island, off the north-westernmost point of Mayo. One of the survivors, Captain Cuellar of the *Labia*, eventually had himself ferried across to the Scottish mainland from County Antrim after nine months of wandering and evasion in the mountains of Connaught and Ulster, part of which he spent in Clancy's Castle, a minute building on a rock in Lough Melvin, County Leitrim.

'Did you know,' I said to Wanda, trying to be cultural while pretending to admire this desperate, watery scene, 'that the inventor of the submarine was born here?'[*]

'If the weather was anything like this when he lived here,' she said, 'inventing the submarine was probably the only way he could keep dry.'

Soon, at a fork in the road, we came to some gates and a ruined lodge. Beyond was all that remained of Birchfield House, the home and birthplace of Cornelius O'Brien, Liberal MP for County Clare and landlord of ten thousand acres. He sat for the County at Westminster from 1832 to 1847, spanning the period of Catholic Emancipation and the Great Famine, and again from 1852 until 1857, dying soon afterwards.

Now in ruins, with its castellations, turrets, squeaky gates,

[*] John P. Holland, Irish patriot (1841–1914). In inventing it he hoped to bring about the destruction of the British Navy by the US Navy.

stumps of once splendid trees now blasted by the wind that howled over it, and carriageways so deep in mud that it was almost impossible to maintain steerage way on our bikes, it was the epitome of Gothick Horror. It was not difficult to believe that a curse had been laid on it and its builder by the local priest, who prophecied that it would become a treeless ruin after O'Brien gave up going to Mass (in fact there is no evidence he ever became Catholic); and it came as a pleasant surprise to find, when we knocked on the door to ask the way out of this labyrinth, that the young farmer who now lived in its adjoining farmhouse was perfectly normal.

It was from this base, the story goes, that 'Ould Corny', as he was known to his tenantry, used to ride out to take stock of his possessions, plan further building operations, and deflower or dispossess his tenants according to their sex and as the spirit moved him. His alleged habit of keeping in close contact with his female tenantry is immortalized in a story still current in Lahinch in which, dismounting from his horse in order to exercise his *droit de seigneur* by the roadside with a young woman who had taken his fancy, she was enjoined by her mother: 'Lift up yer arse now, Mary, that's a good girl, or the gentleman will have his balls in the mud.'

In fact almost all the stories about the man are what contemporaries of his would have described as 'a farrago of nonsense'. As the only man who has taken the trouble to do any research on O'Brien, Henry Comber, a local teacher, wrote 'Cornelius O'Brien has become something of a Bord Failte property and any material published about him is to be found in tourist brochures catering for tourists who thrive on diets of myths, legends and paddy-whackery.'[*]

O'Brien was in truth a Liberal who supported Daniel O'Connell's attempts to repeal the Act of Union of 1800, by which the Irish Parliament had voted itself out of existence. His name has never been linked with rack-renting and evictions, and he was a member of the Ennistymon Board of Guardians and the Liscan-

[*] Source: 'Cornelius O'Brien of Birchfield (1782–1857): Some facts about his life and times as abstracted from the Clare Journal and other sources', *Key Magazine*, n.d.

nor Famine Relief Committee. On one occasion in 1846, in the course of a spirited debate with the agent of Dean Stacpoole, another landowner who accused him of favouring his own tenants in allocating relief work, O'Brien said: 'If Mr Westropp, the agent, had the slightest compassion in such a year as this, he would not have taken rent from his poor tenantry. He would have told them to take back their money and buy bread with it . . .' It was perfectly impossible, he went on, 'for a man with a family of ten to maintain them on ten shillings a week when wheat sold at three shillings a stone. . . . If this was an item of relief, the Government should give wages sufficient to enable the labourer to give his family enough bread, otherwise there is no use in this enormous outlay.'

It must be said, however, that there is no record of O'Brien's parliamentary oratory, which no doubt accounts for Palmerston's verdict on him: 'O'Brien was the best Irish MP we ever had. He didn't open his mouth in twenty years.'

After another mile or so, in which the road skirted the O'Brien demesne, it turned sharply uphill, and I wondered if we would get to the cliffs of Moher before night fell. Here, on the landward side of the cliffs, sheltered from westerly winds, was the holy well of Daigh Bhride, St Brigid's Vat.

If you see an eel while drinking the waters of the Well your wish will be granted. There is a legend that when St Brigid stayed in the vicinity, while on her way from Munster to Connaught in her chariot, an old woman who owned the land where the well then gushed, washed potatoes in the water in order to defile it, so that it would not become a place of pilgrimage. Thereupon it welled up on someone else's property, in its present position on the other side of the road.

The well is fed by a rivulet which emerges in a little white-washed building constructed by Cornelius O'Brien – which itself rather belies his raffish reputation. More like a tunnel than a building, it is filled with votive offerings inscribed with the names of those who received the saint's favours in answer to their prayers and with holy images and sacred oleographs of the Virgin, St Joseph, St Francis, St Anthony, the Infant of Prague, the black saint, St Martin de Porres, Jesus with the bleeding heart and St

Brigid herself. It is also stacked with ancient crutches left by those who were cured of their disabilities, with medallions and swathes of rosaries. In feeling and appearance it is more like a Hindu shrine on the banks of the Ganges than one in the extreme west of Europe – magical.

Outside, on a mound that in spring would be covered with fuschias and other wild flowers, enclosed in two glass cases a bit like miniature telephone boxes, were two images of saints in painted plaster, one life size, the other about three feet high. Both undoubtedly represent St Brigid of Kildare, holy, beautiful and beloved patroness of Ireland, and after Patrick the most famous of Irish saints, each holding a shepherd's crook in one hand and in the other a model of the Cathedral at Kildare. The Cathedral was built on the site of the monastery which she founded in the fifth or sixth century and in which she was buried; thereafter, apart from a brief period when it was extinguished by order of the Archbishop of Dublin in 1220, a perpetual fire was kept burning by the nuns in a circular enclosure forbidden to men. But why then two figures? Is one intended to depict St Brigid of Liscannor, now after centuries of devotion either identified or inextricably confused with her more famous namesake?

There is a tradition that a St Brigid (but which St Brigid?) led the Virgin Mary to the place where she was purified at Bethlehem, after the birth of Jesus, on 2 February, the date which traditionally ushered in the spring, in Ireland at least. But the well has only ever been sparsely visited on that date; its great days are the last Saturday and Sunday in July, Satharn Domhnach Crom Dubh and Domhnach Chrom Dubh (the latter is translated into English as Garland Sunday, though there is no evidence that garlands played any part in its celebration in Ireland). This is the last Sunday before Lammas Day (1 August), known in Ireland as the Festival of Lughnasa, a Church feast commemorating St Peter's miraculous deliverance from prison. In a more pagan context Lughnasa is a harvest festival, marking the last Sunday of summer and the beginning of the potato harvest. In some areas the first Sunday in August, Domhnach Lughnasa, was the day of celebration instead.

Here, at Daigh Bhride, the celebrants spent the Saturday night in prayer, singing, drinking and festivity, and until comparatively recently they were joined there by Aran Islanders from Inisheer, who used to row their *currachs* across to a gap in the cliffs at Doolin* from where they would walk the five miles to the well; it was their singing, according to witnesses, that made the night so memorable. Then on Sunday the *patron* (parish celebration) was continued on the sands at Lahinch and in the town, as it still is today, and it was after this *patron* that the first meal of the new potato crop was eaten.

The scenes on Chrom Dubh Sunday on the strand at Lahinch were described in 1942 by Sean Mac Mathuna, who lived all his life at a townland between the Cliffs of Moher and the cove at Doolin. He referred to it as Cranndubh:†

> . . . it was a real day of sport there on the strand. In the old days there used to be a horse-race on the sand and crowds of people watching it. In the town itself and on the Promenade there were crowds to be seen, and every one seeking some kind of sport. There used to be the whole world of tricksters there, each trickster of them making as much noise as if he were paid for it. The man of the musical instrument was there and the dancing woman, the card-man, and the man that used to frighten us when we watched him dipping a fork in the barrel of blazing tow and putting it into his mouth and down into his throat. And if the tinkers were not there with their women and children it is not yet a day! The world of noise from them by afternoon when the grown tinkers had a good drop past the tooth! Some of them in a fighting humour and more of them without power in foot or hand but lying in a heap after the day. . . . Before my time the man who had the gander in the barrel used to be there. There were

*Doolin is now famous as the home of farmer Micho Russell, who travels the folk festivals of Europe and America, playing on his tin whistles and his flute the jigs, marches, set dances and hornpipes he heard as a child, just as they were played in County Clare 150 years ago.

†Translated from the Gaelic. Source: *The Festival of Lughnasa, A Study of the Survival of the Celtic Festival of the Beginning of the Harvest* by Maire MacNeill (Irish Folklore Commission), OUP, 1962.

'standings' in the street selling a kind of biscuit that is never seen now, a hundred sorts of sweets, lemonade, oranges and many other good things besides. The street used to be thronged with people and the taverns bursting out with those drinking in them. I regret to say that it was not always the Patron of Lahinch passed without a blow being struck amongst those who were drunk or those who had some spite for each other. But probably it was part of the sport and merriment of the day whatever strife would break out amongst the few who would make a show of themselves. It was very seldom that illwill or enmity resulted from a fight people might have on a day of fun and diversion like Cranndubh Sunday at Lahinch.

The vigil at St Brigid's Well and the associated *patron* at Lahinch, together with the pilgrimage to the summit of Croagh Patrick, the holy mountain in County Mayo, on the last Saturday and Sunday in July and the Puc Fair at Killorglin in County Kerry – the Fair of the He-Goat – which lasts for three days are, according to Maire MacNeill, the four most enduring survivals in Ireland of Lughnasa, the harvest festival observed in all Celtic lands.

Close to the well is a burial ground and in it a vault in which the omnipresent Cornelius lay behind a rusty iron door under a Victorian Gothic memorial; and on the hillside stands O'Brien's monument, an elegant Ionic column with an urn on top of it. It was said to have been erected at the expense of his grateful tenantry by compulsory subscriptions; in fact they contributed £36 out of a total of £400. At the base of it a long and fulsome inscription records his many virtues.

Down on the road next to the well there are two pubs, Murphy's and Considine's. Murphy's used to have three fiddles hanging on the wall behind the bar which were available to anyone who fancied playing a tune at any time; but now the lady who used to loan them out was dead, and the pub had been improved and the fiddles packed away or thrown away or given away. There was no one to ask.

By the time we reached the Cliffs of Moher the grey, watery December day was nearly done and it was beginning to grow dark. The Cliffs are among the great wonders of the western world. They are not anywhere near the highest cliffs in the British Isles but they are certainly among the most awesome. A five-mile enfilade of sheer precipices, many of them overhanging a void and highly unstable at certain levels, in places overgrown with moss and other vegetation, they rise from beds of limestone and shale through hundreds of feet of stratified flags to, successively, a wide ledge of yellow sandstone, a narrow band full of beautiful but almost completely inaccessible fossils, and finally a thick band of black shale which extends to the top.

About a mile from the northern end, at the highest point, 668 feet, above the sea, stands O'Brien's Tower, a tea-house and gazebo built by him in 1835 and now restored, from which visitors to the cliffs might admire the unparalleled view. He also provided a piper to entertain them, according to the *Clare Journal* of 5 October 1854, who unfortunately fell over the cliff while drunk. O'Brien also commissioned a three-mile long wall made of upended olive-tinted Lisconnor limestone flags six feet high and an inch thick, and set up by his peasantry along the cliff edge to prevent visitors and their horses being sucked over it by some sudden downdraught. These flags are to be seen everywhere in this region, serving as door and window lintels, roofing slates, floor slabs and most commonly as fencing. Beyond this point the Cliffs gradually descend to a ruined signal tower at Hag's Head where they are still 400 feet high. Beyond that they vanish into the sea.

By now the rain had stopped but it was horribly cold and damp and the wind was still strong enough to blow the waterfalls pouring over the cliff edge high into the air in what looked like long plumes of steam, to fall in the fields behind. By now it was high water and in spite of the wind, except where it broke white on the screes at the base of the cliffs, the sea was about as calm as it was ever likely to be off the Cliffs of Moher in winter.

Altogether it was a sinister scene. A land and seascape completely devoid of colour, like a black and white print of a cemetery; the black cliffs with a pale matching sky and sea above and below them and away to the west across the intervening Sound the three Aran Islands, like black sea monsters swimming shorewards. But it was the birds that made the scene memorable. What they were doing there in December only an ornithologist would know. Some floated closely packed on the surface of the water, forming what looked like great flexible rafts which rose and fell to the fetch of the sea; others hung motionless on the wind; yet more wheeled about a 200-foot high offshore stack, and groups of them perched on ledges on the cliff face as if they were spectators in some vast ornithological auditorium, waiting for the curtain to rise, all setting up an indescribably melancholy wailing, like the cries of lost souls.

'What a place to do yourself in,' said Wanda, echoing my own thoughts, as we looked down gingerly into the depths below, having crossed O'Brien's wall. What a place to do oneself in, and what a landfall. Terrible to look at from the sea as a lee shore, running down as did Ridgway and Bly in their open rowing boat, with the wind strong from the west, having crossed the Atlantic but having failed to make the Aran Islands (they were saved in the nick of time by the lifeboat on Inishmore). Terrible, too, for the crews of the surviving Armada ships which made their mostly inauspicious landfalls there.

And as if O'Brien had been there to chide me for crossing his wall, one of the updraughts that was playing such havoc with the local waterfalls whipped off my Jackie Coogan cap and took it high into the air above us.

'Your Jackie Hooghly!' Wanda cried in Slavonic torment as we both watched it spinning away seawards just like a Frisbee in Marin, perversely obeying some different law to that observed by the waterfalls. 'It's gone, your Jackie Hooghly!' And for a moment I thought she might try and follow it. However, there was no need for alarm. An even more violent updraught caught it and brought it back as neatly as a boomerang to make a perfect landing on the grass inside the wall. As always the luck of Newby had held. How much longer would I be able to rely on it? was something I asked myself with increasing frequency.

'That was your father's cap,' Wanda said severely. I think she was a bit upset that there was now really nothing to chide me with. 'You should put it on stronger.'

Then, after a ride which began with a wonderful two-mile

swoop downhill and ended in total darkness with wind and rain behind us, and men in motor cars no doubt filled to the brim with jars of Guinness in hot pursuit, back to tea at Mrs MacMahon's. She wasn't doing evening meals or high teas in winter; the only place in Ennistymon which was, she said, was the Falls Hotel.

We had already seen the Falls Hotel from the bridge below the falls on the Cullenagh river. In the early part of the century it was known as Ennistymon House, and had been the residence of H. V. Macnamara Esq.; possibly because of his Irish-sounding name or perhaps because he was affable, it had escaped being burned down in the Troubles. His son, Francis Macnamara, was a bohemian character whose daughter, Caitlin, married Dylan Thomas and who himself married, second time round, the sister of Augustus John's second wife, Dorelia.

It was a large eighteenth-century building approached by an avenue of fine trees. Inside an elegant fanlighted doorway the hall contained some rather good *art nouveau* murals and a plaster-work frieze which embodied the ferocious crest of the O'Brien's, a naked arm with a sword in hand.

The bar was like the stage set for the first act of some interminable Irish equivalent of *A Month in the Country*, with the players already in position for the raising of the curtain. Could they have been waiting for us to arrive before starting, I wondered?

Sitting with his back to the other actors, with his feet in the grate, and completely monopolizing what fire there was, was an elderly man with one of those sawn-off noses of the sort that used to be acquired by bare-fist pugilists in the course of practising their art, reading the *Irish Times*. At the bar a wild-looking young man in a 1930s dark overcoat, its collar snowy with dandruff, was drinking – it was difficult to ascertain what. He looked like a spoiled priest, or the dispossessed son of an Irish peer, but when he opened his mouth, didn't sound like either. In a corner a man with a very red face was entertaining his mature and self-sufficient mistress and at the same time trying to do himself in by drinking alternate measures of Smirnoff and Tio Pepe. She had more sensibly asked for the wine list and was slowly drinking rather expensive claret. No one said anything, but when we got up to go in search of dinner they all came too, as if afraid of missing something.

I ordered scrambled eggs and bacon, Wanda a mixed grill. My luck held; Wanda's didn't: I watched her roll her steak up in a napkin and put it in her bag for later disposal. I must say one thing about Wanda – she knows how to behave. Meanwhile I watched the lovers. She was effortlessly eating scampi at £7 a go; he was making heavy weather with one of the steaks. Meanwhile the man with the sawn-off nose and the young man with the overcoat, whom I had by now decided was some sort of commercial traveller (selling what? French letters?) sat at separate tables next door to one another both looking straight ahead, like passengers in a Boeing. When it finally began, by which time I had already asked for the bill, their conversation went something like this:

Young Man: I've heard O'Hara's retiring.

Old Man: He is, is he? And how old would he be?

There was a considerable interval. They were both eating their puddings.

Young Man: Fifty-five. . . . Fifty-seven. . . . Don't know which.

Old Man: Well, I retired when I was sixty-five . . . not surprised he's retiring at sixty-seven.

Interval.

Young Man: I didn't say sixty-seven. I said fifty-five or fifty-seven.

Old Man: (huffily) I don't know anything about that. All I know is that things weren't like that when I was young.

Dinner cost £8 for two, including a pot of tea. With this kind of entertainment we could hardly complain.

Back at Mrs Macmahon's, in the TV Room, separated from us by a hardboard partition, a well-grown schoolboy, presumably Master MacMahon, was crouching surrounded by a wealth of electronic equipment including a high-rise hi-fi that was belting out Led Zeppelin on about Regulo 10.

'No,' he said, when asked, 'I don't mind turning it down at all. In fact I'll put it off. I've still got to do me arit'metic for school tomorrow.'

When he had gone off to do his arithmetic I began footling about with Mrs MacMahon's images and while trying to find out what one of them, who bore a suspicious resemblance to St Brigid, was made of, dropped it. Again my good luck held, and it failed to break (but why do I do such things in the first place?). I wondered what I would have said to Mrs MacMahon if I had bust it – 'Mrs MacMahon, I have broken one of your saints in the TV room, the one that looked like St Brigid', I suppose, but it would have sounded rather lame.

The next day we had planned to begin the exploration of the Peninsula as far south as Loop Head, but it was still pouring at one-fifteen in the afternoon, so we decided to go to Ennis, some seventeen miles to the east, and then home. It was time. Recordings of choirs groaning out 'Holy Night' were already audible over large tracts of Ennistymon and snowballs made of cotton wool were already beginning to look slightly shop-soiled in the shop windows.

We set off for Ennis in a deluge – the rain was fantastic, more like a waterfall than a rainstorm. The road was inundated and there was a fearful cross-wind. Cars and lorries sluiced us down as they roared past. Stopping for a pee was hell. In Ennis, at four in the afternoon, the lights were already on. We wound our way through incredibly narrow streets filled with Christmas decorations and more renderings of 'Holy Night', past a shop where I could have bought a comprehensive selection of St Brigids, and a column commemorating the debut of the great Daniel O'Connell in the House of Commons as soon as the Catholic Emancipation Act of 1829 enabled him to take his seat. The rain had washed away the name of our hotel in my address book, but when we eventually found it we had baths with endless hot water and left our boots in the boiler rooms.

Two days later we were hanging up holly in Dorset. There was no mistletoe.

PART 2

JANUARY

Chapter 7

THROUGH WATERFORD TO CORK

Ireland is dim where the sun goeth on settle.

KING ALFRED. Early English translation of his version
of Orosius, *Geography of Europe,* c. 600

Our next bike ride in Ireland proved to be of a more testing nature. It took place in January and took us from Rosslare along the southern and south-western coasts of Wexford, Waterford, Cork and Kerry, to Slea Head on the Dingle Peninsula (which is only about 40° east of St John's, Newfoundland), ending up in Tralee. It rained every day, sometimes all day, except when it snowed, and when it wasn't blowing a blizzard from the north it blew Force 9 from the west and south-west, the general direction in which we were pedalling. Whichever direction it blew from, it was horribly cold.

It is not difficult to know what the weather will be like on any particular January day in mainland Britain. All we Newbys have to do is to scrape the rime off the inside of our bedroom window to see for ourselves. What is more difficult is to discover what is cooking on the west coast of Ireland, where a lot of Britain's weather first sights land. This is because ever since the twenty-six southern counties of Ireland became a Republic and ceased to be part of the United Kingdom their weather has been studiously ignored by British weathermen. In Britain it is now easier to learn on TV what the weather is like in Banja Luka than at Slyne Head, Connemara. Had we been aware of what was in store for us, we might have thought again.

This time, appalled by the amount of gear I had pedalled through Limerick and Clare before Christmas, I decided to weigh everything I had brought back with me and find out what it all added up to. Wanda, rather smugly I thought, said that she didn't need to avail herself of this service.

Banished to the garden, which was currently filled with snow, I slung a rope over the branch of a beech tree, tied the loose ends together, looped them round the toggle of a Salter Spring Balance for Air Travellers, and with some difficulty hooked the loaded bicycle on to it, very nearly breaking it in the process. Whatever the total weight, it was far in excess of 66 lbs, which was the Salter's limit. I then weighed the bike unloaded. It came out at a rather disappointing 38 lbs, far more than any other bicycle I had ever owned, but this total included the Blackburn carriers and a pump. The four pannier bags and their contents, plus a stuff sac on the rear carrier which held my Gore-Tex suit, a big pullover and front and rear lights for the bike, plus my waterproof camera, strapped to the handlebars weighed a colossal 51 lbs 1 oz. In addition there was the five-foot pre-coiled cable lock made in Germany, which weighed 14 oz. Add to all this on the return voyage from Rosslare to Fishguard a litre bottle of what is laughingly described as 'duty free' Grand Marnier, which weighed 3 lbs 10 oz and the whole lot, including the bike, came to 93 lbs 9 oz.

It was obviously madness to take this lot, even minus the Grand Marnier, to Ireland again and as it was bloody cold in the garden, with more snow in the offing, I decided to weigh everything by category – clothing, tools and spares, literature and sundries, which included medical and washing kit and film – indoors. Clothing came to 15 lbs. The heaviest single items were the warm-lined rubber boots, 4 lbs 10 oz the pair, and a pair of shoes for 'evenings', 3 lbs 10 oz. If anyone thinks these weights excessive I should explain that I take size twelves. Medical and washing kit and sundries came to 5 lbs; tools and spares to 6 lbs; and literature to an unbelievable 15 lbs 14 oz including the six half-inch maps we were going to need. More or less happily engaged in dealing with these minutiae, I failed to notice that Wanda had joined me.

'How much does it all weigh?' she asked in a tone of voice that after forty years of cohabiting with her I have learned to identify with trouble. I told her.

'The trouble with you is,' she said, relapsing into her argot, 'you always take too bloddy much. What I had weighed half of that, *and* I had a litre of whisky for you and a litre of wine for me, and that weighed God knows how much.'

'All right, Mrs Know-All!' I said, not for the first time. 'Next time *you* carry the tools and spares.'

'That's not fair,' she said. 'You know I don't know dese tings. I don't even know how to change gear,' she added pathetically, making me feel a heel, as per usual. 'And don't shout. Anyway,' she went on, changing the subject adroitly, 'why do you want two pairs of long stockings, two thick shirts and a pair of shoes when you're already wearing stockings, a thick shirt and a pair of boots!'

'I thought I might get wet,' I said lamely.

So I didn't take them.

'And as you know so much you might cast your eye over the literature list and tell me what to do about that,' I added.

I had pruned it viciously but it still included *The Shell Guide to Ireland; Murray's Handbook for Travellers in Ireland*, 1912, which nothing would part me from; the *Blue Guide to Ireland*, slightly stuffy but indispensable; Brendan Lehane's *Companion Guide to Ireland; Wonders of Ireland*, which I once participated in writing; the *AA Illustrated Road Book of Ireland*; and *The Genuine Old Moore's Irish Almanack, 1986* – 'Beware of Spurious Imitations' – which not only gave a list of all the horse and other Irish fairs and markets but predicted for me, as a Sagittarian, 'benefits from older people', who would have to get a move on with their generosity or I would be dead; and for Wanda, born under Aries, a glittering future but only if she stayed at home. According to our kitchen scales these weighed 3 lbs 1 oz, 1 lb, 11 oz, 1 lb 10 oz, 2 lbs (even what I had collaborated in writing was overweight), 2 lbs 5oz and ¾ oz respectively. Of these, with the greatest regret, and feeling as if I was dropping the pilot while still on soundings, I now jettisoned the *Shell Guide*, the *Blue Guide*, the *Companion Guide* and *Wonders of Ireland*, all on grounds of weight.

Other books that I would like to have had with me but for their weight were the *Ireland Guide*, published by the Irish Tourist Board (1 lb 7 oz), the *Guide to the National Monuments of Ireland* (1 lb 1 oz) by Peter Harbison, and *Burke's Guide to Country Houses* by Mark Bence-Jones, but how the hell can you carry a coffee-table book weighing 3 lb 1 oz on a bike? I would also have liked Robert Kee's *The Green Flag*, which deals with Irish Nationalism, for me a subject of baffling complexity. But not at 3 lb; the same weight as Maire MacNeill's *The Festival of Lughnasa*. Strange that so many of the best books on Ireland weighed in at around this figure. What I really needed was a *chaise* to follow in my footsteps with my travelling library on board.

The sun was rising astern as we came into Rosslare, dyeing what looked like toy houses on the heights above the harbour a brilliant orange. Otherwise, it was a cold, windy, rain-washed morning and although a south-westerly gale was blowing, here in the lee of the land there was no sea to speak of. Away to the south-east the light on the tower of the Tuskar Rock was still flashing. Here we left our van.

After loading up the bikes, we wobbled away into rural county Wexford. I was feeling ghastly. For some days I had been suffering from sinusitis and while on the ferry I had developed a fatal-sounding cough, which persisted the entire time I was in Ireland and which at night often made it impossible for Wanda to sleep.

At once we found ourselves in a pleasant countryside of winding lanes with hardly any traffic, green fields in which standard, black and white EEC-type cattle were fattening them-selves in a leisurely fashion — as if they, too, knew that no one would really know what to do with them when they were fattened, except to add them to the European meat mountain — and small, single-storey whitewashed farmhouses and barns, many of them thatched, that were beginning to gleam in the emerging sun. Everything was on a small scale, even the trees. Overhead blackbirds and magpies zoomed around in a sky dappled with cirrus, infinitely remote. Gorse blazed in the hedgerows and at Twelve Acre Cross Roads a little band of young men in shirt sleeves, waistcoats and cloth caps were hedging and ditching, using the sorts of implements that are now collectors' items in mainland Britain.

In the course of this ride, which was mercifully flat, we passed no fewer than four castles, including Bargy Castle, home of the unfortunate Bagenal Harvey, leader of the 1798 Peasants' Revolt,

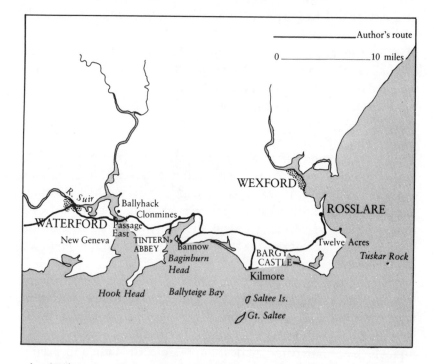

of which more later. We also passed a sign in the middle of nowhere pointing down an arcadian lane which read 'Bicycles Repaired', and the vaneless tower of a windmill. Here, sheltered by the hedgerows, it was like a day in early spring, not January. In spite of feeling lousy I felt extraordinarily happy.

Neither of us felt so happy when we reached the quay at Kilmore, and coming out of the shelter of the hedgerows received the full blast of the freezing south-westerly gale that was roaring in from the Atlantic, piling up the seas on the reefs around the Saltee Islands.

The owner of these two islands, which lie five miles off the coast, is the self-styled, self-crowned Michael I who, when in residence, hoists his standard on his dwelling on Great Saltee. His limestone throne stands on the flank of a hill and bears his coat of arms — a shield supported by two mermaids, each quarter containing a different sort of bird. Nearby a plaque states that the throne was installed in memory of his mother who confided to Michael, when he was ten years old, that one day he would own the island and be its first prince. His heirs are warned that they can only become his lawful successors if the coronation ceremony is properly carried out, using the regalia which he himself has provided for the purpose.

Great Saltee, the largest of the two islands, is about a mile long and is covered with spongy hillocks which in spring are covered with wild hyacinths, sea pinks and campion. Located on one of the principal migration routes, in late May and early June it becomes one of the noisiest places in Ireland when several million birds – in all some thirty different species – gather on every ledge of its cliffs and offshore stacks, filling the air with their squawking. In fact one wondered how the monarch stood it.

'Any news of the monarch?' I summoned up sufficient resolution to ask the little band of fishermen confabulating in the car park.

'He doesn't come here any more,' one of them replied, obviously bored to death by being asked the same question innumerable times.

'What about his son?' I said. I didn't care how bored he was. 'His son comes sometimes,' he said, turning his back on me in a rather pointed way, while the others looked seawards, hoping for a lull in the conversation.

'Ireland of the Welcomes, huh!' I said, but only when I was out of earshot. It was a wild scene – an appropriate place to hear sad stories of kings, even if they were absent rather than dead. There may have been spring in the lanes but here it was a non-starter.

We battled on into the blast for another ten miles to a place called Bannow beyond the far western end of Ballyteigue Strand. It stood, what there was of it, at the mouth of the wide estuary of the Owenduff and Corock rivers; beyond the shallows, over which hundreds of oystercatchers were swirling about, the ebb was running strongly against a south-westerly breeze which was tearing the surface off it. Once Bannow had been an island and it was still marked as Bannow Island on the half-inch map. Once, too, it had been a town but all that remained of it now above ground were the ruins of a thirteenth-century church standing in its graveyard, and of a chantry chapel, called St Brendan's. It was a strange sensation standing among the long straight depressions in the grass, all that remain of the streets of the town, the names of which have been preserved in the rent rolls at Waterford.

It is thought to be here, on what was then an island, that on 2 May 1169 the first landing in Ireland was made by an Anglo-Norman invasion force consisting of thirty men-at-arms, sixty mail-clad horsemen and a large number of archers, jointly commanded by Robert FitzStephen, Hervey de Montmorency (the uncle of Richard de Clare, otherwise known as Strongbow, who himself landed in the area the following year) and Maurice de Prendergast. The Anglo-Normans were recruited in South Wales, most of them young gentlemen in reduced circumstances; the rank-and-file were mostly either Welsh or Flemings.

Others believe that the first landing took place on Baginburn Head on the Hook Head Peninsula, across the Bay from Bannow, and that it was named Baginburn because FitzStephen is said to have disembarked his forces there from two ships, one called the *Bagg*, the other the *Bunn*, which sounds like something concocted by Beachcomber.*

These invaders became known by the indigenous Irish as 'the men from overseas', or as 'foreigners' or 'Franks'. They inter-married, kept themselves to themselves in numerous castles, and were never conquered or assimilated by the local Gaels, from whom they further isolated themselves by speaking their own tongue, an ancient and unique form of English.

A written record of this language, which seems more difficult to interpret the further one goes into it, is an address presented to the Marquis of Normanby in 1836 at Ballytrent, south-east of Wexford, while he was Lord Lieutenant of Ireland, entitled 'Ye soumissive spakeen o ouz, dwellers o'Baronie Forth Weisforthe'. (The English baronies were of Forth and Bargy.) It read as follows:

Wee, Vassales o'His Most Gracious Majesty Wilyame ee 4th, an az wee virilie chote na coshe an loyale Dwellers na Baronie Forthe, crave na dicka luckie acte t'uck necher th' Eccellencie, an na plaine garbe o'oure yola talke, wi

---

*Whatever the truth, Cromwell certainly landed on the Hook Head Peninsula in 1649, where he vowed, it is said, to take Waterford 'by hook or by crooke', Crooke being a small place on the west side of Waterford Harbour. This he failed to do. The phrase is also attributed to Strongbow.

vengem o'core t'gie oure zense o'ye grades wilke be ee dighte wi yer name, an whilke wee canna zic, albiet o''Governere', 'Statesman', an alike.[*]

And so on for another sixteen lines.

In this language, of which there were only a handful of speakers ten years later, there are words long since obsolete in modern English but which appear frequently in the works of the mediaeval poet John Gower and his contemporary Chaucer, and, later, in those of Shakespeare and Jonson. One list of them, compiled by the antiquary Charles Vallancey (1721–1812) who, according to his biographer in *The Dictionary of National Biography*, 'published worthless tracts on Irish philology and history', contained about three hundred such words.

Their continued loyalty to the British Crown and their rejection of the Reformation gave Cromwell an excuse to confiscate their lands, and grant them to some of his military leaders. It is scarcely surprising that in spite of their antecedents these Old English peasants rose against the English in May 1798. Nevertheless, they chose a Protestant landlord, Beauchamp Bagenal Harvey of Bargy Castle, to lead them in what was the only really formidable rising to take place anywhere in the country.[†] They fought with great courage and succeeded in taking Wexford, which they held for a month. When their occupation of the town came to an end, they massacred ninety-one of the Protestant inhabitants by transfixing them with pikes and then throwing them from the bridge into the river Slaney.

When the rising collapsed in July, Harvey and his deputy, John Colclough, were forced to take refuge on one of the Saltee Islands.

---

[*]Translated in Hall, *Ireland, Its Scenery, Character*, &c: 'We, the subjects of his Most Gracious Majesty, William the Fourth, and as we truly believe both faithful and loyal inhabitants of the Barony Forth, beg leave at this favourable opportunity to approach your Excellency, and in the simple dress of our old dialect to pour forth from the fullness of our hearts our sense of the qualities which characterise your name, and for which we have no words but of "Governor", "Statesman", &c.' (Vol. II p. 162).

[†]The Directory of the United Irishmen made plans for a national rising on 23 May 1798, which was to be commanded by Lord Edward Fitzgerald, son of the Duke of Leinster and cousin of Charles James Fox. The Government anticipated the rising by arresting the leaders on 12 March, only Fitzgerald escaping. What followed were disorganized risings in parts of Leinster and north-east Ulster on 24 May, all of which failed.

There they were found hiding in a cave and were taken to Wexford where they were beheaded on Wexford Bridge, Harvey's head being subsequently exposed to view on the Sessions House, and his body thrown into the river.

But to return to the original invasion: in the space of thirty years or so the Anglo-Normans overran large parts of Ireland and when they expired, sometimes without male issue, further reinforcements were sent over to continue their work. For defensive purposes the earlier arrivals contented themselves with throwing up flat-topped mounds of earth and then erecting a wooden tower on top. These mounds were known as 'mottes' and around the foot of them they had a half-moon shaped enclosure in which they kept their cattle and supplies. These almost instant fortifications, built with local manpower, continued to be in vogue until about 1200, by which time the Normans had already conquered nearly half the country. From then on they began to build, in large numbers, castles of stone in the Norman style – most with rectangular keeps or towers surrounded by strong walls. Some castles in towns, such as Dublin and Limerick, had no keep but strongly fortified walls instead; others had a tall keep with a round tower at each of the four corners. With the exception of those sited on rocks, most had a cluster of wooden houses inside their walls. 120 castles or their remains have been identified in the four southern baronies of Forth, Bargy, Skelburne and Shelmalier alone.

By about 1300 some Irish chieftains had begun to realize the threat that these castles offered to their continued existence and began to build castles themselves. There was a tremendous boom begun in the fifteenth century, initiated by the great Norman princes and emulated by the inhabitants of what was known as the Pale, the English part of the province of Leinster, who were offered a subsidy of £10 by Edward VI for every castle built to his specifications on its borders. These were square or rectangular towers of moderate size which also served as dwellings; soon the Irish began to copy them, and a positive wave of tower-house building ensued until around 1650.

And what happened to Bannow, the now lost city? It became the first Anglo-Norman corporation town in all Ireland. According to Holinshed, writing his *Chronicles of Ireland* in the first half of the sixteenth century, the river estuary separating Bannow from the mainland was known as the Pill, a common English West Country name for a tidal inlet. 'The Pill,' he wrote, 'was so quite estranged from Irishrie, as if a traveller of the Irish had pitcht his foote within the Pill [this may also have referred to Bannow itself] and spoken Irish, the Weisfordians would command him foorthwith to turne the other end of his toong and speak English, or else bringe his tronchman with him [what or whoever a "tronchman" was].' And later, in the reign of Queen Elizabeth, Sir George Carew, soldier, sailor, statesman and ruthless suppressor of the Earl of Tyrone's rebellion, wrote of the south part of the county:

> the most civil part, is contayned within a river called Pill; where the auncyentest gentilmen, descended of the first conquerors, do inhabit; the other, also without the river, is inhabited by the original Irishe, the Kavanaghs, Moroghes, and Kinselaghs, who possess the wooddy part of the country, and yet are daylie more scattered by our English gentilmen, who incroche upon them and plant castles and piles within them.

Bannow was still flourishing in the reign of Charles I, but a visitor to it in 1684 reported that it had been quite ruined by drifting sands. In spite of being buried it still continued, as a rotten borough, to return two members to the Dublin House of Commons, whose practice it was to sit by a solitary chimney, all that remained of Bannow above ground apart from the church and chapel, and solemnly re-elect themselves. And when it was finally disenfranchised by the Act of Union in 1800, Charles Tottenham, Earl of Ely, who had a country seat nearby, was paid £15,000 to compensate him for the loss of this privilege, also receiving similar sums for the loss of two other neighbouring boroughs, those of Fethard and Clonmines.[*]

[*]Charles Tottenham, afterwards Loftus (1738–1806), was created Marquis of Ely for some reason connected with the negotiations which preceded the Act of Union. He had previously been made Baron Loftus in 1785; and in 1789 he was created Viscount Loftus, in 1794 Earl of Ely and in 1801 Baron Loftus of Long Loftus in the United Kingdom, 'having thus,' in the words of his biographer in *The Dictionary of National Biography*, 'obtained no fewer than five separate peerage creations within fifteen years. *Prends moi tel que je suis* (Take me as I am),' he concluded, 'was the marquis's motto.'

Inside this silted-up estuary of the Pill was the site of another lost city, Clonmines, where silver and lead were mined. All that remains of the city, which covered twenty acres in its heyday and was surrounded by a rampart and a ditch, are what are known as the 'Seven Churches of Clonmines', actually four castles and three churches, one of them part of a Dominican monastery called St Augustine's. Further downstream a post-Second World War memorial records ten members of a company of the IRA who in 1920 were blown to smithereens in an explosion in a munitions factory – whether a British or an IRA munitions factory is not clear. Close by were the ruins of Tintern Abbey, founded by William le Mareschal, first Earl of Pembroke, to commemorate his deliverance from a storm at sea. He dedicated it to the Virgin and populated it with Cistercian monks from Tintern Abbey in Monmouthshire.

This particular morning had so far presented us with what I considered in my state of health to be an *embarras de richesses* of history and culture, but in suggesting that we should give the Abbey a miss on the grounds that we had already seen six castles, four churches, one chapel and two lost cities with the day practically only just beginning, I encountered unexpected opposition from Wanda, who is normally not averse to skipping a ruin or two, or even three.

'If you skip all the time,' she said severely, 'you will not be able to write your book about Ireland.' We visited the Abbey.

I must say, though it goes against the grain to admit it, that as abbeys go Tintern was marvellous. It had everything one could reasonably demand of an Irish abbey. There were huge, gaunt trees surrounding it and drifts of cawing rooks hanging on the wind. There was a massive tower, and the remains of a nave and transept. And embedded in what had been the chancel was a house built by Sir Anthony Colclough, an Elizabethan soldier who was granted the Abbey after the dissolution of the religious houses, and whose family thereafter laboured under the curse of fire and water, which fell upon all those in England and Ireland who held estates once owned by the Church. The last member of the family to live in the house left it in 1958.

The Colclough curse had at least two other, more exciting

raisons d'être. One was that Sir Anthony found a number of friars still in residence when he took possession and murdered the lot. The second was that another Colclough, Sir Caesar, had flattened an ancient rath (or fort) inhabited by a band of fairies, who proceeded to do away with him in a rather unusual manner. Sir Caesar had boasted to King William (which King William is unclear), with whom he was on intimate terms, of the excellence of the Irish hurlers of Wexford and the King challenged him to bring a team over to England to play a team of Cornish hurlers; and a large assembly of the nobility watched the game at the English court. The Irish were naturally victorious and Colclough then set sail back to Ireland, hoping to make a landfall at Hook Head, where his fiancée, the heiress of Redmond, had promised to keep a light burning in the Tower of Hook, on the Head, to help him sail safely in. Unfortunately, the fairies intervened. They lulled her to sleep with their magic music so that she let the light go out, and the ship was wrecked and Sir Caesar was drowned. After this she converted the tower into a permanent lighthouse, of which a more modern version still exists.

The wind now suddenly shifted to the north, dark clouds obscured the sun and we were glad of our thermal underwear as we plugged on with Wanda gamely leading the field to the ferry across Waterford Harbour from Ballyhack. Personally, I was wondering whether to brave the Irish telephone system and ask Directory Enquiries for the number of the nearest paybed nursing home.

On the far side of the estuary was Passage East, where first Strongbow had landed, and later Henry II, with four thousand men and four hundred ships which, at ten men to a ship, seems a lavish provision. Lying off it were a couple of fishing ships, one Belgian, the other French, taking herring on board from some Irish trawlers. Clouds of gulls were wheeling over them and the air was filled with their cries of frustration at seeing so much good food leaving for the Continent. Also on the far bank, but further downstream, was the site of what was once known as New Geneva, founded between 1782–5 by a band of Swiss Huguenots, a thousand strong, from Geneva. Their enthusiastic patron was Lord Temple, second Viscount Palmerston and father of Queen

Victoria's favourite minister; and a grant of £50,000 was made by the Irish Government to help them found a settlement and to encourage their craftsmen in gold and silver work. There was even talk of building a university, but it all came to nothing and the Swiss went home.

Later it became a barracks and then, after the rebellion of 1798, a prison, from which a number of captive rebels tried to escape by digging a tunnel. The debris which they excavated, always a disposal problem for diggers of illicit tunnels, was taken away by their wives and relatives in the baskets in which they brought in provisions (it sounds as if it was a pretty lax sort of place). Eventually, it was discovered, literally at the eleventh hour, by which time a number of accomplices were waiting outside to spirit the prisoners away, in boats, vehicles, and on horseback.

From Passage East we rode up a really appalling hill in the direction of Waterford. There, the mile-long quays along the south bank of the Suir were choked with parked vehicles, though still highly picturesque. Twenty years ago they would have looked better, as would the north bank of the river where ships now off-loaded their containers at the Bell Terminal, which was now frankly a mess; but then everywhere in the world was less of a mess twenty years ago. Anyway, our interest in aesthetics was for the time being subordinate to our need to find something to eat out of the freezing wind.

We found it in T. and H. Doolan's old, snug and dark pub which contained no one but a mild old man wearing a huge uniform overcoat who was drinking tea and a very grown-up young woman who was into the Irish Paddy and hot water, which seemed a good idea in the circumstances. The old man told us to bang on the bar to summon attention, something I am always loath to do in case the publican is on the bottle and comes rushing out to hit me over the head with it. But I complied, and my bang summoned a sympathetic fellow, a Doolan no doubt, from whom we ordered a large port, whiskey ditto with hot water, and what proved to be delicious helpings of fresh plaice and chips.

The sun had by now gone in and it was growing darker and darker in the pub, as if someone was turning a dimming switch; soon only the old man's pale face was visible and it too was beginning to go out, like that of the cat in *Alice in Wonderland*. By this time, Doolan's was beginning to resemble an abode of spiritualists.

'Is it always as quiet as this?' Wanda asked the girl with the Paddy.

'Not at all!' she replied. 'It's always very crowded three o'clock Saturdays – then there's a fine lot of fellers and girls in from the country.'

Waterford, we later discovered, when we could locate them in the deluge that began the moment we left Doolan's, has two cathedrals, one Catholic, the other Church of Ireland, otherwise Protestant. Both were built by a native of Waterford and a Protestant, John Roberts, great-grandfather of Field Marshal Earl Roberts of Kandahar, Pretoria and Waterford (1832–1914), who was awarded the Victoria Cross in 1858 after leading a cavalry charge during the Indian Mutiny and was known affectionately to the great British public as 'Bobs'.

Christchurch, Roberts' Protestant cathedral, was built between 1770 and 1779, partly destroyed by fire in 1815, restored in 1818 and 're-edified' in 1891 by the architect Sir Thomas Drew, who was noted for his 'robust and virile Gothic'. It was then vandalized in the 1970s. With all this attention lavished on it, it is surprising that it resembles anything at all. The high spot of the interior is the Rice Monument, which shows a body in an advanced state of decomposition with toads and frogs creeping out of it. It hardly left one asking the way to the dining car.

The Roman Catholic Cathedral of the Holy Trinity, known as the Big Chapel or the Great Chapel, was built later, between 1793 and 1796, in what for Catholics were still Penal Times. It cost £20,000 and the money is said to have been collected from the faithful entirely at the doors of other churches. A complete statement of what the Penal Laws entailed is impossible here, but among other things Catholics were forbidden to buy land or take leases for more than thirty-one years; they were forbidden to teach in school, teach their own children or educate them abroad; mixed marriages between people of property were forbidden and any child of such a union might be brought up as a Protestant. No Catholic could be a guardian and all wards in

Chancery were brought up as Protestants. It was a pretty savage system.

Architecturally, Roberts had Waterford wrapped up. He also built the Exchange and Assembly Rooms (1788), which later became the City Hall and Theatre Royal respectively, and an elegant town house with a splendid staircase (1795) in Great George Street, now used by the Chamber of Commerce and the Harbour Commissioners.

'What are you going to do now, Author?' Wanda asked as we stood on the steps of Christchurch, having absorbed the horror of the monuments within, and contemplating what one could see of the deluge outside in the pitch dark.

'Why don't you tell me?' I said huffily, knowing that she had already formulated some plan and disliking having to try to answer questions I can't answer, something which happens with increasing frequency.

'Because you have to decide,' she said triumphantly. 'You're the breadwinner.' If we hadn't been standing on consecrated ground, I would have put the curse of fire and water on her. 'You haven't forgotten,' she went on, 'that we have to be in Cork tonight? We're being put up in that hotel with a famous restaurant so that you can write about it.'

'Oh Lor,' I said, 'I thought it was tomorrow. Well, we can probably get a train, or a bus. The timetables are with the bikes. We'd better go and have a cup of tea and look at them.'

As soon as we were able to do this it became apparent that so far as we were concerned the train was a non-starter. Years ago a railway line, delineated on the map in the 1912 *Murray's Guide*, had wound its way innocuously through the countryside from Waterford to Mallow in County Cork, a spa famous for the foulness of its youth:

> Beauing, belling, dancing, drinking,
> Breaking windows, damning, sinking,
> Ever raking, never thinking,
> Live the rakes of Mallow.

From here it was only twenty-one miles on the Great Southern and Western Railway to Cork. But since then the aforementioned

Irish equivalent of Beeching had torn a lot of it up. Now, anyone foolish enough to make by rail what is by road a journey of seventy-eight miles, is taken out through the back-blocks of Waterford, Tipperary, Limerick and County Cork on an immense 114-mile semi-circular peregrination.

The timings were horrific, too: the evening service, of which I had thought we might avail ourselves, left Waterford at 20.50 (no refreshment facilities), reached Limerick Junction at 22.24, where there are no refreshment facilities either, to connect with a train which finally reached Cork at 23.55. On Saturdays the connection involved a wait at Limerick of 40 minutes, before arriving at Cork at 00.20 on Sunday morning; and Sunday was the great day when for the first leg of the journey there was no train at all, only a motor coach, appropriately indicated in the timetable by something that looked like a hearse.

The bus timetable was much more cheering and we had already decided to take a bus due to leave Waterford at 18.00 arriving Cork 20.15, when the proprietor of the café, who had become interested in our future, predicted rightly that the driver, who was approaching pensionable age and grumpy with it, would not take our bikes, exercising his right on an Expressway service to reject them, if he so wished.

'We'd better cancel the hotel in Cork and stay the night here.'

'Listen,' said Wanda, which was her favourite preamble, whatever the subject, 'if you think I'm going to give up a night in a nice, comfortable hotel for a bed and breakfast with a forty-watt bulb at the wrong end of the bed for reading with, you're mistaken. And what about the dinner? That book you didn't bring said, "One of Ireland's greatest kitchens and cellars". You read it out to me yourself. How far's Rosslare? If there is a train, one of us should go to Rosslare, get the van and drive back here, then go on to Cork.'

To our amazement there was a train to Rosslare that didn't first make a point of going to Limerick Junction. If everything went well we might just reach Cork in time for dinner. We telephoned our hotel. They were very nice and said that it would be all right for a late dinner, as long as we didn't make a practice of it.

'Let's toss to see who doesn't go to Rosslare,' Wanda said. I won.

'Oh hell,' I said. 'We've got our old-age Eurail half-price passes. What happens if you get lost, or the van breaks down, or you just decide not to come back? I'll be stuck here for ever. Let's be devils. Let's both go.'

And so we said goodbye to gallant little Waterford, without even laying eyes on a cut glass wine decanter; and goodbye to its distinguished sons, among them the young Irish leader Thomas Meagher (1823–67), condemned to death for his part in a rising in 1848. In fact his sentence was commuted to transportation to Tasmania, whence he eventually escaped to America to fight with great gallantry in the Irish Brigade of the Union Army, and eventually to become acting Governor of Montana, before falling overboard from a river steamer and drowning in the Missouri. And goodbye to Dorothy Jordan (1760–1816), notable comic actress and mistress, among other recipients of the honour being the Duke of Clarence, later William IV, by whom she had ten children, all of whom took the name of Fitzclarence. (When the Duke proposed, at the suggestion of George III, that her allowance from him should be reduced from £1000 a year to £500 she sent him the bottom part of a playbill for one of the productions she was taking part in which read, 'No money returned after the rising of the curtain'.) And goodbye Charles Kean, actor (1811–68), second son of Edmund Kean; and to William Vincent Wallace (1813–68), a voluminous composer and author of the operas *Maritana* and *Lurline*, both performed at Covent Garden with great success. An adventurous traveller, he visited Sydney, where the Governor paid him a hundred sheep to take part in a concert; Tasmania; and New Zealand, where he narrowly escaped being murdered by Maoris, thanks to the intervention of the daughter of a chief. Later, he took part in a whaling cruise in the South Pacific, in the course of which the crew murdered every European on board with the exception of himself and two others. In India he was made much of by the Begum of Oude, and visited Kashmir and Nepal; in Santiago he gave a concert for which he was paid partly with gamecocks; in Lima he was paid £1000 for a single appearance and in Mexico he wrote a

Grand Mass for a musical fête. He put a lot of money into piano and tobacco factories in America but lost it all, before returning to England where he wrote his operas and became famous. Before embarking on this odyssey he married a Miss Kelly of Blackrock, near Dublin, but she left him in Sydney and he never saw her again.

Goodbye Miss Kelly and goodbye Waterford. I love you, I think; but I would have loved you even more if you had not been under water.

Arbutus Lodge, Cork, at which we eventually succeeded in arriving at ten-thirty after an 130-mile drive from Rosslare, was a two-storey mid-nineteenth-century Italianate house, with touches of Romanesque here and there, perched on the side of a hill in the labyrinthine suburb of Montenotte. Architecturally, Montenotte resembled parts of nineteenth-century Torquay and Newton Abbott. Far below were what had once been lush pastures on the banks of the river Lee, downstream from the city, and in more recent times became the site of the Ford automobile and Dunlop tyre works (both now only of interest to industrial archaeologists), a power station, oil tanks, distillers, chemical works, etcetera.

Fortunately, distance lent enchantment to what had become a pretty ignoble view. The Lodge, like dozens of other residences in Montenotte, was the sort of place one expected to find oneself drinking Lapsang Souchong in company with some Irish Jane Austen and spreading crumpets with Gentleman's Relish. Dinner was delicious, as promised; the beds were comfortable and the breakfast excellent; anticipating a long day I had porridge, scrambled eggs, bacon, drisheen (black pudding), soda bread with very good marmalade and gallons of tea.

We left the van at the hotel and walked into the city along the quays that line the river Lee, which flows through the city in two main streams, making part of it an island. It was swathed in mist and spectral swans floated on it, motionless. These quays, which once sheltered dozens of ships, had an air not only of departed glory but of departed activity, having lost their traffic to the car ferry terminal downstream, and to the deepwater port at Rin-gaskiddy in Cork Harbour, where the transatlantic liners used to come in. Even a short list of signs on some of the now semi-decrepit buildings that line them suggest another age – 'The Cardboard Box Factory', 'The Cork Button Company', 'Drummys', 'Booth For Tools' – but some of these quays seen across the water were beautiful; and there were fine Georgian houses at the upstream end of the island on which the main commercial part of the city stands. Down at its eastern end, where the North and South Channels meet, there is a fine classical Customs House built at the end of the Napoleonic Wars, in a similar position to that occupied by the Dogana di Mare, the Custom House of the Sea, in Venice, at the junction of the Giudecca with the Grand Canal, but not looking so good being, now, unfortunately partly obscured by more modern constructions.

In Cornmarket, off Coal Quay, was the Old Market, according to those trustworthy compilers of the *Shell Guide*, 'Cork's only example of the Grand Style of the 18th century'. It was not market day, but some desultory selling was taking place of assorted junk and cast-off clothing, some of it cast off a great many times. And there were empty stalls by the roadside, between a couple of which a beat-up old van was parked, containing a couple of tinker men, two tinker women with thin, lined faces and a band of tinker children of indeterminate number, all with runny noses. Sud-denly, as if obeying an unpremeditated summons, the two men got out and made for one of the empty stalls, where one of them without preamble began laying out the cards for the three-card trick, while the other stood close by keeping a look-out for the police and at the same time putting down stakes to encourage the rest of the crowd.

Almost at once the owner of the stall appeared, a big, tough woman of about fifty with her hair in a greasy, grizzled bun and with a big apron out front; the sort of woman who would enjoy a good fight with another woman outside a pub on a Saturday night.

'Get to hell off my place!' she said, breaking through the crowd to the tinker and brandishing a big red fist under his nose. 'May you die roaring! Get off it!'

And although the tinker looked as rough as she did he didn't stop to argue. He simply picked up the cards and moved off to a nearby open site covered with rubble, and the crowd re-formed around him, rather like a swarm of bees about a queen.

Cork was famous for its beggars, who were reputedly as noisy and good-humoured as their counterparts in Dublin were insolent and unattractive. Back in the 1830s Mrs Anna Maria Hall, author of *Ireland, Its Scenery, Character &c*, described how difficult it was to resist them:

> If you have no halfpence the answer is ready, 'Ah, but we'll divide a little sixpence between us.' The language in which they frame their petitions is always pointed, forcible and, generally, highly poetic: 'Good luck to your ladyship's happy face this morning – sure ye'll lave the light heart in my bussom before you go?' 'Oh, help the poor craythur that's got no childer to show yer honour – they're down in the sickness, and the man that owns them at sea. Darling gintleman, the heavens be yer bed, and give us something.'
>
> One beggar, on receiving nothing from one known to be a Poor Law Commissioner, addressed him with, 'Ah, then; it's little business you'd have only for the likes of us.' Another, soliciting charity from a gentleman with red hair, thrust forward her child with, 'And won't ye give a ha'penny to the little boy? Sure he's as foxy like yer honour.' And when one of the customers in an attempt to commiserate, said, 'You've lost all your teeth,' to one of them, the reply came back, 'Time for me to lose 'em when I'd nothing for 'em to do.'[*]

Cork, in parts like a Dutch city before they filled in the Zuider Zee, had a sad feeling about it; something to do with the weather, no doubt, but more perhaps to do with the horrors that were perpetrated in it during the Troubles: vile, senseless murders

---

[*] At Nass, in County Kildare, where the number of native beggars was said to be twice the population of the town, a person in a stage coach, pestered beyond endurance, told the applicant to go to hell. At this, the woman turned up her eyes and said, 'Ah, then it's a long journey yer honour's sending us; maybe yer honour'll give us something for our expenses.'

committed by both sides, including that of the Lord Mayor of Cork, an ardent supporter of Sinn Fein, all culminating in the burning down by the Black and Tans on 12 December 1920 of a large part of the eastern, downstream part of the city, for which they made use of hundreds of gallons of petrol taken by connivance from military depots, and in the course of which the Carnegie Library and a large part of the shopping area was destroyed.

One of the nicest but not the warmest places in Cork in winter is the covered English Market which lies between St Patrick Street, Grand Parade and Oliver Plunket Street. Both St Patrick Street, which was one of the first to be set ablaze by the Black and Tans, and Grand Parade were created in the eighteenth century by filling in a channel of the river Lee, so that shoppers now shop where ships formerly tied up alongside quays. Unfortunately, what was architecturally the finest part of the market had been recently destroyed by fire; the last of a series of misfortunes that has dogged Cork since its beginnings.

It all started off sedately enough in 600 AD when one of the islands in the river (the *corcaigh*, or marshy place, from which the city took its name) was selected as the site of a monastery by St Finbarr, the son of a master metal worker to a Prince Tigherach. Finbarr had already founded another monastery on an island in the lake of Gougane Barra, at the feet of the Sheehy Mountains in West Cork. By the end of the ninth century the monastery and the town that had grown up round it had become such a popular target for raiding parties of Norsemen that in 917 a band of them decided to settle there, so as to be nearer to their work, as it were, and they themselves eventually became Christianized.

When Henry II arrived on the scene Cork was ruled by Dermot MacCarthy, who unwisely submitted to him and immediately found himself out on the streets. In 1378 the Irish set fire to the city, by which time it had been an English possession for some ninety years or more.

Cork always had a predilection for supporting revolt, but almost invariably chose to support the wrong side, often with dire consequences. One such example was Perkin Warbeck, pretender to the English throne in the reign of Henry VII. In 1497 he sailed from Cork to Cornwall, where he proclaimed himself King as Richard IV; he was hanged at Tyburn two years later, having made a thorough nuisance of himself, together with the Mayor of Cork, who had been silly enough to conspire with him, and the town lost its charter. It also supported Charles I during the Civil War and was taken by Cromwell's forces. In 1689 it welcomed James II and victualled his forces before his departure for the North where he was defeated at the Battle of the Boyne. In recognition of this assistance John Churchill, first Duke of Marlborough and William's commander-in-chief in England, took Cork and Kinsale, and Cork was set fire to once more and its walls and fortifications destroyed. In the civil war which followed the signing of the Anglo-Irish Treaty of 1921, Cork was the only city occupied by the Republicans, the anti-Treaty members of the IRA, and that, too, was lost to them when units of the Sinn Fein Free State Army under Michael Collins and a couple of generals landed at Passage West in the narrows north of Cork Harbour and took the city without much trouble.

In spite of all this, which would have floored a less resilient lot of people for evermore, the shoppers in what remained of the English Market seemed full of fight, milling around a fountain ornamented with cast iron pelicans, and nattering away at the butchers in their brightly lit stalls who were doing big business in what their placards described as 'bodice of beef', and drisheen. Drisheen, the black pudding I had been given at Arbutus Lodge for breakfast, is larger in diameter than most other black puddings, and used to be made with sheep's blood (in Tipperary they used turkey or goose blood, and the results were said to be spectacular), breadcrumbs or oatmeal, pepper, a pinch of mace and a sprig of tansy. Now it is usually made with pig's blood and liver and thyme. Cork men and women apparently never forget the pleasure of eating drisheen and many of them return from wherever they may be in exile for the pleasure of tasting it again.

And so we said goodbye to Cork; true we had not seen much of it, but we both felt that we had been able to absorb some of the *genius loci* of the place, which in my case was assisted by having absorbed two memorable pints of Murphy's stout. Brewed in

Cork, Murphy's is different from Guinness, more velvety, and a taste for either, if over-indulged, can lead to smiles all round for the shareholders and for the consumer a dramatic change of profile and/or a visit to the bankruptcy court.

Chapter 8

THROUGH THE REALMS OF
MOVING STATUES

'When I complained to an Irish soldier of the length of
the miles between Kinsale and Cork, he acknowledged
the truth of my observation; but archly added, that
though they were *long*, they were but *narrow*.'

PHILIP THICKNESSE. *A Year's Long Journey
Through France and Spain*, 1789

Since we now had a van surplus to our requirements, we set off northwards to see some of the places that would have been impossible to see had we been on bicycle, with limited time and energy at our disposal. The first was Lismore, a vast, now largely Victorian castle, high on a rock above a narrow bridge spanning the river Blackwater, which looked nice in the rain.

The castle was originally built while he was Governor of Ireland by Prince John, son of Henry II and later himself King of England from 1199–1216. He was a most unpleasant fellow, unpopular with almost everybody in the country – with the indigenous Irish for his insolent manners (he used to pull their beards and encouraged his sycophants to do the same) and equally unpopular with his mercenary soldiers because he spent what was intended to be their pay. No one shed a tear when he died of dysentery, having just lost his treasury in the Wash.

Later the castle became the property of Sir Walter Raleigh but he could not afford to keep it up so he sold this and his other extensive Irish possessions, which he had come by in pretty dubious circumstances, for a paltry sum* to Richard Boyle, first Earl of Cork, an Englishman of indefatigable deviousness, known to some as 'The Great Earl' and to others, less admiring, as 'That ******* Earl'. One of the Earl's sons was Robert Boyle, known as 'the father of chemistry' and propounder in

*Altogether this was a bad time for Sir Walter. He had recently made pregnant Elizabeth Throgmortòn, one of Queen Elizabeth's ladies-in-waiting, and although he married her after she had given birth to a fine boy, the Queen had him committed to the Tower. It may well have been this particular seduction which John Aubrey described so vividly in his *Brief Lives*.

1662 of Boyle's Law, by which he was able to prove, experimentally, that the pressure and volume of a gas are inversely proportional.

By the marriage of the Fourth Duke of Devonshire to a Boyle in 1753 the castle passed to the Devonshires. On succeeding to the title in 1811 the sixth Duke, known subsequently as 'the Bachelor Duke', commissioned William Atkinson to restore in the mediaeval manner that part of the castle which overhung the river. The Duke entrusted further work to Joseph Paxton, who had been Superintendent of the gardens and woods at Chatsworth, the ducal seat of the Devonshires in Derbyshire, and who had by this time become a personal friend of the Duke, whom he had accompanied on his extensive travels in Europe and Asia Minor, and to Lismore in Ireland in 1840. Ten years later, having completed the great conservatory at Chatsworth, which was 300 feet long and which to some extent was the prototype of the Crystal Palace, and having the satisfaction of knowing that his plans for the Great Exhibition of 1851 had been accepted by the organizers, Paxton embarked on the reconstruction of Lismore. The stone to rebuild it was brought all the way from Derbyshire.

Hoping to be allowed an unofficial visit to this fascinating place which, apart from the grounds, is rarely if ever open to the public, we presently found ourselves in a courtyard, one side of which housed the Duke's agent, another side an austere, high Victorian estate office. Glad that we weren't wearing our bicycle clips we entered it and found, not as I had imagined an old man called Mr Fothergill standing at a high desk scratching away at eviction orders with a quill pen and chuckling to himself the while, but a pair of formidable ladies, Irish versions of Bond's Miss Moneypenny. They looked as if they probably had a computer or two locked away in a roll-top desk.

For a moment I thought we might win through but it was not to be. The agent was elsewhere, and not expected back until the following morning; would we telephone for an appointment another day, one of them said in tones which somehow contrived to mingle concern for our future with complete indifference and to create a feeling of pessimism as to the outcome of any telephone conversation we might succeed in having with him. Both the Duke and his agent are well served by these ladies who, while only having two heads and not three, make Cerberus look like a lap dog.

What had we missed? The mediaeval chapel of the Bishops of Lismore, restored as a fantastic ballroom or banqueting room for the sixth Duke, some of its furnishings, such as the great chimneypiece, designed by Augustus Pugin (1812–52), who played an important part in the design of the new Houses of Parliament. These works at Lismore must have been among his last, for the re-modelling did not begin until 1850 and in 1851 he was appointed a Commissioner of Fine Arts for the Great Exhibition. By the end of that year overwork had induced a nervous breakdown of such severity that in 1852 he became a patient in a private asylum, from which he was removed to Bedlam, the great public asylum in South London (now the Imperial War Museum), and subsequently died at Ramsgate that same year. Those who saw the interior after Atkinson's re-modelling say that it was not particularly exciting. 'Vast apartments full of battered furniture and gloom' was what Lady Caroline Lamb hoped to find at Lismore, when brought to Ireland in an attempt to make her forget Byron by her husband and her mother, Lady Bessborough. She was disappointed. The rooms proved to be small and, to her taste, bijou.

In 1814, however, workmen had discovered, hidden in the walls, two objects of inestimable value. One was the Lismore Crozier: made of pale bronze ornamented with gilt and lapis-lazuli over an oak core, it bore an inscription asking for prayers for Nial, son of Aeducain, who was Bishop of Lismore from 1090 to 1113, and for Nechtan, the artist who made it. The other find was *The Book of Lismore*, a manuscript on vellum, compiled in the fifteenth century by various scribes from the long-lost *Book of Monasterboice*, which contains accounts of the lives of the saints together with historical and romantic tracts. [*]

The village outside the walls of the Castle was a pleasant place with a wide street flanked by shops, some of which had windows dressed with merchandise that looked as if it had been acquired in

---

[*]Dog-eared and damaged by damp, it was painstakingly copied in 1839 by the Gaelic scholar, Eugene O'Curry, Professor of Archaeology at the Catholic University in Dublin, and the copy is now in the Irish Academy.

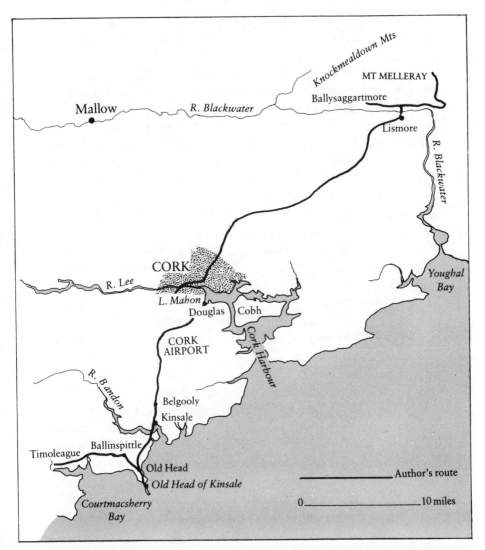

the 1930s. It was early closing and the place was one of the most deserted of all the villages we had so far seen, at least in broad daylight, or what was currently serving as broad daylight in these parts, which wasn't much. Even the pub, quite a lively-looking place from the outside, was closed. In every way, in its neatness and well-keptness, Lismore announced itself as something which is still quite common in England wherever Dukes exist but which

129

is almost impossible to credit in Ireland, given the building horrors that have taken place in the last few years: a Ducal appendage.

The village has two 'cathedrals': St Carthage's Cathedral (Church of Ireland) and the Roman Catholic St Carthage's Church, built in the 1880s (this too is known as 'the Cathedral', but the See is really at Waterford). The Protestant cathedral had been destroyed by some warlike ruffian at the beginning of the seventeenth century and rebuilt at the end of it. In 1827 it was given a spire by George Richard Pain, one of two English brothers (the other was James) who originally worked as assistants to John Nash. It is not surprising, given these Nashean antecedents, that it has a somewhat frivolous appearance.

Carthage, otherwise Charthaigh, Cuda or Mochuda, was the son of a shepherd. He became a monk at the age of twelve, and spent forty years as an inhabitant of Rahan Abbey in County Offaly before being expelled at Easter 635 for abandoning the traditional date of Easter celebrations. Carthage finally reached Lismore, where he was offered a tract of land on the banks of the Blackwater by the Prince of Waterford, on which he founded a monastery which became known as the 'Holy City'. His order survived there to reach the height of its importance in the eighth century, when it became a place of pilgrimage and retirement for Irish kings and princes who had had enough of the rude, rough world outside, after which it was sacked five or six times by the Vikings, but always rebuilt. Its golden age finally came to an end when Strongbow's son plundered and burned everything – the church, the abbey, the convent for women and the leper hospital; and it was on this site laid waste that the beastly Prince John built the first castle.

The next surprises in store for us were some constructions in a wooded valley upstream from Lismore on the left bank of the Blackwater, at a place called Ballysaggartmore. We found them by chance on the way to see something else which we never got to. The first buildings we encountered (although abandoned, they are certainly not ruins, and show every sign of having been built to last for ever) were two Gothic gatehouses hidden away at the foot of the demesne near the main road, forming an extraordinary castellated complex of archways, towers and turrets, pierced with windows with leaded panes, and built of blocks of yellow sandstone. The whole thing was the epitome of Gothick melancholy. What could it have cost to build? From the gateway a long drive led away through dense woods to another magnificent set of follies, a castellated bridge pierced by three Gothic arches with gatehouses at either end in the form of miniature castellated castles, each with a two-storey round tower defending it, all executed this time in rusticated red sandstone of local origin. Beyond all this one expected to see a moderately sized castle, or at least a continuation of the drive; but there was nothing, only a very muddy track leading away among the dripping trees along the side of the hill, and another which led steeply down through the valley to the main road. With the little stream purling along and the rain hissing down on us and the miniature castles that looked as if they would never grow old Ballysaggartmore was a place to remember.

It was not until I got back to England that I was able to find out anything much about it, and that was pretty sketchy. These wonderful constructions were the work of J. Smith – not even his first name seems to have been recorded – who was head gardener to a gentleman named Arthur Keily, on whose property they were built. He married a Miss Martin and it was she who is said to have persuaded him to build a castle in emulation of his brother's castle, Strancally, at Knockanore, south of Lismore, which was designed and built by the Pain brothers sometime around 1830.

The Ballysaggartmore Gothic gatehouses and castellated bridge were intended to be architectural appetizers on the way to the *pièce de resistance* – the castle itself. Had it been built, they would have ceased to be follies and would simply have formed part of a grander design. Unfortunately, so much money was expended on these *hors d'oeuvres* that there was none left for the castle itself, and the Keilys – he changed his name to Ussher in 1843, as did his brother at Knockanore – were forced to continue to live in their not very grand eighteenth-century house nearby. It is a sad story, but at least the Keilys (or Usshers) could console themselves with the thought that although they didn't have a castle, they did have the most wonderful follies.

After Ballysaggartmore we drove to Mount Melleray, high on the slopes of the Knockmealdown Mountains, an abbey built by Trappists in what was then a wilderness after all the foreign members of the order were expelled from France in 1822. Here we hoped to stay the night in the abbey guest house in which the monks offer free hospitality, but unfortunately for us this service was not operating in winter. The abbey church was rather grim and bare; it was built in the 1920s, a largely infelicitous time for architecture, particularly ecclesiastical architecture, and was the sort of building in which it is always Sunday afternoon. Even the conifers that had been planted along the terrace, possibly as a windbreak, were calculated to obscure the magnificent views from it to the south and west, where the sun had finally managed to break through, bathing everything in a stormy, ochreous light. It is strange how impervious so many members of the Church appear to be to the surroundings in which they perform their everyday acts of faith, a Church which in the past has inspired some of the greatest artistic masterpieces the world has known.

Down in a little wooded dell by the bridge over the Monavuaga river, the upper parts of which were still touched by the sunset, there was a painted concrete statue of the Virgin, which had been set up there during 1954, the Marian Year. It was a pretty place, very quiet except for the sounds of rushing water. Kneeling before the statue were half a dozen women and one elderly man. Vases filled with artificial flowers, and admonitions and instructions on how to comport oneself, some of them written in coloured ink which had run a bit, stood amongst the still dripping greenery.

In August 1985 this particular statue had ceased to be just another Marian image and became what some now refer to as the Miraculous Virgin of Mount Melleray. For it was then that she was first seen to smile, and to move her head, now surrounded by a blue halo, and other parts of her body. On one occasion she actually descended from her place on the side of the dell in order to admonish some small boys who were behaving in a rowdy fashion, which gave them a bit of a turn. She is also said to have announced that the world would come to an end on 28 or 29 September, the latter date being the Feast of St Michael and All Angels (Michaelmas). Well, there was no action on this particular afternoon. If ever a statue looked immovable, this one did. Maybe something would have transpired if we had stayed on for a bit, but we had no time.

We went on to spend the night in a very comfortable B and B on what were still the arcadian shores of Lough Mahon except where the local authorities, with that delicacy of taste that characterizes local authorities everywhere but which nowhere reaches its full flower more than in Ireland, had decided to build a sewage plant on them. Mrs Walsh, our hospitable landlady, told us that we could leave our van with her as long as we liked, and thinking we might be short of reading matter she very kindly presented us with Georgina Masson's *Italian Gardens*, a magnificent coffee-table work which weighed 5 lbs 4 oz, and which we left in the van as ballast after ascertaining that her feelings would not be hurt.

Not far off was Castle Mahon, now a golf club, a fortress house with towers at each of its four corners, built by Anastasia Gould in 1836 as a surprise for her husband while he was away overseas. When it was completed and she balanced the books she found that as the result of an advantageous deal she had struck with the workmen whereby she was their sole supplier of food and clothing, the net cost came to 4d. In spite of this she apparently incurred the displeasure of her husband, who thought she had mismanaged the business.

The nearest place to eat was Douglas, which at nine o'clock on what was now a nasty, cold, wet night was still the scene of frenetic activity, with people tottering out of the shopping precinct, some of them in pairs bent double under the weight of huge cardboard containers that contained washing machines, Toshiba Microwave ovens, Hitachi 26" Teletext TV sets ('Offer Price £449.99. Save £30') and/or Philips Twin Deck Midi System Hi-Fis with Graphic Equalizers ('Offer Price £189.99. Save £20'). After a nice dinner of grilled sole Wanda bought a pair of Taiwanese gloves from a shop in the precinct in which entire outfits of clothes lovingly crafted in South Korea and Taiwan came out at only £14 a set; then we went back and had lovely hot baths at Mrs Walsh's B and B.

The next day started with everything except my sinuses being frozen solid. Then it began to pour with rain, and by the time we got going it was so dark that flocks of birds were going to roost, under the impression that night was falling. I felt we had been a bit dotty to abandon the van.

We left for Kinsale, having asked the way from the kindly driver of a juggernaut container lorry loaded with bananas. The somewhat erratic route he proposed took us through an industrial estate full of banana warehouses and suchlike, and it was in this unsuitable area for such a purpose that we both developed the urge to pee, which is not all that easy when one is wearing Gore-Tex trousers over other trousers over thermal underwear, not to speak of Bike Brite Retro-Reflective Sam Browne belts. When Wanda finally found a spot that seemed to be to her liking she discovered, too late, that it was infested with stinging nettles. In spite of these difficulties we presented a brave face to the world and actually succeeded in raising a cheer from a little band of heroes who were clearing dense, rain-sodden scrub from the roadside, as we plugged up an interminable hill past Cork airport.

We reached Kinsale, having crossed two parallel ranges that were for us the equivalent of the Karakoram, via a beautiful, wooded estuary where brown swans floated in the puddles that the tide had left behind and a few oystercatchers were scraping a living on expanses of steely-coloured mud which looked as if they were jumping up and down under the rain that was bombarding them. In fact there was more water in the atmosphere than there was air.

The lower part of Kinsale, with its tile-hung houses disposed around the main square, had a strange, operatic, foreign feeling about it, even in the rain. (The upper parts of the place, on the other hand, were Georgian English.) The Valmoule Restaurant was even serving Crabs Guadeloupe, although the place next door was reassuringly Anglo-Irish, offering a three-course meal, choice of beef, pork or lamb, at £3 a head, including tea. Perhaps it was the influence of Spain that made it look as it did. In September 1601 a Spanish fleet commanded by Don Juan d'Aguila sailed up the Brandon estuary on which the town stands and disembarked some 3800 foot soldiers, who immediately proceeded to occupy the two castles which commanded the entrance to the harbour.

The Spaniards' plan was to bring help to Hugh O'Neill, Earl of Tyrone and to Red Hugh II O'Donnell, Lord of Tyrconnel (an ancient territory in north-west Ireland now County Donegal). Since 1594, in what was known as the Nine Years War (1594–1603), the pair of them had had a series of spectacular military successes against the forces of the English Governor of Connaught on the borders of Tyrconnel and Tyrone and in Munster, where 210,000 acres of the best land had been confiscated in order that they might be settled by Protestants in what was known as the Plantation.

It was unfortunate that the Spaniards had chosen to make their landings at the furthest possible point from where the forces of O'Neill and O'Donnell were at that time operating. And there, at Kinsale, d'Aguila and his Spaniards waited for the Irish armies to arrive from the north, besieged meanwhile by an English force of twelve thousand men, commanded by Lord Mountjoy, Elizabeth's Lord Deputy in Ireland, whom she had sent there with the task of crushing the rebels for good and all.

It took the rebel armies ten weeks to reach Kinsale, but when they arrived Mountjoy found himself in a precarious position between the guns of the Spaniards in the town and the encircling Irish forces. On 24 December it was decided that the Irish and Spanish should launch a simultaneous attack on the English. What followed was a disaster. The Irish lost their way to the starting point, and instead of attacking were completely routed by the English. Meanwhile the Spaniards did nothing but watch the outcome of the battle from the town.

Nine days later, on 2 January 1602, the Spaniards surrendered and were subsequently allowed to leave the country. O'Neill succeeded in escaping but was forced to make his submission to the English throne in March 1603, six days after the Queen's death, and the following month to make a further submission to James I. O'Donnell sailed for Spain where he was given a cool reception by Philip III until the truth emerged about d'Aguila's cowardly behaviour, at which time his stock began to rise. But it was too late: on 10 September he died, having, it is thought, been poisoned by a Scotsman. He was buried at Valladolid. He was only twenty-eight. Although the last rites were postponed for another five years, these events at Kinsale marked the end of the old Gaelic order, which had survived from the earliest times in Tyrone and Tyrconnel.

For in spite of a pardon from James I for both O'Neill and O'Donnell's successor, Rory O'Donnell, the former having his earldom of Tyrone restored to him and the latter being created Earl of Tyrconnel, they both lost their power as independent rulers, which must have influenced them in their decision to leave the country. This they did at midnight on 14 September 1607 from Rathmullen in Lough Swilly; a total of ninety-nine persons, including family and retainers. Bound for Spain, after a fearful voyage in what was a small vessel, 'having little sea-store and being otherwise miserably accommodated', they were driven ashore at the mouth of the Seine, and eventually arrived at Rome after much wandering and with a much reduced retinue. There they lived as pensioners of Pope Paul V until their deaths, O'Donnell's in 1608 and O'Neill's in 1616, and both Earls were buried in the church of San Pietro di Montorio.

In fact, like Cork, Kinsale continued to be a rather unhealthy place to be mixed up with unless you happened to be English and Protestant. After Mountjoy's victory no Irishman or Catholic was allowed to live within its walls. James II landed there in 1689 to begin his unsuccessful campaign to recover his throne. After his defeat at the Battle of the Boyne it was from Kinsale that he sailed into exile. John Churchill, later Duke of Marlborough, took the town after reducing Cork, and having a Churchillian eye or nose discovered a thousand barrels of wheat and eighty pipes of claret in one of the forts. It then became an English naval base, which it remained until the latter part of the eighteenth century when ships became so large that they could no longer be easily accommodated there. The base was moved to Cork, and after this Kinsale ceased to be prosperous.

Of course neither of us knew all this when we arrived in Kinsale on our bikes, but then the disadvantage of riding bikes in the rain is that you can't consult guide books while awheel, and when you're not awheel you are too busy eating, drinking, squirting oil on your chain, changing your wet socks, sticking plaster on your bum, writing your notes or just slumping or sleeping to do much improving reading. At least we were. So much for Kinsale *in tempi passati* – perhaps too much.

Chapter 9

A NIGHT IN BALLINSPITTLE

'He was talking very excitedly to me,' said the Vicar, 'about some apparatus for warming a church in Worthing and about the Apostolic Claims of the Church of Abyssinia. I confess I could not follow him clearly. He seems deeply interested in Church matters. Are you quite sure he is right in the head? I have noticed again and again since I have been in the Church that lay interest in ecclesiastical matters is often a prelude to insanity.'

EVELYN WAUGH. *Decline and Fall*, 1947

Our first stop at Kinsale was at the premises of a friendly garage proprietor and bike-repairer who operated his business single-handed in a building which resembled an airship hangar with the heating switched off. I asked him to adjust Wanda's faulty back brake as I had left my pliers back in England and had never acquired what is known as a Third Hand Tool; it took an eternity because we were part of a queue which included the owners of a pre-war Ford tractor that was in need of re-animation and a car that looked as if it might have passed a millennium or two in the Labbacallee wedge-shaped gallery grave, Ireland's largest and finest. And from time to time the owner had to trot across the road to work his petrol pump which was out on a limb next door to the town's principal department store, located in the former Community Hall. In it every assistant had her own individual Calor gas heater, and there was a large enough stock of Irish handicrafts to last until the end of time. Here Wanda, less interested than I in machinery on the verge of dissolution, took refuge, moving from heater to heater and chatting up the girls, from one of whom she received a leaflet entitled *Ballinspittle in the Night: Some Facts about the Statue*. Having described the construction of a grotto there and the erection in it of a statue of Our Lady in 1954, it went on as follows:

> Isolated unusual sightings have been reported over a ten to fifteen-year period. One of these was reported by two young girls in January, then on the 22nd of July 1985. Members of the Daly and O'Mahony families on an afternoon walk stopped to pray at the Grotto. At the end of the prayers two of the group, one aged 17, the other

aged 10 years, told the others that the statue was falling or going to fall. All seven saw as did others before nightfall. Various other manifestations were reported by 13 persons on that first night. Movements, alterations, even visions are reported by a minority daily, and about 80% nightly (Peak Social Hours). There is some evidence of sudden cures and many reports of spiritual conversion.

About 500,000 have visited so far.

Among the gas heaters, all the girls were for the phenomena.

'It was five visits before I saw her move,' the garage man said, having adjusted the brake and refused payment, which made us feel bad about being impatient. 'I'd almost given up hope. And when I did see her move, I didn't want to believe it.'

'You've chosen a terrible day if you're on your way for the Statue,' said one of two men sharing a food-free lunch in the Anchor Inn, where we were enjoying a degustation of soup and pie. 'I don't believe she'll be obliging at all.'

'And why shouldn't she oblige,' said his companion, 'whatever the weather? Would she be getting even a drop of moisture on her, even spiritually?' And they both went off into a rambling theological discussion, some of which was about why they had never been able to see it move when it had obliged for their wives and daughters, the rest of which was impossible to understand, or disentangle from their heavy accents and inversions of syntax such as 'It is on my way home I was.'

Until now neither of us had any idea that we were anywhere near Ballinspittle. This was because it was situated on the folds of our half-inch map of the area, which had been folded and unfolded so often in the prevailing damp that its location had become nothing more than pulp. Now we decided to leave at once, and try to see the statue in one of its Peak Social Hours.

And so to Ballinspittle along the shores of the Brandon estuary, past decrepit buildings that looked like barracks, and forts, and decrepit quays with fishing vessels that looked as if they would probably never go to sea again tied up alongside, with the rain still coming down like anything on everything. Then we crossed a bridge and climbed steeply into thick, freezing fog. The surface of the road had an awful lifeless quality, as if it was covered with porridge, and our brakes were permanently on. I was behind Wanda who was battling away, making things impossible for herself in a gear of 51.3″, which was much too high for her in the circumstances, having locked herself on to a 38-tooth chain ring and a 20-tooth sprocket.

'Change down!' I shouted, with no effect at all. Anyone wearing a Gore-Tex hood can hear practically nothing, not even a passing juggernaut. '*Change down!*' I shrieked in the direction of her right ear, coming up alongside her, a hazardous business in the prevailing conditions of nil visibility. 'Push the right lever forward and pull the left one backward!' I shouted.

'There's no need to shout,' she said huffily, at the same time pushing and pulling the levers so that up front the chain mounted on to the mighty 48-tooth ring and at the back descended on to the 14-tooth sprocket, producing the highest gear of the lot, a colossal 92.6″, at which point the machine stopped moving and Wanda dismounted.

'This is too much,' she said. 'I'm going to walk.'

'It's easier riding,' I said. 'You're just in the wrong gear.'

'I don't care what gear it's in,' she said. 'I'm not a superwoman. You ride, I'm walking.'

After which, because we were on the pulped section of the map and obeyed a crazy signpost, we made what proved to be a wide detour before descending to Ballinspittle.

Ballinspittle was two streets and a small square, and the reader will be relieved to know that I am not going to run on about the Norsemen, the Anglo-Normans and the Anglo-Saxons, and their influence on Ballinspittle. I don't even know what the significance of the rather extraordinary name is.

We put up in what had been the schoolhouse, built in 1833, and was now the home of a Mr and Mrs O'Donovan and their eight children: one boy and three girls, big; two boys and two girls, small. We were cold and wet, our climbing boots were like sponges, and kind Mrs O'Donovan gave us a nice pot of tea before we set off for the statue.

'I saw her hands moving,' she said. 'And some of the children, but not all, saw her turn her head sideways, the first time. Besides ourselves there were two ladies there. They said "Hail Marys" but nothing happened until they began the rosary. It was the rosary that clinched it.'

The Grotto was about half a mile uphill from the village and about thirty feet above the road, in the face of what was really more of a steep bank on the hillside than a cliff, although here and there outcrops of rock protruded from it. How much of the Grotto was natural and how much was constructed was difficult to say, but according to the pamphlet issued by the Committee, which also took the opportunity to announce a new cassette on sale, a lot of work had been put into it. Someone irreverently has compared it to a sentry box. The site had been donated by a local man, and was planted with dwarf conifers and shrubs and further embellished with vases of artificial flowers and rosettes. Below it, down near the roadside, there was a small enclave in which there were benches on which one could either sit or kneel while contemplating the statue. On a night such as this, when there were only three other visitors besides ourselves – a middle-aged nun in a severe pale grey gabardine raincoat which matched her complexion, what looked like her middle-aged brother, in pale grey ditto, and the driver of the taxi in which they had come here, who had nothing on but a suit – there was plenty of room. This little enclosure was separated from the bank and the Grotto by blue and white cement railings with the words 'Immaculate Conception' cast in the upper part. On the opposite side of the road rose a steeply sloping field, its surface covered with sand, which was said to be capable of holding between six and seven thousand spectators, rather like one of the terraces behind the goal posts in a football stadium.

The statue itself was what is known as a Five Foot Eight Lourdes. It was made in 1954 from half a ton of concrete, its hands reinforced with wire, by the Barnardi Brothers in Cork, known there locally as Chalkey God's, and the man who made it, Maurice O'Donnell, is still alive. According to him, the demand for statues to be made that year was so great that they often used to leave the statues unpainted to be finished off on site. The correct colours were white for the robes and blue for the scarf, which was how the Virgin appeared to the fourteen-year-old peasant girl, Bernadette Soubirous, at noon on 11 February 1858 in the Massabielle Grotto at Lourdes. The fingertips of the statue were pressed together across the breast in an attitude of prayer and a rose had been placed between them, a daily offering made by Catherine O'Mahony, one of the seven girls who first saw the statue move. A long rosary made up of large beads hung from her wrists. The face was slightly upturned and the expression it wore, which was intended to suggest piety, could only be described as vacant, partly due to the treatment of the eyes which were nothing but blobs of bright blue paint. Above the head was a halo of eleven electric light bulbs, which strongly illuminated the face.

Three days after the first manifestations took place, on 25 July 1985, Teresa O'Donnell from a village near Skibbereen in south-west Cork, visiting the shrine with her family, saw the statue appear to grow larger and clearer. The following night she saw 'a small silver cross shining very brightly' on a nearby hill. Others present saw it too, but enigmatically said that 'in reality it was not there at all.' A party of Bavarians who were in the field that night, when questioned by a reporter, said they had seen the statue move but that they thought it was due to the halo of electric lights. 'We shan't be coming again,' they added, a little ungraciously.

On 31 July a 37-year-old housewife and mother of four from Cork city, Mrs Frances O'Riordan, had her hearing restored during a night visit to Ballinspittle, having been completely deaf since contracting measles at the age of four. In 1982 she had visited a Cork hospital where an ear, nose and throat specialist had told her that both eardrums were irreparably damaged. She not only saw the statue move but experienced strange choking sensations and a feeling that her body was about to explode. She then heard the first sounds she had heard for twenty years: the crowd singing 'Ave Maria' (it was too dark for her to lip read). The doctor to whom she subsequently went to have a hearing aid fitted said she now had almost 30 per cent hearing. Although not a regular churchgoer she had made three pilgrimages to Knock in County Mayo, where a series of apparitions were seen on the gable of the parish church in August 1879, hoping for a miracle, but without success.

Another cure, this time of arthritis, was apparently effected on a Mrs Kathleen O'Loughlin, the wife of a taxi driver, Gerald O'Loughlin, who told the journalist June Levine how it happened:

> He had gone to the Grotto four times at night and stood in 'huge crowds' but did not see anything unusual. His wife was in great pain with her feet and legs and 'it was fierce for her getting down to pray' – but she got up without a bother. The pain was gone. It took a few days for the swelling to go, but the pain went like that. . . .*

On 15 August, the Feast of the Assumption, three weeks after the events witnessed by girls of the Daly and O'Mahony families, fifteen thousand people from all over Ireland descended on Ballinspittle by car and special bus and coach services, and the tradespeople of Knock, who are deeply into the religious memento business, were said to be beginning to be worried about their future livelihood. In anticipation of this influx a sixty-strong Shrine Committee had been formed and prayer-masters and mistresses selected to lead the recitals of the rosary and other prayers, punctuating them with edifying commentaries on the dire state of everything. A car park had been opened, for which tickets cost £1 each. The field had been bulldozed free of dangerous protuberances and covered with sand brought from Courtmacsherry Bay. A nearby stream had been piped underground. Lavatories were in position. The road past the shrine had been closed to vehicular traffic and the little enclave immediately below the statue roped off for the use of the aged and infirm between two and four in the afternoon, at other times for those with enough push to get into it, such as newspaper reporters.

The day began with a Mass conducted by the Bishop of Cork at the Diocesan Shrine in Cork, for he would not allow Mass to be celebrated at the shrine itself. Hymns, however, were sung at the shrine by various choirs, including the Our Lady of Lourdes

*Source: June Levine in *Seeing is Believing. Moving Statues in Ireland*, ed. Colm Toibin, Pilgrim Press, 1985, to which I am indebted for this and much other information.

Choir; sixty people also recited the rosary outside the gates of Our Lady's Hospital; and at eleven o'clock that night the Riverstock Folk Group performed. Meanwhile proprietors of burger and chip vans did big business, and the Ladies' Committee made tea. Most of those who came for the night brought baskets of food. This was the night that a policeman from Blarney, Jim O'Herlihy, took a number of pictures with an Olympus camera and zoom lens which, when he got the film processed in Cork, showed the hands and arms in a succession of different positions, in spite of the fact that no movement was visible through the lens.

Ten days later, on 25 August, during which attendances at the Grotto averaged five thousand a day despite cold and wet weather, three thousand people recited the rosary and sang hymns. Three quarters of these said that they saw some movement, though one, a steward in charge of mustering the crowds, said he was 'damn slow to admit it'. With the onset of winter the number of visitors dramatically declined, but the phenomena showed no signs of diminishing.

What was remarkable was the variety of ways in which the statue was seen to move: 'sometimes in a series of inelegant jerks, rocking and quivering, as one might expect during an earth tremor' (by Dennis Barnett, a reporter for the *Sunday Tribune*); sometimes swaying; sometimes constantly moving. Others saw the face transformed into that of Christ or St Joseph, Padre Pio or a Jewish rabbi. The statue was also seen to have a glint in its eyes, to gesture with the arms, to twist its body, to smile and look around, to open and close its eyes, to move from side to side, to attempt a genuflection, or to be about to fall.

And what of the demeanour of those present, so many of whom had witnessed something or other? No observer noticed any signs of ecstasy or delirium, in fact the reverse. When one of the girls who first saw the statue move on 22 July was asked what she was thinking of when the incident occurred, she replied, 'If I was thinking of anything it was about the good time we'd had in Cleo's Disco in Bandon the night before.'

However, there was a good deal of disorganized opposition to the idea of a moving statue at Ballinspittle, the silliest of which came from the government press secretary Peter Prendegast, who was quoted as saying, 'three quarters of the country is laughing heartily at Ballinspittle', which was one thing it certainly wasn't doing. Anything more likely to rally support for the statue would be difficult to imagine. More solid criticism came from the local builder who had laid the foundation stone thirty-one years previously, Mick O'Reilly. 'It's as solid as a rock. The actual statue isn't moving. It's an illusion, but it looks like a calling to prayer to counter the ills of the world.' And on the evening of 3 October 1985 the statue was attacked by two men armed with hammers and hatchets, while a third took photographs and exhorted the visitors to the shrine not to 'adore false statues'. They were members of a Californian Christian sect. The statue was severely damaged, but was repaired by Maurice O'Donnell, and on 11 November it was lifted back into position in the Grotto to cries of 'Three Cheers for Our Lady in Heaven!'

It was still not yet dark, and having failed to elicit any movement from the statue we dawdled up the road in the direction of Kinsale for about half a mile before turning back. What with the rain hissing down it was a thoroughly lowering evening, and not one on which one would have expected anything of the statue, unless one knew of its previous outstanding form in bad weather. When we got back to the Grotto the three people who had been there had left and there was no one else present.

It was by now quite dark and the only illumination was that shed by the eleven electric lights which made up the halo. They strongly lit the upturned face, less strongly the upper part of the body, and left the lower parts of the statue in almost complete darkness. As we knelt there before it I prayed that I wouldn't see it move. I didn't want it to move, not because I didn't believe it really could move – whoever or whatever made the world and the universe would not have much trouble activating a statue – but because I didn't think it ought to move for me. Nevertheless, just as during the war I had gazed out fixedly into the darkness of the night so many times while acting as a sentry, eventually imagining I saw movement, so I gazed at the statue of the Mother of God in Ballinspittle, waiting for a sign. And suddenly, when my eyes had begun to ache with the effort of concentration, it began to move, not just backwards and forwards, but from side to side. It was extraordinary, but no more extraordinary in its way than seeing movement taking place in the darkness as a sentry, and sometimes actually shouting, 'Who goes there!' I looked away, looked again, and it wasn't moving any more.

'I've seen it,' I said to Wanda, and told her what I'd seen.

'Some people have all the luck,' she said. The trouble was I didn't feel lucky, nor did I feel excited, or spiritually uplifted, or anything.

After this we stayed on for a while but I didn't see it move again, nor did Wanda. I felt rather awful having seen it, not even being a Catholic, but I was not by any means the first non-Catholic to see it. So far as one can make out the Ballinspittle statue favoured no particular creed: it was equally likely to oblige for a Mussulman.

Back in Ballinspittle things didn't look so good from the point of view of food, so we drank hot whiskey and water in our bedroom and then sallied out into the rain, bought sardines, cooked pork and soda bread and ate them in Hurley's pub in the company of four friendly men who made room for us by the fire, which the landlord kept stoked with a mixture of what is known as slack (small coal) and cement – a strange mixture, but it burned well, and was apparently very economical. There was also a very drunk, carefully dressed old man left over from a funeral that had taken place that afternoon, who was still on his pins, rocking backwards and forwards, preparatory to leaving the premises. 'Moike, are you practithing to take on the stathue, now?' one of the others called out after him as he moved out into the night. No one present was anything but reserved about the various abilities the statue displayed, and all of them were extremely modest about what they themselves had seen. No one talked about the phenomena in a religious context, but rather as if they had been on parade, as it were, in its presence.

The next morning was much warmer, in fact it was muggy, but it still continued to rain. We had breakfast in the front room which was very bright and full of religious pictures and pictures of the family and lots of shiny athletic trophies which they had won and were still continuing to win at school. Breakfast was extensive, with lots of porridge, and while we ate Noreen O'Donovan told us how, until the previous year, she had been crippled with arthritis and had been in agony, hardly able to walk – a terrible affliction, especially for a woman with a large family, but not altogether surprising in a place as damp as Ballinspittle appeared to be. 'Then one day,' she said, 'there was an excursion to Knock and all the way there in the coach I was in terrible pain, but whatever it was, the bumping in the coach or Knock itself, I was cured. I'd love to go to Lourdes in August but there isn't much chance of that.'

Just as we were going to load the bikes up she suddenly said, 'Would you like to see Our Lady of Fatima? She's away down at Mrs Pat Bowen's place. It wouldn't take long. She's only there for a week.' So we set off in the ancient O'Donovan family motor.

Mrs Pat Bowen was Secretary of what everyone round here called the 'Com-it-tee'. She was young, dark-haired, attractive and very devout and she herself had seen the face of Our Lord shining through that of the statue; and I wouldn't have liked to have been the one who suggested to her that what she had seen was anything less than supernatural. In her front parlour, surrounded by burning candles, was a facsimile statue of Our Lady of Fatima, who on 13 May 1917 appeared to three peasant children, only one of whom survived beyond the age of twelve, at what was to become the Lourdes of Portugal. Fatima attracts hundreds of thousands of pilgrims each year, both in May and on 13 August, when peasants from all over Portugal take advantage of the end of the wheat and barley harvests to visit the shrine, as do parties from the towns, some arriving by coach, others with donkeys, their panniers loaded with provisions, to camp out in the stony surroundings of the shrine.

This particular statue, which was of painted plaster, had been provided by an organization known as the Blue Army of Fatima, based in Cork, which supplies what are known as 'pilgrims' statues' (statues that have been blessed by the Pope) on a weekly basis, from Wednesday to the following Wednesday. The only proviso is that the statue must never be left alone, and indeed there was a lady kneeling before it when we arrived. It was an impressive thing to see in someone's front parlour, surrounded by candles, and we, too, knelt while Mrs Bowen recited part of the rosary.

Afterwards Noreen took us on a tour which included a visit to the lighthouse on the Old Head of Kinsale, from which nothing at all could be seen in the fog and rain, and for a drive along the shores of Courtmacsherry Bay, where her husband, who had retired from managing a creamery at the age of forty-six due to ill health, had his daily bathe. Looking at the icy seas thundering onto it, I decided that wild seahorses would not have dragged me into them. After this we said goodbye with genuine regret to this good, kindly, humorous woman who, with her eight splendid children, her faith and her courageous endurance of what in Britain would have been regarded as poverty, had all the virtues that the Catholic Church in Ireland, run by men who often have only the haziest idea what they are demanding, demands of its women.

What did the sudden reoccurrence of such phenomena as moving and speaking statues and visions, all in the space of a single year, signify? Were they of supernatural origin or were they, as suggested by a team of psychologists from University College, Cork, an optical illusion? When the savants came up with this explanation there was widespread belief that the Bishop of Cork had persuaded them to do so in order to stop the whole thing getting out of hand, presumably pursuing the same train of thought as that of the vicar in Evelyn Waugh's *Decline and Fall*, who observes that a lay interest in ecclesiastical matters is often a prelude to insanity.

Was it something to do with the really enormous changes that had taken place in the everyday lives of the Irish, especially in the rural parts of Ireland, since the early 1960s, when we had last been there? During those twenty-odd years there had been an economic boom which had fizzled out completely, but which had changed the face of Ireland: whereas previously it was common-place to see people walking many miles along the roads on their way to work, to school or to market, now most people had cars, or knew people who would give them a lift; tractors had come into widespread use on the farms and many people had stopped planting potatoes, as it was easier, though much more expensive, to buy them in a shop, imported from Holland. In the same way attractive but insalubrious cottages were abandoned for those ugly but comfortable bungalows. During this time TV became widespread and gradually destroyed the habit of conversation. The price of Guinness had soared, to £1.50 Irish a pint by the time we left Ireland, putting it out of the reach of the old and unemployed. Many of the bars were now called 'lounges' and were as flash as their counterparts in the United States. Taxation was crippling, except for the farmers who made up 25 per cent of a population the younger and more talented of whom were draining away overseas, like water from a leaky barrel. Since our last visit, we felt the Irish had certainly lost a good deal of their sense of humour, a priceless attribute that many Western peoples have never really possessed, and one that depended on their ability to turn a unique phrase, something that the ever-increasing use of what might be described as English Irish of the sort now taught in schools and heard widely on television was, presumably, largely responsible for.

Chapter 10

ON THE ROAD TO SKIBBEREEN

My son I loved our native land with energy and pride
Until a blight came on the land and sheep and cattle died,
The rent and taxes were to pay, I could not them redeem,
And that's the cruel reason why I left old Skibbereen.

It's well I do remember that bleak December day,
The landlord and the sheriff came to drive us all away;
They set the roof on fire with their demon yellow spleen
And that's another reason why I left old Skibbereen.

Irish song, 'Skibbereen'

BIOLOGICAL WIND THRESHOLD*

Force	Description	Human Activity	Birds	Inverte-brates
7	MODERATE GALE	Walking becomes difficult	Small perching birds grounded	Butterflies & deerfly grounded
8	FRESH GALE	General progress impeded	Swifts, ducks, swallows, few raptors flying	Only dragonflies still airborne
9	STRONG GALE	Children blown over	Only swifts airborne	All insects grounded
10	WHOLE GALE	Adults blown over	All birds grounded	—

*Source: LYALL WATSON, *Heaven's Breath*, 1984.

Looking back on our travels in Ireland in January 1986, it would be almost impossible to credit the weather we encountered, if I did not have before me as I write the Irish Meteorological Services summary of the weather for that period. There was only one place, Rosslare, where less than twenty rain days were recorded and even that managed to come up with a very creditable 97mm of total rainfall for nineteen of them; its best or worst day, according to whether you are a subscriber to the *Guinness Book of Records* or simply want to go cycling, registered an awe-inspiring 17.8mm. Snow, hail and sleet were frequent, as were gales, particularly on the coast where we were. According to the weathermen the depth of snow never exceeded 2cm, which is simply not true. We saw a 6-foot snowman on the Dingle Peninsula. On 29 January the temperature in south-east Mayo fell to −7.1 centigrade.

In the second of two periods of gale force winds – of up to 70 knots in some places – we got as far as the west side of the Beara Peninsula, part of which is in County Kerry, part in County Cork. On the first day out of Ballinspittle we skirted the estuaries of rivers, some of them too small to be named on our maps, passing sandbanks and villages of identical cottages painted in brilliant turquoise, imperial yellow and *sangue de boeuf*. At the head of the Arigadeen estuary, at Timoleague, what at a distance looked like a battleship çast up on the shore turned out to be the gaunt, grey, extensive ruins of a Franciscan friary, smashed up not during the Reformation, which spared it, but by English soldiers on a visit in 1642, who found thousands of barrels of wine in its vaults.

Then into a region of marshy land further south and west, with a few poor farms and cottages. Lost in this wilderness, I tried to ask the way at a cottage surrounded by electronic debris and savage dogs. With torn curtains and a long wire trailing out of the letter box like an unlit fuse it was difficult to believe that it was actually inhabited, but it must have been because a naked electric bulb was burning in its unimaginably horrible front parlour. No one answered the front door, though. It was a wet Saturday afternoon and there was not a living soul on the roads; everyone was inside guarded by savage dogs rendered even more savage by not being allowed to watch TV. Finally I found a dogless farmyard with a man in it carrying a dung fork but when I approached him he, like all other Irish apparitions, simply faded away.

At dusk we came into Clonakilty, a town founded by Richard Boyle, the great effing Earl of Cork, passing a couple of tinkers' caravans down on the foreshore and what was left of a bungalow given to them by the local council, after they had stripped off all the useful bits, so that it looked as if a shell had burst in it. From one of the caravans two tinker girls emerged, bound for a night out in Clonakilty, as smart as bandboxes. The rain was truly awful and we took refuge in a hotel with hat racks made from deer antlers and had tea while drying out among farm ladies and their daughters in for the shopping.

We stayed in a B and B kept by a truly formidable lady who had massed bands of relatives on the premises, and a maid to put coal on the fire, as if it was the 1930s, and woke up on Sunday to a dark scene: violent squalls were hurling themselves on Clonakilty from a sky the colour and consistency of ebony. Then suddenly it was clear, the orange street lights went out and everything was brilliant and rainwashed. As we went into the town we saw men standing on the corners reading the lubricious bits in the Sunday papers and houseproud women polishing their door knockers. While Wanda went to Mass in a church with a tall, slender spire, I hung about outside, studying the graves of eleven priests, all buried cosily together in a single vault, in company with other male black sheep who interpreted attending Mass as standing outside in the church-yard. Perhaps it was our imagination, but we didn't feel that people were as friendly here in Clonakilty as we were accustomed to.

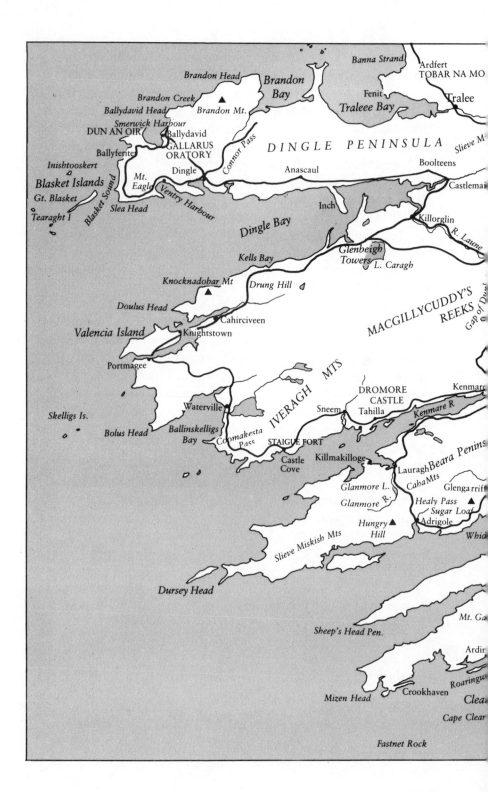

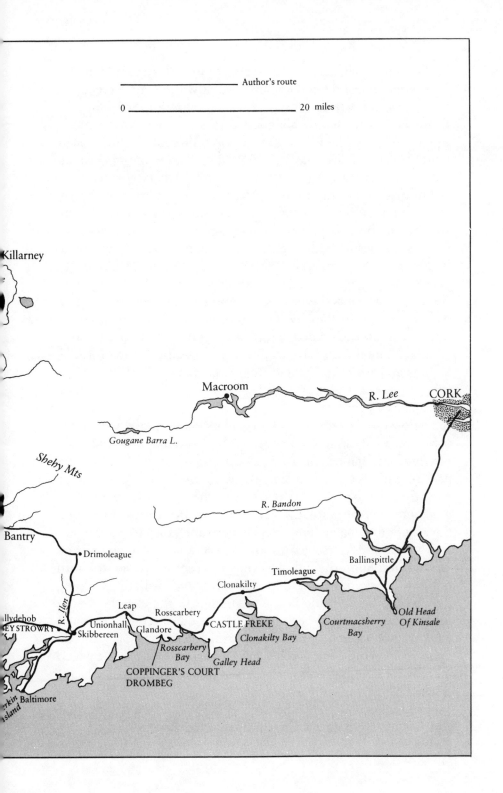

Author's route

0 ——————————— 20 miles

Killarney

Macroom

R. Lee

CORK

Gougane Barra L.

Shehy Mts

R. Bandon

Bantry

Drimoleague

Ballinspittle

Timoleague

Clonakilty

Leap

Rosscarbery

CASTLE FREKE

Courtmacsherry
Bay

Old Head
Of Kinsale

lydehob
EY STROWRY

Unionhall

Glandore

Clonakilty Bay

Skibbereen

Rosscarbery
Bay

Galley Head

COPPINGER'S COURT
DROMBEG

rkin Baltimore
sland

We then embarked on what seemed a long, long ride (in reality only seven miles) up endless hills and down to Castle Freke, the wondrous and extensive ruins of a house built in 1780 by Sir John Evans-Freke and finally abandoned in 1952, with castellations, square and polygonal towers and a portcullis that still functioned. Gutted by fire in 1910, it was rebuilt in time for the coming-of-age ball given there in 1913 for the tenth Lord Carbery.

Although now almost completely hidden from view by encroaching vegetation on the gatehouse side, where the portcullis still hung, there were still long, magnificent views across the wooded demesne to the lighthouse on Galley Head, and westwards over Rosscarbery Bay. We followed the wall of the demesne, beautifully made with slates laid vertically, past entrance gates topped with what looked like whipped cream walnuts, down to the bay itself, where the surf boomed on the sands, the air was filled with flying spume and there was a gimcrack motel with forty rooms with broken windows for sale, already an Irish ruin. Then to Rosscarbery, a small place above a spacious estuary with sandbanks covered with green veg, and reached by a causeway.

There were six pubs in and around its main square, which was only 100 yards long. We chose Nolan's Lounge, the only one offering sustenance on a Sunday afternoon, which was jam-packed with people. Suddenly, as we were downing powdered mushroom soup and damp ham sandwiches (this was no *route des gastronomes*), the landlady got the message that the Garda was on the way (it now being long after closing time), the lights went out, and we found ourselves in the street still clasping uneaten sandwiches. Soon the pub was empty except for some stubborn old hardliners, quivering and quavering and dribbling, hoping they would be invisible in the gloaming. In the end the Garda never came. They had been right to hang on: there was rain and huge rainbows and on a long straight stretch of road an apocalyptic wind – it had to be at least Force 10 – a blast of which literally blew Wanda off her bike and into a ditch, from which I rescued her crying with vexation.

Hereabouts in a deep valley, out of the terrible wind, was what was left of Coppinger's Court, an ivy-clad seventeenth-century fortified house occupied by an amber-coloured donkey with eyes to match which was groaning away wanting sympathy, and a he-goat that didn't want any. Then up a horrible hill past the Drombeg Stone Circle, Hut and Cooking Place that neither of us felt inclined to visit; then a lovely swoop down to Glandore Harbour, where we wanted to stay the night but found all the hotels were shut.

So out of Glandore, with the sun gone in, past a pretty Protestant church hidden among the trees with a tunnel leading up to it through solid rock, and along the shore of the inner estuary and past a bridge leading to Unionhall across the water, where Swift stayed in 1723 and liked so much that he wrote a Latin poem in praise of it: 'Carberiae Rupes', or 'The cliffs of Carbery'.

Leap, at the end of the estuary, also had six pubs within 100 yards, of which the biggest, the Leap Hotel, was bulging at the seams with members of the local hunt who had been having a Sunday meet and were all dressed up for it, and another party, equally dressed up, recovering from the effects of a funeral they had attended, sipping away like anything at Irish whiskey and hot water. By this stage both parties had become somewhat inter-mingled. In this hospitable place we each had two set teas with scones, two hot whiskeys with water, two high teas and more hot whiskeys and water, while an Irish group played and sang Irish airs. All this was served like lightning by Mrs Ann Sheahan, wife of the proprietor, and together with two bed and breakfasts came to just £25.

It poured all night and was still pitch dark when we woke, but it cleared a bit later, when we took the road to Skibbereen, six miles to the west, at first uphill past gorsey tussocks, rocky outcrops and, to the right, little loughs. While we were exercising ourselves in this fashion a van passed us, the driver of which dropped a bundle of newspapers outside a small shop. A dog emerged, and having sniffed it and looked it over thoroughly in case it contained any pornography or contraceptive apparatus, none of which is well thought of in this part of the world, bore it back into the shop to be given a further going-over by the proprietor. The buildings on the outskirts of Skibbereen were rendered in bright turquoise, acid green, vivid yellow and orange. It was sale time: one shop had a close-out lot of Makita angle grinders on offer, but we did not allow them to detain us and pedalled on along the bank of the River Ilen en route for Schull, passing Abbeystrowry, an ivy-clad monastic cell built by the Cistercians, even in such weather beautiful and mysterious. The road was now beginning to traverse what were some of the poorest parts of Ireland, whose inhabitants had suffered the most terrible privations in the years of the Great Famine – more poor tussocky land with slatey-looking stone pushing up through it. Ahead of us now was Mount Gabriel, a bleak mountain, bare apart from the pale dome of some warning system on top of it; to the left fleeting views of a castle on Mannin Island, one of the 127 assorted rocks, islets and islands in Roaringwater Bay.

Schull (it means School) had a rocky foreshore, a small jetty which was in the process of being dug up, a fish factory and a pair of dank but commodious public lavatories which we both patronized, a positive treat after performing in the rain, as we usually found ourselves doing. Half mad with thirst we pedalled up its hilly main street past a pub which also sold coal and went in for undertaking, to the Bunratty Inn, Irish Pub of the Year 1983, at which we finally came to rest. The only other customer was an ex- Fleet Air Arm navigator who had come to Schull to make arrangements for his wife's ashes to be scattered here, the place where she had been born.

Mrs Mulvaney, the innkeeper's wife, was, unfortunately, seriously ill and it was her husband from whom we ordered drink and sandwiches. He had worked for the American Tobacco Company in a previous incarnation, both in Shanghai before the revolution, and in Singapore; and he had an extraordinary collection of cigarette packet labels (which he had extracted from the firm's copyright department), one of them for a Chinese brand that had been the world's biggest seller. Here we ate delicious crab and smoked salmon sandwiches – the best pub food we had so far found – and that night we slept above O'Donovan's Grocers on Main Street, now the premises of Mrs Mary McSweeney.

Our room had been papered with large-scale maps of the area by some archaeologists who once stayed there, and these provided a lot of fascinating information about this part of the Mizen Head

Peninsula, including the whereabouts of a number of children's cemeteries which dated back to 1846, the worst year of the Great Famine.*

Skibbereen and the surrounding countryside suffered fearfully during the Famine. The only employment was on public works, which paid a man 8d a day, a sum wholly insufficient to support a family; this was reported to the British Government in London by two local Protestant clergymen who specially went there for this purpose, but no food was sent. On 15 December 1846 Mr Nicholas Cummins, a Cork magistrate, visited Skibbereen and as a result of what he saw wrote a letter to the Duke of Wellington, who was himself an Irishman, sending a copy to *The Times*:

My Lord Duke,

. . . Having for many years been intimately connected with the western portion of the County of Cork, and possessing some small property there, I thought it right personally to investigate the truth of the several lamentable accounts which had reached me of the appalling state of misery to which that part of the country was reduced. I accordingly went on the 15th inst. to Skibbereen, and to give the instance of one townland which I visited, as an example of the state of the entire coast district, I shall state simply what I there saw. . . . Being aware that I should have to witness scenes of frightful hunger, I provided myself with as much bread as five men could carry, and on reaching the spot I was surprised to find the wretched hamlet apparently deserted. I entered some of the hovels to ascertain the cause, and the scenes that presented themselves were such as no tongue or pen can convey the slightest idea of. In the first, six famished and ghastly skeletons, to all appearance dead, were huddled in a corner on some filthy straw, their sole covering what seemed a ragged horse-cloth, and their wretched legs hanging about,

*In Skibbereen Workhouse more than 50 per cent of the children admitted after 1 October 1846 died 'due to diarrhoea acting on an exhausted constitution', according to the workhouse physician. I am indebted to Cecil Woodham-Smith, *The Great Hunger, Ireland 1845–9*, Hamish Hamilton, 1962, for this and much other information on the Famine quoted here.

naked above the knees. I approached with horror, and found by a low moaning they were alive, they were in fever, four children, a woman, and what had once been a man. It is impossible to go through the details, suffice it to say, that in a few minutes I was surrounded by at least 200 such phantoms, such frightful spectres as no words can describe. By far the greater number were delirious, either from famine or from fever. Their demoniac yells are still ringing in my ears, and their horrible images are fixed upon my brain. My heart sickens at the recital, but I must go on.

In another case, decency would forbid what follows, but it must be told, my clothes were nearly torn off in my endeavours to escape from the throng of pestilence around, when my neck-cloth was seized from behind by a grip which compelled me to turn. I found myself grasped by a woman with an infant, just born, in her arms, and the remains of a filthy sack across her loins – the sole covering of herself and babe. The same morning the police opened a house on the adjoining lands, which was observed shut for many days, and two frozen corpses were found lying upon the mud floor, half devoured by rats.

Sir Randolph Routh, Chairman of the Relief Commission, blamed the landlords:

The proprietors of the Skibbereen district, he told Charles Edward Trevelyan, Permanent Head of Treasury, 'draw an annual income of £50,000'. There were twelve land-owners, of whom the largest was Lord Carbery [of Castle Freke], who, Routh declared, drew £15,000 in rents; next was Sir William Wrixon-Becher, on whose estate the town of Skibbereen stood; Sir William, alleged Routh, drew £10,000, while the Reverend Stephen Townsend, a Protestant clergyman, drew £8000.[*]

In the county of Cork alone the desperate state of Skibbereen was

[*]Source: The Irish Crisis, quoted in Cecil Woodham-Smith, The Great Hunger. I remember reading a letter in a magazine or newspaper, some time after the publication of Cecil Woodham-Smith's book, from someone who had found the book in a university library in the United States filed under the heading 'Gastronomy'.

reported to be paralleled in Schull, Bantry, Brandon, Baltimore, Crookhaven and Castlehaven. During all this time fever was raging and by March 1847 it was epidemic, carrying off thousands more.

The most accessible of the six children's cemeteries appeared to be the one in Ardintenant, east of Schull Harbour, and with the sun now shining brilliantly we set off to look for it. Marked on the map north of the Harbour was the workhouse and on the same site, the fever hospital, and we went to see them on the way to look for the cemetery. The buildings, or what was left of them, were hidden behind huge, high ivy-clad walls and stood in a morass of mud churned up by the cattle which grazed around the place. A gateway fitted with iron gates led to them: one, an amorphous construction covered with ivy; the other, a larger, two-storey building with what might have been one big lofty room with an open fireplace at both ends. The roof and upper floor had collapsed and a dense growth of ivy covered this too. Which had been the workhouse and which the fever hospital was difficult to say. It may have depended on who outnumbered whom, the living or the dying. A stream ran through the field in which they stood, the waters of which, besides being used by the occupants of the workhouse, had been used to work a carding mill, and possibly other mills, down near the shore where there was a miniature harbour.

It took a long time to find the cemetery. A man building a very ugly stone wall for someone's bungalow down on the road to Ardintenant – 'Me labour's costing him two thousand pounds, let alone the materials' (someone to be avoided like the plague) – had never even heard of it. A farmer who lived within sight of it among a very dangerous collection of disused copper mine shafts thought he knew where it was, but was wrong. Most vehement was a woman living in a bungalow who said 'it wasn't anywhere at all nearboy'. Finally, an old man living alone in a very small whitewashed cottage told us where it was: in the field which belonged to the vehement woman, immediately opposite her house. It was thickly overgrown with brambles and gorse and only one stone was visible above the undergrowth but the rest, innumerable small stones, could be felt underfoot. It was horrible: I felt as if I was treading on living children. Our interest in children's famine cemeteries evaporated.

Back in Skibbereen, having cycled there with the wind astern, a novel experience, we lunched in Brendan McCarthy's pub under a poster advertising 'Monster Card Drive – Prizes: Bull Calf, Half Ton of Coal, A Ham, Four Bottles of Whiskey'. The local head of Bord Failte kindly did some brisk telephoning on our behalf and arranged for us to get to Clear Island (offshore Irish islands being difficult to reach, especially in winter), so after tea in a caff we set off for Baltimore, from where the island boat sails. We followed the river Ilen on its last laps to the sea, past old demesnes, one of which had a Gothic church tower rising picturesquely among deciduous trees. One of the good things about the Church of Ireland was that they certainly were dab hands at choosing beautiful situations for their excellent, mass-produced churches. Further downstream the Ilen suddenly became an estuary, and a lovely one, with minute grassy islands apparently floating in it, all flooded with a stormy, magical, lemon-coloured light. Who is responsible for these miraculous effects, so much more satisfying than meretricious moving statues constructed of cement?

We got to Baltimore about four-thirty, passing the decrepit Gulf Stream Hotel which was for sale – hardly surprising if what we were now sampling was representative of the weather. It was now raining and blowing hard from south-west and Baltimore was very, very cold, in spite of being hemmed in on all sides by islands of various shapes and sizes; but it was nice down by the harbour, which was overlooked by a little castle of the O'Driscolls. We were now in O'Driscoll country: it was here in 1537 that one of the O'Driscoll lords took for himself the contents of a ship loaded with Spanish wine bound for Waterford, which had taken refuge from the weather. This led to the burning of the town by an expeditionary force of Waterford men, and the ruination of the castle. It was here, too, that a force of Algerian pirates put ashore on the night of 19 June 1631; they, too, sacked the town and carried away 117 of its inhabitants of both sexes as slaves, introducing what may well have been the first female O'Driscolls into the harems around the Mediterranean. The man who piloted them in, a fisherman called Hackett, was later tried and executed at Cork.

We found accommodation in O'Driscoll's Corner House Hotel

above the harbour. The hotel was being repainted and the owner himself, who was getting married shortly and was also involved in running the post office, was existing in a state of some confusion in a kitchen, the principal ornament of which was an enormous American gas stove suitable for cooking mammoth steaks which were not on offer on this particular p.m. All night it blew like hell, the wind rattling the casements and the rain battering them. Outside, chocked up on the waterfront, was a yacht with a single occupant who must have felt rather like St Simon Stylites on his column. Inside we had an electric heater, a rather frightening electric blanket, the O'Driscolls' answer to the electric chair, and lots of nice cold water to wash in, but you can't have everything and at least we had a roof over our heads.

In the morning we rode out to a huge white sugar-loaf beacon known as Lot's Wife which looks across a narrow sound to Sherkin Island. The rain had stopped and the sun was shining but the wind was blowing so strongly that we could lean out on it without falling over, which meant it was Force 9. Gouts of froth streamed up the face of a precipice on the extreme edge of which a herd of cattle stood grazing, accompanied by an enormous, wily-looking goat; apparently the cattle often fall over, having neither apprehension nor fear of heights, but never the goat. Having done this there was not much else to do, the mail boat not being due to sail for Clear Island until half past two in the afternoon.

'I'm afraid I can't go on with much more of this,' said Wanda, as we sat in a deep valley leading down to the sea next door to an abandoned Morris done out in jungle camouflage with nothing inside except seatbelts. 'The winds and the rains are simply killing me.' And she shed a tear or two. Nevertheless she promised to delay her decision about abandoning both me and Ireland until our return from Clear Island.

We put to sea in the good ship *Naomh* (Saint) *Ciaran II* (Ciaran or Kieran being the island's patron saint.[*]) The only other

---

[*]St Ciaran of Saighir (to distinguish him from his more celebrated namesake St Ciaran of Clonmacnoise) was of the royal blood of Munster. He lived in the fifth century, and studied at Tours and Rome, from where he returned to Ireland a bishop. He inhabited a cell in upper Ossory around which grew the monastery of Saighir.

passenger was the representative on the island of the Cape Clear
Development Co-operative, set up in 1970 in an attempt to arrest
emigration from the island, the population of which had fallen
from 1000 to 180 in a century. While courteous enough, he was
not exactly a fount of free information about his kingdom. Maybe
he thought we were going there to erect a casino, a tower block or
something similar.

The skipper of the *Naomh Ciaran*, a steel-built vessel of about
38 tons, was Conchubar O'Driscoll, and there was yet another
O'Driscoll among his crew. They had just finished loading a large
tractor, and the ship was full of other produce ordered by the
islanders from Skibbereen. The skipper took her out round the
west side of Sherkin Island, past more O'Driscoll ruins, and into a
patch of nasty short, steep sea into which the *Naomh Ciaran*
smashed with vigour, throwing spray over her deck-house, as if it
was bath night. Once across the Sound between Sherkin and Clear
Island he turned her to go inside the Bullig reef off Illauena Island,
a manoeuvre which threw us all over the place and broke my
glasses. It was clear now and across the Sound the cliffs of Clear
Island with the seas breaking on them and the green, stone-walled
fields above them were brilliant in the sun.

It took a little under an hour to reach North Harbour. It has a
labyrinthine entrance which makes it practically impossible to get
out of when something known as 'the draw', a nasty sort of
undertow, is working. The jetty was crowded with islanders,
together with a few specimens from what, apart from the
Australian Outback, must be the world's largest concentration of
beat-up motor vehicles. There is no insurance, no need for a
licence and no driving test, and the mainland is scoured for
vehicles suitable for use on the island by the twentieth-century
equivalent of grave robbers. The surroundings of the harbour,
above which rises a big hill, were disordered and picturesque.
There were a number of old houses and sheds used by fishermen,
heaps of lobster pots, boats in various stages of decay, the power
station, out of sight round a corner; and the ruined church of
Trawkieran, otherwise Teampall Ciaran, built around 1200 on
the site of an earlier monastery said to have been founded by St
Ciaran. And down by the beach was Tobar Ciaran, his holy well,

with a solitary palm tree growing on it, from which water is still procured for blessing the homes of the islanders and the sick. Next to this was a Grotto occupied by Our Lady and St Bernadette, with what looks like a lingam in front of it but is really the stump of a cross.

In search of somewhere to stay we set off up the hill past a stone building with the sign 'Club Chleire Heineken', that was in the process of being converted by the island co-operative into a very agreeable social club, with a bar that was unfortunately closed; past a grocer's shop with a bar inside it that was a bar no more, past a line of picturesque cottages on a ledge carved out of the hillside, all now abandoned, and past Bourke's pub, also closed.

We put up in the commodious modern bungalow of Mrs O'Reagan. It was still only a quarter to four so we decided to walk to the Bill of Cape Clear. The scene from the cliffs above the Bill was awe-inspiring. Four miles off to the south-west was the Fastnet Lighthouse, a tall, angular granite tower rising 147 feet from its foundations. It was now blowing Force 10 and huge seas were battering against the tower, leaping up the side of it from the boiling cauldron below. Beyond it a big slab-sided container ship was punching out into the storm but it was soon lost in the murk. The air between the Bill and the Cape was full of what looked like Ping-Pong balls: gouts of spume generated at the base of the cliffs which were now floating inland on the wind. At four-thirty the light on the Fastnet came on. By now the sky to the north-east was clear, with a big moon riding high in it, but everywhere else it had closed in, except when the cloud opened up for a moment to allow an unearthly yellow light to illuminate the rock.

The only time I had seen the Fastnet from the sea was in June 1939, when we had raised it fifteen miles to the north-east at eight in the evening, coming up to it in a four-masted barque. We had been within an ace of making one of the fastest sail passages from Australia to Europe between the wars, but now, ninety days out from Spencer's Gulf, South Australia, baffled by contrary winds, we had long since lost out to the *Parma*, which had made it in eighty-three days in 1933. As night came down the wind fell away and all through the night the light flashed at us mockingly every five seconds. By the next morning there was still no wind and we were closer in to the land, making a lot of leeway. The air was full of haze and what we first took to be a dredger with a white funnel resolved itself into the angularities of the Fastnet seen in strange perspective with the white lighthouse on top of it.

All that day we hovered near the rock. Later in the afternoon a boat approached, with five men in it rowing like demons, and an old man in the stern sheets looking like Coleridge's Ancient Mariner. They had rowed nine miles from the village of Crookhaven on the Mizen Head Peninsula. We invited them aboard and the Captain gave them rum, and soon a light breeze began to stir and the ship began to rustle through the water. It was time for them to go and the last we saw of them they were drifting away into the sunset, very drunk, towards the New World, with the Ancient Mariner sitting erect in the stern. They were the first strangers I had talked to for ninety days. Some twenty-five years later I went to Crookhaven and got drunk with the survivors.

Back at Mrs O'Reagan's we had bacon and eggs and whiskey. She had come to live on the island from the mainland with her husband, who was a mechanic. He had died twelve years previously, leaving her with a daughter who had first of all gone to school on the island and then, when she was old enough, to a boarding school on the mainland, which was the usual arrangement. The school on the island now had twenty-five children on the roll. She didn't speak Irish herself, and said the families on the island were very self-contained. The majority were O'Driscolls.

When her husband died Mrs O'Reagan continued to keep about a dozen heifers for fattening. She tried to grow green vegetables but the island is infested with rabbits which makes it difficult; the latest news was that someone had introduced myxomatosis. Like all the offshore islands I had ever visited, the economy of Clear Island verged on the dotty. Milk, or most of it, came from the mainland. Only one family had sheep and only one person knew how to butcher them. Some people grew potatoes; one man grew wheat for his own use. But most food was ordered from Skibbereen.

After the bacon and eggs we decided to go to a pub, not knowing that none of them opened until nine or after. We were in bed by eight.

The next morning was one of cold, violent rain squalls, and we learnt that 'on account of the draw', the *Naomh Ciaran* wouldn't be able to leave at least until noon, if at all. So we decided to walk to the Old Lighthouse which was high up on the east side of the island. Whoever built it had obviously failed to notice that the site chosen was shrouded in fog for the greater part of the year, rendering the light quite invisible. The road climbed steeply through a stone-walled landscape, its houses either ruined or secretive-looking, like their occupants. There was not a dog to be seen. Had the islanders eaten them all? All along the road and in the fields and farmyards were numbers of what appeared to be parked cars, but were in fact cars that would never move again. Far off we could see the Fastnet still getting a battering, and the Ping-Pong balls of froth continued to drift in across the fields. From time to time we were whipped by hail. It was a melancholy scene. I tried to imagine what life would be like for us if the *Naomh Ciaran* didn't sail, or had already sailed and never came back – and failed.

Back in Bourke's pub near the North Harbour which for some inscrutable reason known only to himself Mr Bourke had decided to open, we listened to Mr Bourke's tale of woe in what even by Irish standards was a remarkable orange and yellow interior, lit, a bit early in the day for it, by one gas mantle, and so old that the stone that separated the front from the back part of the premises had almost been worn in half by the passage of innumerable booted feet. 'Sixty years in the Bourke family,' he said, 'and I can't open in the evening anymore because the custom doesn't pay for the fire.'

We eventually sailed at twelve-thirty in a wind Force 8. When a beam sea hit the *Ciaran* just after we left the harbour I nearly broke my other pair of glasses. The following sea, when we got on course, was not all that nice either. Again we sailed inside the reef, which was displaying horribly spikey rocks on either side of it which I hoped the skipper had noticed; from time to time everything was obliterated by heavy hail. There was no doubt that these were dangerous waters; even a *précis* of ships lost in them had made chilly reading.

Baltimore was cold and miserable, but a bus was leaving for Drimoleague on the Bantry Road at two o'clock, and the driver let us put our bikes on board. Travelling with this kindly driver was his daughter, a solemn little girl of four, and 'a great one for the buses'. He was a mine of information, some of it on the most recondite subjects; passing a place called Caheragh, invisible from the road in the rain-sodden greenery, he volunteered the following: 'At Caheragh there is a cemetery. It was three years ago now they were disinterring a girl aged fifteen or sixteen who'd been buried for sixty years, to make room for an additional one, and when they opened up her coffin they found her in it, uncorrupt.'

'Dead, dead,' said the solemn little girl, having presumably heard the story when travelling the same route on a previous occasion, being a great one for the buses, and looked even more solemn. 'She was dead.' As a result of all this, Caheragh had become a place of pilgrimage.

It was not surprising that when the time came to leave this pair, we did so with genuine regret. Especially as the driver of an Expressway bus which was due to leave Drimoleague for Bantry at 15.07 was an old fellow of near pensionable age who would not allow our bikes on his bus. The next twelve miles to Bantry, with the rain beating down on us, were pretty boring, most of them being up rather than down.

Bantry, with its huge square full of pubs opening out on to the Bay, should have been nice, even in the rain, but it wasn't really, even though there were no huge tankers discharging oil at the Terminal in the Bay. There was no problem about coming to a decision about whether or not to visit Bantry House, built in 1765 by the first Earl of Bantry and filled with treasures by the much-travelled second Earl, because it was closed. By now it was dark. Neither of us wanted to stay in Bantry but the next place was Glengarriff, eleven miles off around the head of the Bay by a road which on the map looked like a snake in its death throes. It was no time for false economy. Feeling musty and dilapidated we chartered a large taxi, and followed the driver's recommendation to stay in the Bay View Guest House. It was jolly good, not the least of its charms being a huge cast iron bath in mint condition which the landlady, Mrs Heffernan, wanted to get rid of on the grounds that it 'uses too much hot water. Not all the people who come here being educated like yourselves.'

Unfortunately, Mrs Heffernan drew the line at supplying supper so, being ravenous, we were forced to re-robe ourselves in our Gore-Tex suits and sally out into the terrible night for the mile-and-a-half walk into Glengarriff, where Mrs Heffernan had said she was 'by no means sure that you will find a bite of food at all.' She was nearly right. Of the six pubs we found there only one, called Perring House, had anything, and that was a choice of stew or re-heated roast beef, but at least they meant well. Behind the bar was a Cockney mulatto girl from Kilburn of about sixteen whose uncle played in a local folk group. She was bored out of her mind, she said, by winter in Glengarriff. The owner, who also spoke Cockney, was Irish but had spent six years in England, putting in foundations for houses, first living in Kilburn – 'Kilburn's all right' – then Stanmore: 'Stanmore's a sort of death in life. I met my friends either at the Cricklewood Tavern, full of Irish, or the Welsh Harp Inn, which had an Irish landlord, that is until it went and got burnt down, didn't it?'

Then we went back for a go in the huge bath, sharing. Educated people like ourselves know the value of water, especially hot water. Downstairs Mr Heffernan, an otherwise cheerful fellow, was immobilized before the TV, bored to death.

The next day dawned, when it did, long after eight o'clock, wet and cold with a very strong wind and snow on the 2000-foot tops of the Caha Mountains. We left the nice, warm haven of the Bay View Guest House with extreme reluctance, and on the way out of Glengarriff we met an Australian dressed like an imitation Irishman in a long black overcoat and a woolly hat with a bobble on it, waiting by the roadside for a bus to Bantry. He told us that he was living in a cabin on the mountainside on property belonging to a friend, and that he passed the days gathering wood in an enclosure of oaks which once formed part of the demesnes of the Lords of Bantry. Given the kind of weather we were having it sounded a rather joyless occupation. He was going back to Australia in February. How we envied him. Then we set off westwards along the south side of the Beara Peninsula on the road to Adrigole, crossing an arcadian, wooded river on the banks of which flourished an assortment of wonderful trees and shrubs, with a view downstream of the ruins of Cromwell's Bridge, said to have been built for him in an hour. Here, in the surroundings of Glengarriff, the vegetation was extravagantly rich – giant fuschia up to twenty-five feet high, escallonia, eucalyptus, tree ferns, oak, holly, yew, mountain ash and Chilean myrtle – while *clethra arboreus*, pink saxifrage, Irish spurge, pale pink English heather and greater butterwort were some of the flora that clamoured for attention in due season.

The sun chose this moment to make an appearance, illuminating the little tree-clad rock islands in the Bay, and the snow-covered mountains behind. Then it began to rain again. What followed was the very steep ascent via Furkeal Bridge, more or less at sea-level, to the Avaul Loughs 400 feet up, in a distance of only a mile and a quarter. To the right of the road was a wilderness of bogs which turned orange when the sun came out, and above them huge expanses of dead grass with waterfalls of shiny stones pouring down from the slopes of the Caha Mountains, the highest of which in view was the Sugar Loaf, which gave the impression of being a perfect pyramid and looked as inaccessible as a peak in Tibet. The air was filled with the sounds of innumerable, invisible brooks, but there was not a bird in sight; those with any sense were down near the Equator. The loughs were near a pass from which there was a stupendous view over Bantry Bay, with Cooleragh Harbour immediately below and, across what was now a shimmering expanse of water in which a solitary fishing boat floated motionless, the Whiddy Island oil terminal, the long, black finger of Sheep's Head Peninsula pointing into the Atlantic, and, far away to the northeast, what were probably the Sheehy Mountains on the Cork – Kerry border, also covered with snow. Then a steep descent – what a waste of hard-gained height – to Cooleragh, a hamlet above the Bay, followed by a stiff climb from 281 feet to 415 feet in half a mile. Ahead now were the extraordinary contours of Hungry Hill, at 2251 feet the highest peak in the Caha Mountains. When it wasn't blotted from view by the elements it looked like a whipped cream walnut. I mentioned this to Wanda and she reminded me this was the comparison I had used of the gateposts at Castle Freke, what now seemed a lifetime ago, and that if I wanted to have whipped cream walnuts in my book either the gateposts or Hungry Hill would have to go.

From this dizzy height we flew downhill among bogs, expanses of gorse and bracken and small walled fields in which little groups of black and white cattle stood around, no doubt discussing the absence of tourists and the dreadful weather, which was keeping them away in the fleshpots of Glengarriff, and wishing that they themselves were under cover in the white *clachans* (or small groups of dwellings) of their owners on the hillsides of Curragh and Curraduff.

Chapter 11

RETURN TO KILMAKILLOGE

To westward where the avenue approaches
Since they have felled the trees of my demesne,
And since I'll not be visited by coaches,
I'll build a mighty wall against the rain.

JOHN BETJEMAN. 'Sir John Piers. IV: The Return',
Selected Poems, 1948

Now Ireland has her madness and her weather still.

W. H. AUDEN. 'In Memory of W. B. Yeats', 1939

Adrigole, the village at the foot of the Healy Pass, would have been quite nice if it hadn't been pouring with rain. As it was now twelve-thirty, as well as raining, it seemed to be time for a drink and something to eat before facing up to the rigours that lay ahead of us; I had tried to make light of them to Wanda, but she no longer believed anything I said about roads and how hilly they were. Anyway she was now so cold, in spite of her Korean gloves, that she had lost all feeling in her fingers. In the first two pubs we entered no one seemed to have even heard of food, let alone provide it, and treated us like a couple of loonies when we opened our mouths, pointed our thumbs down our throats and went through the motions of chewing. The third pub had a somewhat depressing interior and clientèle, but at least there were sandwiches on offer.

'At Adrigole Bridge we may turn right for the winding ascent of the Healy Pass, completed in 1931 under the aegis of Tim Healy, at the summit of which (1084 ft) we enter County Kerry . . .', intones the *Blue Guide to Ireland*, so we did. The road to the Pass across the Caha Mountains was begun during the Famine years to give occupation to the needy; the remuneration was 4d (the equivalent of about 1½p) for a twelve-hour day, which gave rise to such a high death rate that work on it was abandoned, and only resumed in 1928 at the instigation of Tim Healy, the leader of the Irish Party at Westminster, and Governor-General of the Free State from 1922 to 1928.

The first couple of miles of road from sea level were easy enough, with the snowy-white Adrigole Mountain to the left with waterfalls pouring down its slopes, and to the right the steep cliffs which fell away from the outlying parts of the Sugar Loaf to the glen of the Adrigole river. It was when we rounded the big bulge of Adrigole Mountain that we found ourselves riding into a succession of freezing squalls that came roaring down on us from the head of the Pass, now just visible high above a wilderness of peat bog at the top of an uncountable number of hairpin bends. It took us an hour and a half to cover the four and a half miles to the Pass from the bridge (one of the old men in the pub where we'd had lunch said he had done it in half an hour but I bet he hadn't). For the last two and a half miles or so Wanda had to walk, and I walked with her, afraid that she might pass out.

By the time we reached the Col, where there was a big white crucifixion group and a shut-up tourist shop, evening was coming on. A bitter wind was funnelling through it and MacGillycuddy's Reeks, the mountain range beyond the Kenmare river, and the Iveragh Mountains on the Ring of Kerry, were all white. Then a violent hailstorm enveloped us and, our faces stinging, we began what would otherwise have been a lovely, four-mile freewheel downhill to sea level in County Kerry. To the left were the huge, steel-coloured cliffs of Tooth Mountain with a long glen running back into it. By the time we reached the bridge over the Glantrasna river, which was in full spate, the hail had stopped but it was raining buckets, and from there we had a miserable ride among what were now the funereal rhododendron thickets in the demesne of Dereen House.[*]

Then, all of a sudden, we were out on the shores of Kilmakilloge Bay, to be greeted, as if by magic, by a brilliant orange sunset under our first cloudless sky of the whole trip, although the mountains and Healy Pass behind us were shrouded in black cloud. The wind had dropped completely and it was very quiet, apart from great flocks of oystercatchers out on the mud, making a tremendous whistling.

[*]Home of the Marquesses of Lansdowne, and noted for its great collection of trees, some of them of huge size, rhododendrons and other shrubs and ferns. Now the property of the nephew of the Seventh Marquess, who was killed in action in 1944. The Lansdownes were descendants of the adventurer, Sir William Petty, who acquired enormous estates during the Cromwellian confiscations.

There was a stone jetty with a kink in it, an Edwardian ocean-going steam tug named *Stentor* up on the foreshore, from the interior of which the noise of hammering could be heard, an English King George V letterbox painted Irish Republican green with a palm tree rising above it, and across the road a yellow and white painted pub with a slate roof and a sign which proclaimed that it was Teddy O'Sullivan's.

Frozen, we parked our bicycles outside and opened the front door, and there was Mrs Joan O'Sullivan selling a little girl some sweets. She looked up and gradually a slow smile of recognition spread over her face.

'You've been a long time away,' she said with a certain hint of reproach. 'You missed a fine funeral today – Mrs Lyons from the shop at Lauragh. There was a great turn-out. Some came all the way from Dublin in a Mercedes. Some are still in the bar; they won't go home. You'll stay the night, of course.'

It was eighteen years since we had last been to Kilmakilloge. Insofar as we have any rules as travellers, there are two that we try to obey, not always with success. One is never to fail to make a detour to see something of interest on the grounds that the opportunity to visit it will occur at some future date. It rarely does. If you see a signpost that reads 'Source de la Seine, 6 kms' and you feel impelled to visit it, you should do so. The other is never to go back, on the grounds that nothing will be as good second or third time round.

Altogether, this was our third visit to Kilmakilloge. The first time had been more than twenty years previously when, just as for the funeral, the bar had been crowded, and that time Joan had been in tears.

'Why are you crying?' Wanda had asked her. 'Is someone dead?'

'No one is dead, at all,' she said. 'It's the schoolmistress at Lauragh, she's leaving us,' and began to howl again. That night, after the schoolmistress had finally taken her departure, we dined on the most delicious skate. 'You'll come again,' the O'Sullivans both made us promise the next morning before we left.

Two or three years passed, then, just before Christmas, Wanda ricked her back and was in agony that no doctor could relieve. We decided that the only thing to do, in order to avoid an exhausting Christmas in England, was to skip it and leave the country. My daughter said she would like to come, too. I rang the O'Sullivans at Kilmakilloge and got a surprisingly unenthusiastic response when I suggested that we should spend Christmas with them. Nevertheless, I went ahead with arrangements to ship our Land Rover to Cork on the 23 December. The only memorable thing about the voyage was that a very drunk man, on his way to Ireland for Christmas, managed to blunder into our cabin in the middle of the night and be sick in the washbasin under the mistaken impression that it was a convenience.

On the morning of Christmas Eve, even as choirs were giving renderings of 'Holy Night' in Cork, I got the tourist office to telephone the O'Sullivans and announce our immutable intention of arriving on their doorstep. 'They will take you,' the tourist official told us eventually, 'but they don't sound very excited about it.'

It was dark when we arrived. Mrs O'Sullivan looked at Wanda when we entered the bar and a look of ineffable relief appeared on her face. 'Oh,' she said, 'I thought it was another Mr and Mrs Newby. We had another woman with a name something like that. She was a dreadful sort of woman, the sort of woman who has forty frocks.'

That night we all went to midnight Mass at Lauragh and on Christmas morning while it was still dark outside drank a bottle of champagne in bed, which our daughter had thoughtfully provided for this purpose. Then, after rashers and eggs we set off for nearby Lough Mackeenlaun, a holy lake nearby, named after St Mo-Chionlan, otherwise St Cilian or Kilian, which has the peculiar property of drying out when it rains, and was, in the past, famous for its floating islands formed of tussocks of vegetation. On its shore there was a grassy mound with some stones sticking out of it, all that was left of the church of St Kilian, who was martyred at Würzburg and whose *patron* is held here on 7 and 8 July.

Christmas lunch was a great success: turkey accompanied by a magnum of red Hermitage we had brought with us was preceded by a soup into which Joan had introduced the best part of half a bottle of sherry. After the pudding we joined a great press of people in the bar, all drinking whiskey or Guinness, or both. Later I went for a walk in the gloaming and went to sleep in a ditch for a bit. On the following day, Boxing Day in England, the Wren Boys arrived, one of seven parties of boys and girls from the school at Lauragh who case the area on their annual Christmas visitations. They wore strange, home-made masks, funny hats and their mothers' old dresses, irrespective of whether they were boys or girls, and they sang the following:

> The Wren Boys
> The wren, the wren
> The king of all birds
> St Stephen he was caught in the bush
> And we have come here to Your Honour
> Give us a treat to bury the wren
> And you know what that means, don't you?

That afternoon, out for an airing, we met an elderly farmer with a brand new motor car, something pretty remarkable in the vicinity of Kilmakilloge Bay at that time. Would I have the kindness to turn it round for him, he asked, as otherwise he would have to drive it all round the Beara Peninsula and over the Healy Pass, about eighty miles, to get it turned the other way as he hadn't yet 'got the trick of going backwards'. After all this Wanda found herself miraculously cured and we went back to England, but we knew that wherever else we might go in the world, this was one place to which we would want to return.

Now, in January, in a beautiful sunset over a golden sea, we visited what remained of the ancient church of Kilmakilloge, a short distance from the holy lough, in the graveyard of which Mrs Lyons had just been laid to rest, not far from the monument to the O'Sullivan Chieftain Mac Finghan Dubh O'Sullivan, who died in 1809. By the time we got back to the pub the hammering noises that had come from inside the good ship *Stentor* had ceased, and the man responsible for them had emerged – a Mr Langford who divided his time between demolishing the *Stentor* in Kilmakilloge Harbour and demolishing other things in Shaftesbury, England, where he owned an enormous scrap dump and employed a squad of seven men to bust things up. And that night we had mussels and scallops fresh from the Bay, followed by Christmas pudding, vintage 1985, in memory of our last visit. Overhead a full moon swam in a star-filled sky.

The next morning, a Saturday, was as foul and dark as the previous evening had been clear and golden. It required all one's determination to get up and pack.

'How far do you think we're going on this trip?' Wanda said, while we were eating an O'Sullivan breakfast. 'And when do you think we're going to get there?'

'I don't know,' I said. 'It's difficult to say. I'd really like to go round the Ring of Kerry. That's about seventy miles. (I was hopelessly out — it is more than a hundred.) And then there's the Dingle Peninsula. And there's Killarney, too. With luck we might make Tralee by next Saturday.'

'Do you really have to go round all these bloody peninsulas?' she asked. 'They all look about the same in this sort of weather.'

'I don't see how I can just ignore the Ring of Kerry *and* the Dingle Peninsula.'

'In that case I'm going back to Mrs Walsh's to get the van. I can just see us stuck in Tralee, wherever that is, on a Sunday, waiting for a train on Monday.' In fact, for once, she was maligning the Irish Railways which run two trains from Tralee to Cork on Sundays.

'I don't want to use the van,' I said, becoming heated. 'It's against the spirit of the venture.'

'*You* don't have to use it,' she said, 'but I wouldn't feel immoral about it. We're not trying to break any records. We can leave it in Kenmare, if you want to be heroic. It only means we can go home when we want to without biking all the way to Cork. Meanwhile you can go and look at tings.' She left at one-fifteen, having been very kindly offered a lift back to Douglas. I wondered if she would ever come back. I don't think I would have done had I been her.

So I set off to 'look at tings' astride my bicycle which, minus its customary load, felt as if it was fitted with wings. I trespassed recklessly in the demesne of Dereen House, home of the Lansdownes, among rhododendrons, plantations of bamboo and skyscraping conifers, over which the spirit of Sir John Betjeman's

Irish poems would have hung like a fog, if it hadn't been foggy already. Then past Lauragh Old School, still in use, training up further reinforcements of Wren Boys, and up the glen of the Glanmore River to Glanmore Lough, with islands floating in its absolutely still waters, one of which had some sort of ruin in it.

It was an impressive place. To the left a thick mist enveloped the sides of Knockastumpa and Knockowen, down which we had freewheeled from the Healy Pass, and below them were stone-walled fields filled with cattle and a scattering of white farmhouses. Around me on the lake shore were large rocks, expanses of brown, soft ribbon-like grass, birch trees with branches the colour of red wine, and clumps of rhododendrons and holly, the leaves of which a number of cattle were tucking into as if they were some kind of delicacy and not a short cut to a post-mortem examination. The air was full of the sounds of running water and of birds, some of which to my untutored ear sounded like 'weet wee', 'queou queou' and 'peopeep'. There was also an unseasonal abundance of gnats.

Across the lake to the west the steep cliffs of Lackabane fell to the shore, populated by tall clumps of pines, their boles free of branches which added to their stature, and by rhododendrons which flourished among the rocks. It was more like a cliff in Kwantung Province than in County Kerry. For the next couple of miles or so the road followed the Glanmore, which either hurried down over stones or drifted slowly through deep, peaty pools. I saw a good salmon lying under Glanmore Bridge, facing up-stream. The glen was very narrow now and steep-sided, with long waterfalls pouring down into it from the upper parts of Claddagh-garriff, the mountain to the east of the Healy Pass. The last house was a farm high up at the end of the road in a big cirque of mountains dotted with innumerable sheep – Derryclancy, Hun-gry Hill, Knocknagree and Eskatarriff. Behind this building a series of falls, spectacular now that they were in spate, poured down the rocky flanks of the various peaks to make the Glanmore, even here, a roaring torrent.

On the way down from the falls I met the farmer, who had just arrived in a taxi, presumably not having a motor car. His name was Florence O'Sullivan. His wife was dead but he had two sons and two dogs to help him, a collie and a fox terrier. He said he enjoyed the TV programme *One Man and His Dog*, which is all about sheep dog trials in Britain, and is immensely popular, but added without any suggestion of showing off, 'It's a bit different here, a bit more up and down as you might say.' When I asked him the name of this place, he said he called it 'The Pocket', which seemed appropriate. However, the map showed another 'Pocket', this one up another glen immediately to the north of where we were, the Drimmin, standing in a similar cirque of mountains, two of which, Eskatarriff and Lackabane, it shared with Glanmore.

This valley, to visit which involved cycling almost all the way down to the shop at Lauragh and then climbing up again, proved to be a graveyard of defunct motor vehicles, in spite of its magnificence. The road up it expired by a farmhouse, beyond which a track of exceptional squelchiness led away in the direction of a steep, rocky prominence, with the narrow gorge of the Drimmin to the right and to the left the way up to a small pass between the Eskatarriff and Coomacloghane mountains.

I was in a place called Cumeengadhra, although I did not know it at the time. This was the land, in the 1800s, of a family named Sullivan Rabach, and it was here that a sailor, a fugitive from a ship in Berehaven, was murdered while spending the night in their farmhouse. His throat was cut, with the connivance of the rest of the family, by the elder son, Cornelius, as they suspected that he had money on him. Their neighbours and joint tenants were the Sullivans Caoch who, like the Sullivans Rabach, were butter-makers, and that evening Maire Caoch, the wife, happened to look in through the Rabachs' gable window and saw the body. She told her husband and he warned her never to mention the matter again as his sister was the mother of Cornelius and it would certainly lead to trouble. He died soon afterwards. From this time onwards the widow ceased to enjoy, if she ever had enjoyed, a good relationship with the Rabachs and eventually, goaded beyond endurance by various disputes with them, she rather unwisely allowed Cornelius to know that she knew about the murder. One morning in June 1814 he followed her up to the upper grazing ground, where she had gone to milk the cows, and there, with a milk can still in her hand, thirteen years after the original murder, he strangled her.

There was, however, even in this remotest of remote spots, a witness: Daniel Sullivan, aged about twenty, who made his living by cutting off cows' tails and selling them for twisting into rope. He witnessed the deed from the top of a cliff, but being in his own words 'not a stout fellow' he kept quiet and subsequently moved away from the area.

Sixteen years after this second murder Daniel Sullivan, thinking himself to be on his deathbed, confessed to a priest what he had seen. In the event he didn't die and the priest persuaded him to give the information before a magistrate. A warrant was issued for the arrest of Cornelius Rabach in March 1830, by which time he was nearly fifty years old. It took the best part of ten months to apprehend him. He was a good man on the hills and his hide-out, or one of them, was a cave, the mouth of which provided an extensive field of view over the approaches. Eventually he was taken in his own home while in bed with his wife; one of the constables who arrested him was the son of Maire Caoch, the murdered woman. Cornelius was sentenced to death. The principal witness for the prosecution was Daniel Sullivan, and so Mafia-like were the ramifications of the Rabachs that, to save his life, the authorities felt constrained to allow him to spend a year in protective custody.[*]

It was now growing dark. In the last of the light I went up through the soggiest of bog land past the gaping hole in the rock that had been Cornelius Rabach's hideout and into the high, wide marshy pastureland where Maire Caoch was strangled. It was a weird spot; a place where if you twisted your ankle you might remain for ever, or at least until someone brought up sheep or cattle to pasture in the spring. Then I went down along the side of the astonishing cleft that the Drimmin had carved for itself through the rock and splashed through the bog back to my bike. It was now quite dark and by the time I got back to Kilmakilloge at six o'clock Wanda had arrived with the van. We dined on mussels and steaks, which we both in our different ways felt we had

[*]Source: *Kenmare Journal*, 1982.

earned, and the next morning we quitted Kilmakilloge and the O'Sullivans with some emotion, as it was unlikely that we would be passing this way again for some time.

It was nice being in a van, whirling along the shores of the Kenmare River. Kenmare itself was rather nice too, despite the rain; originally founded in 1670 by Sir William Petty as one of the English Plantations, it was laid out in its present form about a century later by his descendant, the first Marquis of Lansdowne. Macaulay wrote of its origins:

> Scarcely any village built by an enterprising band of New Englanders, far from the dwellings of their countrymen, was more completely out of the pale of civilisation than Kenmare. Between Petty's settlement and the nearest English habitation, the journey by land was of two days, through a wild and dangerous country. Yet the place prospered, forty-two houses were erected; the population amounted to 180; the cattle were numerous; the supply of pilchards, mackerel and salmon was plentiful, and would have been still more plentiful had not the beach been, in the finest part of the year, covered by multitudes of seals . . .

Petty also had the equivalent of the final solution to what was known as 'the Irish Problem', which was to import twenty thousand English girls into Ireland and export twenty thousand Irish girls to England. In 1688 the English settlers were driven out, a new experience for English Protestants, after being besieged by a force of three thousand Catholics, part of the army raised by Richard Talbot, Earl of Tyrconnel, in support of James II. They made their last stand on a little peninsula in the river from which, after capitulating, they were allowed to embark in two vessels, each of only 30 tons, 'packed like fish one upon the other', eventually reaching Bristol fourteen days later, after an exceedingly rough passage. And Kenmare, like all these regions of south-west Ireland, had a fearful time during the Famine. Between 1831 and 1841 the census returns show that the population increased significantly and small tenant farmers adopted an illegal system of subdivision of land in their anxiety to provide means of subsistence for their descendants. Thus a holding which formerly supported a single family as well as providing enough cereal crops to pay the rent, now had to support many more households, all dependent on the potato crop which failed to some extent one year in five. Thousands of people existed under these conditions in the huge demesnes of the Lansdownes whose agent, named Hickson, a kindly but some say neglectful man, allowed this practice to take place; while the British Government, although aware of these conditions, took the view that 'necessity alone could not justify artificial interference, with the regular order of providence and society'. By February 1846 smallholders and squatters were facing starvation and were forced to eat the diseased potatoes which led to a widespread outbreak of fever. This spread to the recently completed workhouse in which there were large numbers of paupers. Work was started on a fever hospital but this was not ready until March 1847.

The medical officers' reports, reproduced in the *Kenmare Journal* of 1982, make harrowing reading:

> 19.12.46: Nearly one sixth of the entire number in the house are in fever. The nurse Biddy Sullivan has taken the disease and is lying down severely affected. Hot coffee continues to be given to these patients instead of milk and nothing could be more improper or cruel, as they are tormented with thirst, which coffee will not quench. This drink also retards recovery and promotes a fatal termination.

> 9.1.47: Number in fever 119. Up to four patients are put into one bed, for want of straw, and the convalescent patients cannot rise for want of fire, sometimes for want of clothes. There being a shortage of beds the sick lie on the ground. . . .

> 22.5.47: During these past two months, the number of those suffering from fever, dysentery and measles averaged 220 per week and 153 inmates died during that same period. The Workhouse is not only a great hospital for which it was never intended or adapted but an engine for producing disease and death, as a

fearful proportion of those admitted in health fall victims of the fever in a few days, due to the crowded state of the house.

It was not until July that the epidemic began to subside.

Our stay in Kenmare was not a great success. Having acquired the English Sunday papers on which we were relying to keep us going as bedside reading in whatever B and B we might find ourselves in the week to come, I managed to get them thoroughly sodden while trying to jam them into our pannier bags. While I was doing this Wanda made an excursion to the Church of the Holy Cross for early Mass, only to find it still shut. Our last act was to confide our van to the care of an honest-looking fellow with much the same trepidation as one has when handing over one's child for the first time to a boarding school.

From Kenmare we set off to encompass as much of the Ring of Kerry as we felt we could put up with, along the southern shores of the Iveragh Peninsula, by a dank, dead straight road. Eight miles along it the walls of the huge demesne of Dromore Castle began, and continued without a break, except where the road crossed a tributary of the Kenmare River, for a distance of four miles. Through a gateway flanked by a mock mediaeval gatehouse of the 1830s, at the end of an interminable processional ride flanked by moss-grown deciduous trees and enormous conifers now being cut in great swathes, stood the castle, stark and rather forbidding, on a terrace above the Kenmare River. It was a lofty two storeys high with narrow windows, heavily castellated and machicolated. Inside a turreted porch was a huge door that looked as if it was closed for ever, furnished with a modest bell-push. This we rang but there was no answer, which seemed scarcely surprising as there was no sign of life anywhere. Nor were there any exterior signs of dilapidation: the castle simply appeared to be asleep, waiting for someone to claim it. That it was not was made abundantly clear when I rudely peered in through one of the ground floor windows into a lofty room that might have been a library, furnished with huge drapes and early

Victorian furniture, and saw a paper of recent date lying on a small table. At this we rode away in a panic.

At Tahilla, on Coongar Harbour, about twelve miles out from Kenmare, the sun came out fleetingly and the black waters of the Kenmare estuary were brightened with long ribbons of gold. Hereabouts we stopped at The Rambler's Rest, Prop. T. O'Sheehan, a pink painted cottage with a pre-War or even pre-First War Cyclist Touring Club sign in the form of a wheel in relief on the front of it. Inside, four elderly people, including Mr and Mrs O'Sheehan, had just put their Sunday lunch on a fine old cast-iron peat-burning stove. Laughing and shouting and generally full of beans, Mrs O'Sullivan, whose son lived next door, 'which is a grand thing for us, indeed, God Help Us!' produced tea and two delicious cakes, one fruit, the other with butter on. They had a TV in the kitchen but only watched the news – 'We can't get on with the rest of it at all.'

Still only 12¼ miles from Kenmare, but determined to reach Waterville, another twenty-five miles or so to the west, or bust – 'The sooner we get this bloddy peninsula over the better,' was how Wanda put it, a sentiment with which I thoroughly agreed – we left these hospitable people in what was now pouring rain. Nevertheless, at Castle Cove we made a heroic 3½-mile detour uphill to Staigue, one of the largest and finest of Ireland's stone forts. There the road, which in warmer times would have been edged with fuschia and bog iris, ended outside an isolated farmhouse by a babbling brook with a sign that read, 'Staigue Fort. Trespassers 10p. Children Free'. Beyond this the fort, with unmortared walls between ten and eighteen feet high and thirteen feet thick at the base, rose out of the fog like the abode of Cyclops. Inside, flights of steps made of jutting, regularly spaced slabs enabled the occupants to ascend the walls.

The next five miles or so, conducted in thick, yellow Sherlock Holmes-type fog of a sort long extinct in Britain, were absolutely ghastly. The road, which was said to offer some of the Ring of Kerry's finest views over the islands in Darrynane Bay, now invisible, wound round the edge of the Cahernageeha and Farraniaragh Mountains and culminated in the ascent of the 683-foot Coomakista Pass. There followed a steep descent, still in swirling fog, until suddenly the sky opened up ahead to reveal stone-walled fields sweeping down to Waterville on the sandy shores of Ballinskelligs Bay, and beyond it the sheer cliffs of Bolus Head with the sun setting behind them.

Waterville had all the distilled melancholy of a seaside resort out of season. The Butler Arms, The Smuggler's Inn, the Waterville Beach and the Waterville Lake Hotels, the owners and managers of which smiled so welcomingly from the pages of *Discover Ireland, Hotels and Guest Houses*, were all shut, and I only hoped that they themselves were in warmer climes.

'Let's get out of here,' Wanda said.

Recklessly we hired yet another taxi owned by yet another O'Sullivan – in Ireland you can travel for days through regions in which all the inhabitants appear to have the same name. How does one distinguish between fourteen Mike O'Sullivans, apart from having casts made of their teeth? We asked O'Sullivan where he would stay if it wasn't in Waterville and preferably not somewhere that meant going backwards, and when he had got over the shock of anyone not wanting to stay in Waterville he suggested a place on Valencia Island away to the north that might be just the thing, and said he would take us there for a consideration, but wouldn't we like to see the sunset over the Skelligs on the way? We said we would love to and we set off at breakneck speed with our bikes – 'Now those are the finest boikes I ever saw' – on the roof rack, through a flat landscape at the feet of the Ballinskelligs across which a band of beaglers with five or six couple of shagged-out beagles were wending their way home. We could see why they looked tired when we crossed the ridge of the Ballinskelligs and saw another pack, this one in full cry up the steep hillsides (or as full cry as a pack of beagles can be on a 60° slope after a long day), with a hare with the situation well in hand way ahead of them. 'There'll be no kill today,' said one of the followers, a phlegmatic man armed with a stave and wearing a cap.

Eight miles offshore were two conical black shapes silhouetted against the dazzling light of a stormy sunset: Little and Great Skellig, rock islets composed of grit and shale veined with quartz, rising sheer out of the Atlantic, and the home of seals and innumerable puffins, stormy petrels, fulmars, shearwaters, nesting gannets and many other seabirds. Together with the Great Blasket and its attendant islands further north, off the Dingle Peninsula, these were at one time the westernmost inhabited spots in the whole of Europe.[*] If one counts the lighthouse keepers on the Great Skellig and on Tearaght Island in the Blasket group, both manned at the time of writing, they still qualify. At Portmagee, small fishing village of orange, pale green, white and ochre houses where the boats were sheltering inside the jetty, there was a pub in which the proprietor, a young man who ran trips to the Skelligs in the summer months, told us that if we wanted to go out to them in winter it would cost us £70, weather permitting. 'Come back at Easter,' he said. 'It might be cheaper.'

On Valencia Island, of which it was difficult to form any opinion in the prevailing conditions, it now being pitch dark, we stayed in a pub in which the landlord went on and on while we were eating plaice and chips, dizzy with fatigue, quoting extempore from guide books about the island – 'Contrary to general belief its Spanish-sounding name is an anglicization of the Irish *Bheil Inse*, pronounced *Val Inshe*', he recited, and 'Knightstown, the principal settlement, has a Western Union cable station at which the first cable messages from America were received in 1858.' But he made us feel a couple of heels when he got on to his early life. Born Cardiff, 1919. Mother died when he was aged two. Abandoned by his father aged seven. Brought up by aunt in Cardiff. Cycled here from England in three days in 1937 on beautiful lightweight bike, of which he still has the frame, etc. And he turned out to be positively angelic when we discovered the next morning that we were short of money, upon which he cashed an English cheque for us, backed by a now defunct Eurocheque card, giving us £100 for £90.70 English.

That morning, with a ghastly grey light suffusing the landscape, we made our way over a foul hill to the abandoned Geokaun slate quarries, now a shrine: an enormous cavern, dripping with water,

[*]The Great Skellig was also the site of the westernmost religious foundation in Europe until the ninth century, when the monastery founded there by St Finan in the seventh century was raided by Vikings, from whose attentions it never really recovered.

in which Our Lady of Lourdes was perched high up among slates that looked as if at any moment they might fall on our unworthy nuts, with St Bernadette below, standing in front of an altar and a fountain and gazing up at her. Below it was a lighthouse at the entrance to Valencia Harbour, and away to the north, out beyond Doulus Head, was the Dingle Peninsula. 'We're getting there,' I said, in parody of British Rail's ridiculous slogan, but my partner didn't think it very funny.

Knightstown, to which we now descended, the capital of the Island, was a really attractive place: a lot of fishing boats in and out of the water, the old lifeboat station with all the rescues recorded on boards, the old fishermen's huts, an old-fashioned hotel with a palm tree growing outside it, and a post office with a very friendly postmistress who had a miniature gondolier's hat with *Venezia* inscribed on it, one of the most westerly postmistresses and gondolier's hats in Europe. Then all the way back to Portmagee, and out on the road to Cahirciveen. Cahirciveen (c. 1550 inhabitants and shrinking), birthplace of Daniel O'Connell 'the Liberator', had a very, very long main street and apart from being asphalted and having a lot of cars in it, it was exactly as it had been before 1914, if the old photographs displayed in a shop window were anything to go by. Altogether it had between fifty and sixty pubs, according to various independent witnesses, although one reckless young fellow said there were sixty-two. Whatever the real number, for the size of the place they must have constituted some kind of record. The most amazing was The Harp, which had a facsimile of this instrument outside it and an old-fashioned exterior which didn't prepare me for the interior, a labyrinth which housed a squash court in which the thud of ball on rackets could be heard, a sauna and a huge, pitch dark ballroom with cunning steps concealed in it, on one of which I tripped and fell flat on my face. After this I inspected a restaurant which had roast chicken lunches at £1.95, and a nameless shop illuminated by one single, bare electric bulb, perhaps until that morning a drapery, its shelves filled with empty cardboard boxes, and at the far end a screen from behind which strange rustling noises proceeded. Meanwhile, Wanda took tea at the Tower Tearoom in front of a cosy fire. Before she went in there was sign in the window which said 'No Cyclists', but when she parked her bike outside and went in the proprietress took the sign down, replacing it when she left.

We left Cahirciveen by the road to Killorglin, up what was the estuary of the river Ferta. To the left of the road, beyond a steam power station, rose Knocknadobar, a holy mountain, the Hill of the Wells. A great festival used to take place there on Lughnasa, the last Sunday in July, a pilgrimage with singing, dancing and athletics. Fires were lit, and special cakes were cut either by a young couple about to marry or, failing such a pair, by the couple who performed best in the dancing contest. The pilgrims and revellers stayed on the hill until midnight and before they left the summit was strewn with wild flowers. They then went down to the houses and *shebeens* (drinking places), where those too infirm to climb the mountain were already gathered, and there passed the rest of the night in dancing, card-playing and story-telling.

There are several wells on the mountain; the water from one (Fionan's Well) was reputed to cure sick cattle, and a cattle fair was held nearby. The pool at the foot of Knocknadobar, called Glaise Chumra (the Fragrant Stream) and dedicated to St Fursey,* was visited in particular by pilgrims with eye trouble for its healing powers.

A similar festival took place on Drung Hill, north of Knocknadobar, at the summit of which is Leacht Fhionain (Fionan's Cairn). Fionan is the patron saint of this parish. A number of legends are connected with this hill: that St Fionan is buried under the cairn and the well sprang up there for this reason; and that three nuns for three years in succession, and on the same day, saw a round stone rise out of the hilltop and descend the slope, which led them to conclude that an annual pilgrimage should be made to the summit. There was also a custom recorded by the historian Charles Smith, who travelled in these parts in the middle of the eighteenth century, that anyone who passed the mountain should compose some verses in its honour, or risk misfortune. 'All the verses that I heard,' he wrote, 'were about as rugged and uncouth as the road on which

---

*St Fursey, a nephew of St Brendan, had wondrous visions of the other world and founded monasteries at Yarmouth and at Lagny in France.

they were made, for which reason I shall not trouble the reader with them; although I had several copies given me for that purpose.'

At about one-fifteen we reached the heavenly warmth of the Falcon Hotel, in which three Frenchmen dressed in long rubber boots and Barbours, who had been shooting woodcock, were drinking whiskey and eating a picnic put together in France from a wicker hamper. We asked the gillie, who was excluded from the feast, who came shooting in these parts of Kerry nowadays.

'There used to be a lot of Germans shooting,' he said, 'but now they all go to Kenya. The Italians like to come but they're terribly dangerous and no one wants them. The only good shot is what they call a 'Conte' from Milan; but he's a terrible man, too, a terrible fussy man.'

'He is that,' interjected a boy from behind the bar.

'With this man everything has to be just so. The drinks must be right, the food must be right – he gets very angry sometimes about the food' (I can't blame him, I thought) 'and the bed must be just right, not too hot and not too cold.' ('What that Conte needed was a week in the bed and breakfasts; that would break his spirit,' Wanda said later.)

I asked him if there were any deer.

'Only Japanese Sitka deer,' he said.

'What do you do with them?' I said. 'Shoot them?'

'No, we export them.'

'Where to?'

'To Japan.'

We continued on our way. It was now very cold. We passed the ruins of a huge folly built high above the road, backed by mountains – Glenbeigh Towers, built 1867–71 and burned down in 1922 during the Civil War. It was designed by Edward William Godwin, the architect of Dromore Castle in County Limerick, for Roland Winn, fourth Lord Headley of Aghadoe, a landlord notorious for his ill-treatment of his tenantry. He later threatened to sue Godwin, who had already run off with the actress Ellen Terry, because the Castle let in water in authentic mediaeval fashion, and because the cost was too high. The fifth Lord Headley, his successor, having married three times, then became a Muslim and made the pilgrimage to Mecca, after which he assumed the title of *Al Hadji* and became President of the British Muslim Society.

We rode the next twenty-five miles or so to Killarney by a minor road that skirted Lough Caragh and the northern flanks of the now snow-covered MacGillycuddy's Reeks in the sort of rain that would have made Noah batten down the hatches, and arrived long after dark. Although we felt pretty miserable, the lights burning inside St Mary's, the great Gothic Cathedral that is Pugin's masterpiece in Ireland, lured us into its soaring interior and there, in a pew remote from public view, we listened to Benediction while two enormous pools of water spread about our feet, as if we were incontinent.

Killarney, with all the lights on in its narrow streets, was full of life in spite of the oceans of water that were falling on it, everyone except ourselves being quite content under the umbrellas which the inhabitants of Cork and Kerry, not to speak of Limerick, Galway, Mayo and Sligo, are presumably born with already open. After the places we had visited, being in High Street, Killarney was a bit like being in the rue du Faubourg St Honoré. But all of a sudden the lights began to go out, at which point Killarney became a city of dreadful night.

We had tried five different pubs and B and Bs which either didn't want us or we didn't want them before we finally washed up on the front doorstep of The Orchard, Props. Mr and Mrs Roger and Joan O'Donoghue, whose eight sons had provided eight-elevenths of the local football team before four of them emigrated to America. Then to bed after the hottest bath anyone could possibly imagine. The following morning after breakfast we talked to Joan O'Donoghue, a ball of fun despite being crippled with arthritis, a complaint that seems particularly prevalent among the devout ladies in Ireland, especially those with large families. I asked her, in an unguarded moment, what she did besides running a guest house and having four sons more or less on the premises, upon which she went off into peals of laughter.

After this we penetrated what were now the snowy fastnesses of the Gap of Dunloe, battling through it up a series of hairpin bends to what is called the Madman's Seat from which a view of what looked like Siberia was obtained. Then we took the road along the bank of the River Laune – strong, deep, wooded and silent – to

Killorglin, passing en route Liebherr's German Crane Factory and a Bavarian delicatessen and butcher's shop installed in an apartment block that might have been transported block by block from Munich.

Killorglin, where we ate the *würst, sauerkraut* and *dunkelbrot* we had acquired there, is the place where on 10 August, what is known as Gathering Day, a male goat is hoisted to the top of a high stage where it remains, presiding over an extensive market in cattle, sheep, horses and goats, until Scattering Day, 12 August. That evening, he is taken down and carried round the town on the shoulders of four men to the premises of the town's shopkeepers, most of whom have benefited from the fair and are consequently asked to contribute to the attendant expenses of maintaining a goat up in the air. When the goat is finally released into greener pastures (one would imagine that it would have had its throat cut as the climax to what is an extremely ancient ceremony), the horses, cattle and sheep are taken away too, but at all the exits from the town there are road blocks at which men armed with sticks enforce a toll on every animal's head. The proceeds all go to a family named Foley, who have an ancient and unique charter which entitles them to it and, if hindered, gives them the right to use force to gain it.

We set off for Dingle in driving sleet, past the road that led to Ballyskissane Pier, from which a car-load of members of the IRA, on the way to meet the *Aud*, a two-masted sailing vessel loaded in Germany with arms for the cause, plunged into the waters of Dingle Bay, drowning all the occupants, on the night of Good Friday, 19 April 1916.* By now we both felt unequal to the remaining twenty-nine miles to Dingle and at Castlemaine sought out another taxi man, who was willing to take us on for a consideration. I didn't catch his name or much of the other extraneous information he purveyed about what he felt about atomic bombs, AIDS, drugs, contraception, etc. – he was the most boring man we had met in the whole of Ireland. Anyway, I was busy scribbling down notes such as the following about our surroundings: 'Bolteens, bungs, one or

---

*At noon the next day, the *Aud*, with its German crew, was given chase to by an English patrol vessel, and at six-thirty that evening she was surrounded by English warships and escorted into Queenstown Harbour where her Captain, Spindler, ordered the crew to abandon her and blew her up.

two rnd hses, some boogy (sic) towards water. Clears enough to see snow on Slieve Mish Mts,rt. Washing hung on outbldngs by hswives despairing of ever drying it.' At Dingle, delivered from this mastermind, we boarded our bikes and fled the town, knowing that wherever we went westwards on this remote peninsula, unless we had waterwings or were going to walk out over the high tops, we would be coming back this way.

Down near the shore of Dingle Harbour stood the once fine eighteenth-century Burnham House, the property of the Lords Ventry, descendants of a Cromwellian trooper, John Mullins, who struck it rich. It had been given the Catholic Educational Institution treatment, from which it had emerged a bilious shade of yellow, together with other humiliations, but it had retained its demesne, and some of the inmates, healthy-looking girls in tracksuits, were puffing round the grounds.

'What happened to the last Lord Ventry?' I asked a man driving a gigantic lorry full of stones, when we emerged.

'He'll be across the Jardan now,' he said.

Then to Ventry Harbour, a huge oval expanse on the steel grey sands of which Daire, 'King of the World', and Finn McCoul fought a great battle which lasted a year and a day and which resulted, as all the best battles do, in the extermination of the opposing forces and the salvation of the homeland. Here, after the battle, Crede, the wife of the warrior Cael, sang a dirge for her dead husband, part of which goes as follows:

> Moans the bay –
> Billows grey round Ventry roar,
> Drowned is Cael MacCrimtann brave,
> 'Tis for him sob wave and shore.
>
> Woe is me!
> Dead my Cael is fair and free:
> Oft my arms would ward his sleep,
> Now it is the deep, dark sea.
>
> Woe, the roar
> Rolling round from sea and shore;
> Since he fought the foreign foe,
> Mine the woe for Cael no more.

Drowned was Cael MacCrimtann brave,
Now I've nought of life my own:
Heroes fell below his glaive,
His high shield has ceased to moan.

Ahead of us now was Mount Eagle, and from this point onwards I experienced a feeling of unreality about the twentieth century that I had hitherto experienced nowhere else in the western world. I find it impossible to analyse, or even begin to write about it, but the memory remains with me still. Here we entered an area which contained within it one of the greatest concentrations of ancient remains in Ireland, an area so rich in them that even the minds of scholars must reel: *clochans* (dry stone beehive huts), ogham stones, some of them cross-inscribed,* promontory forts, ringforts, some of them with souterrains, pillar stones, prostrate stones, one of them with cup-and-circle and other prehistoric markings, cross slabs, ruined churches, oratories and *bullauns* (stones with a depression in them, probably used as mortars). I hope I haven't missed any out. According to Killanin and Duignan, numbers of them 'have been cleared away by farmers, local authorities and other vandals'.

Now out along the road to Slea Head, blasted out of the mountainside with explosives, it began to snow with incredible violence but the wind was so strong that it was all blown down the cliffside into the sea. Offshore big seas were running with a full gale from north-north-west, creating long parallel ribbons of foam downwind that stretched for miles across the mouth of Dingle Bay, a phenomenon I had never witnessed before. The Great Blasket, which from here resembled a long, narrow upended sliver of rock with cliffs in some places 1000 feet high, was separated from the mainland by Blasket Sound, a mile wide but with a navigable channel reduced to less than 1000 yards by various underwater reefs and a huge conical rock that jutted out of it. With a three-knot tide running through it it now resembled a cauldron of water on the boil.

---

*Ogham stones are commemorative Christian gravestones, with inscriptions in the Ogham alphabet, a fourth- and fifth-century adaptation of the Latin alphabet, originally used for carving inscriptions on sticks.

It was through this Sound that the first Armada ship to make a successful landfall, Admiral Juan Martinez de Recalde's *Don Juan*, together with two small despatch vessels, was brought in a similar gale on 15 September 1588. This superb feat of seamanship would have been impossible had her pilot not had local knowledge,[*] especially as the *Don Juan* had been shot through close to the waterline during fighting in the English Channel in early August, in which de Recalde had greatly distinguished himself.

Another large ship, the *San Juan Bautista*, flagship of the Castilian Squadron, succeeded in following in to safety, but a third, the *Nuestra Senora de la Rosa*, was less fortunate. She tried to enter, struck a rock but continued to run on, firing her guns to attract help, and anchored in the Sound near Recalde; but at two in the afternoon she dragged her anchors, hit a rock and sank, taking with her everyone on board except the pilot's son. He was washed ashore on some flotsam, taken prisoner and sent to Dingle, where one wonders what fate awaited him. Also lost were 50,000 ducats in gold and silver and twenty-two brass cannon on land mountings. Two hours later the *San Juan de Ragusa* also came in with her mainmast down; she subsequently sank but her crew were saved. Here, under the lee of the Great Blasket de Recalde, very ill, and the surviving ships remained for thirteen days before sailing for Spain.

Out across the desolate waters of the Sound, the Great Blasket is the biggest of that group of islands which for their size must be among the most written about and best written about islands in the world. Reading these books (the majority written either by inhabitants of the islands or by people who lived on them and knew them and their people intimately), one is struck by how

---

[*]For centuries before the reign of Queen Elizabeth I, and during it, hundreds of Spanish fishing boats were operating off the Irish coasts, which at that time were as productive of fish as the Grand Banks of Newfoundland were subsequently to become. There was therefore no shortage of skilled pilots in the Spanish Armada. What is surprising was how dependent some of them were on the very inaccurate charts of the north coast of Mayo. Perhaps they were overruled by their superiors. Inaccuracies were still appearing in maps published in 1610, despite the fact that Mercator's charts, published twenty years before the Armada set sail, were extremely accurate.

vividly they record almost everything that one could hope to learn about the islanders: not only the details of their daily lives, but of their aspirations and fears for the future, and above all of their liveliness and humour. Having read them so recently, it was almost with a feeling of horror that I looked at these now-abandoned islands, the descriptions of a little Blaskets world that is no more still ringing in my ears:

> Men have set out east and west; one currach is at Tiaracht fishing for lobsters and two are in Dingle, one with lobsters, the other with mackerel. The latter sell for four shillings the hundred and lobsters for a shilling apiece. A currach from Dunquin has gone west to Inishvickillaun with a gentleman on board – a man who is learning Gaelic in Comineol. . . . There are some people gathering turf, others are at school and others again are by the hearth, cooking for themselves – they have the best of it, I believe. They will have the tasting of everything.
>
> When the men meet together around midday they ask each other the news.
>
> 'Were you out fishing last night, Séamas?'
>
> 'I was, my sweet man.'
>
> 'Did you have a good catch?'
>
> 'Two boats caught more than we did and two caught less. Six hundred we had.'
>
> 'Well, if you were short of relish with the potatoes for part of the year,' says Tadhg, 'maybe you haven't that to say today. It will be a long time now before you are so short of something tasty.'
>
> 'Upon my soul, my darling man, ten of them was all I brought home because we had no salt to preserve them,' says Séamas, 'and I let the two hundred of my share go to Dingle to pay for the salt. It is not the end of the world yet, with God's help.'
>
> June 1919 [*]

[*]Source: Tomas O'Crohan, *Island Cross-talk. Pages From a Diary*, trs. Tim Enright, OUP, 1986.

It was bitterly cold. From the Head we pedalled – it was impossible to freewheel – downhill into the paralysing wind to Coumeenoule Bay, where a scattered settlement of about a dozen houses, one of them with a beehive *clochan* standing next to it, stood on the steep slopes of Mount Eagle, here divided up by stone walls into fields that no man would probably ever till again. Down below, on the rocks out towards Dunmore Head, pounded by the sea, was the wreck of a Dutch ship. Above it on the cliff, hanging over the void, a big crane was being used to haul the engines out of it bit by bit.

We had been told by the boss of the tourist office in Killarney that one of the only B and Bs to be open at this end of the Peninsula at this time of year would be that of a Mrs Hurley at a place called Kilcooley near Ballydavid. It was by now pitch dark and snowing hard. Away to the west the loom of the light on Tearaght Island, the westernmost point of the Blaskets, was just visible through the flurries, but not the light itself. Miles before there was any chance of encountering Mrs Hurley's B and B we saw the first of several signposts pointing to it, but unfortunately some local joker had swivelled them round. The result was chaotic. In such circumstances the Irish half-inch map, even in broad daylight somewhat capricious in the information it chooses to furnish, was quite useless. Every time I wanted to look at a signpost I had to take my feeble Everready light off the handlebars and flash it on the sign, which invariably gave its information in Irish. In this fashion we twice passed the Gallarus Oratory, the most impressive of the remaining smaller Christian edifices in Ireland, without seeing it.

We had already visited the shop in Ballydavid to ask directions, without success. It was on our way back there, to find out if they really meant what they said, that I descried a low building. Desperate, I banged on the door and waited. After some time the door was opened to reveal an unlit void.

'Excuse me,' I said, 'do you happen to know the way to Mrs Hurley's Bed and Breakfast?'

'Well, I do know,' came the reply, 'it's just the other side of Ballyferriter. All you have to do is . . .' and went off into the sort of crazy spiel that had already had us circling the neighbourhood in increasing desperation.

'And where are ye fram?' or words to that effect, said this invisible figure.

'From England.'

'Glory be to God!' he said, and shut the door.

Eventually we found the abode of Mrs Hurley. She wasn't feeling too good, she said (neither were we), but she did have the kindness to direct us to another B and B not more than three miles away before shutting the door on us.

Next morning snow lay thick o'er hill and dale, causing a serious hold-up in what might be called culture: projects such as climbing Brandon Mountain, the second highest in Ireland at 3127 feet. We did however manage to get to the Oratory, which looked for all the world like a beautiful, perfectly preserved stone ship set upside down in the wilderness, its hull – in this case its steep, pitched unmortared roof – made of stone slabs of such perfect fit that it was still completely rainproof after a thousand years.

Brandon, or more commonly Brendan, was born in about AD 486. A great light is said to have shone over the area on the night of his birth, and when he was baptised at a well east of Ardfert, three castrated rams leapt from it – known as Tobar-na-Molt, it is a place of pilgrimage in May and June to this day. He was educated by St Erc, ordained at Tralee, and became one of the Twelve Apostles of Ireland. It was these apostles who, having seen a wondrous flower from HyBrasil, the Isle of Paradise, chose Brendan to go in search of it. This he did, setting out in about 525 from Brendan Creek below the mountain which bears his name. From reading the modern translation of the *Navigatio Sancti Brendani*, published in about 800, two centuries after his death, we know that he may well not only have reached the Canaries but the American seaboard as far south as Florida, using a form of *currach*, 'a wicker boat with ox-skins covered o'er', seeing en route Icelandic volcanoes, and icebergs on one of which a decidedly frigid Judas Iscariot was allowed a cooling-off period from the flames of hell on Sundays and festival days. Tim Severin's account of his own voyage to Newfoundland in just such a vessel shows that it is indeed perfectly possible that Brendan could have travelled that far. He died in 578 and was buried in his cathedral at Clonfert, now a Protestant establishment.

With much greater difficulty we moved on to Dun an Oir, the Golden Fort (or Forte del Oro), on a promontery on Smerwick Bay, a long couple of miles in the snow north of where we had been staying. Forte del Oro was built on the site of the Iron Age fort by a force of eighty Spaniards headed by the Papal Nuncio Dr Nicholas Sanders, and James Fitzmaurice Fitzgerald, known as 'the arch traitor', to assist Gerald Fitzgerald, first Earl of Desmond in a large-scale revolt against the English in defence of Catholicism. The following year six hundred Italian reinforcements arrived, but in November a powerful force under the English Admiral Winter captured their ships and Lord Grey of Wilton, the English Lord Deputy, attacked the fort with eight hundred men. After three days' bombardment it capitulated. The officers were spared, but more than six hundred of the unfortunate rank and file were massacred, as well as a number of local Irish women. Before the surrender the Italian commander of the force, Sebastiano di San Giuseppe of Bologna, yielded up Father Laurence Moore, Oliver Plunket and William Wollick, an English Catholic, all of whom refused to acknowledge the religious supremacy of Queen Elizabeth I and were subjected to torture with an expertise not unknown to the Inquisition, before being hanged. At the time these events took place Fitzmaurice Fitzgerald was on his way to pay a vow at the monastery of the Holy Cross in Tipperary, but was slain in a skirmish before arriving. By 1583 the revolt had collapsed and Gerald, Earl of Desmond had been captured in a wood on the borders of Cork and Kerry, and killed.

We now directed our bikes towards Dingle, crossing a miniature pass between two mountains with the snow streaming across it in the wind; and from there to Anascaul, from where another road led over the mountains to Tralee Bay, on the north side of the Peninsula, by way of the 1354-foot Connor Pass. It was under eight inches of snow, so we had to give up, and got a lift to Tralee in an empty removals van.

In Tralee it wasn't snowing, only pouring with rain, and we chartered a taxi to McKenna's Fort, a lonely ringfort in which Sir Roger Casement was captured on Good Friday 1916. He and two companions landed from a German submarine on the vast expanse of Banna Strand, which stretches away for miles north of

Tralee Bay. While doing so their rubber boat overturned and they were soaked. After walking inland for some distance they came to the fort where Casement remained, exhausted, while the other two went on to Tralee in order to make contact with Austin Stack, Commandant of the Kerry Brigade of the Volunteers. Casement was arrested in McKenna's fort that afternoon, with sand on his trousers and a used railway ticket from Berlin to Wilhelmshaven in his pocket, as was Stack when he later went to the police barracks in which Casement was being held, to try to speak to him. Casement did however manage to send a message out of the barracks, which was taken to Dublin by a Volunteer, telling the rebels that arms but not men were being sent to help their cause. By this time the *Aud*, in which the arms had been shipped over, was lying on the bottom of Queenstown Harbour together with 20,000 rifles, ten machine guns and a great quantity of ammunition. Two months later Casement was convicted of high treason and in August 1916 he was hanged at Pentonville, going to the scaffold with great courage. Stack was also sentenced to death but his sentence was commuted to twenty years' penal servitude; he survived a hunger strike and forcible feeding, and was released in July 1917.

The fort was almost invisible, completely covered with brambles, as it had been when Casement hid in it. On the way back to Tralee I discovered from the driver that there was also a memorial nearby, which he hadn't bothered to show us as he 'didn't think you would be interested in that old stuff, being English'.

Later in bed we read *The Kerryman*, dated Friday, 24 January 1986, which had the banner heading:

COUNTY COUNCIL REJECTS NORTH AGREEMENT
CIVIL WAR GHOSTS PARADED AT ASHE HALL

Councillor John Joe O'Sullivan welcomed the Agreement and said that Michael Collins signed the Treaty as a stepping stone. He was not surprised with the current attitude of the Fianna Fail party which in the Civil War made brother wade in the blood of brother. de Valera hanged Irishmen, including Kerrymen, and these are now the people who were claiming to be republican.

Councillor Kiely: Did ye not shoot them?
Councillor McEllistrim: Ye blew them up.
In the vote which followed, the motion to welcome the
Agreement was rejected.

The next morning we took the bus back to Killarney, and
another to Kenmare to pick up the van. We caught the night boat
from Rosslare to Fishguard in a Force 10 wind, which smashed all
the glasses in the bar when the ship cleared the breakwater. By one
o'clock the following afternoon we were back at home in Dorset.
It was Friday, 31 January, the last day of what had been an
altogether memorable month. As someone said to me while high
in the rigging of our four-masted barque, taking in sail early in the
morning of New Year's Day 1939: if things continued as they had
done in January, the year to come looked like being 'a focking
no-good year'.

PART 3

JUNE

Chapter 12

DUBLIN UNREVISITED

My intention was to write a chapter of the moral history of my country and I chose Dublin for the scene because that city seemed to me the centre of paralysis.

JAMES JOYCE. Letter to Grant Richards, 5 May 1905

Have a facial in a lofty room with marble fireplace . . . and rococo ceiling . . .

Vogue. October 1986

It was March before the terrible winter of 1986 released its grip on us sufficiently to allow us even to contemplate biking in Ireland once more, and June before we actually got around to doing it, by which time the weather, at least in southern England, had gone into what looked like a terminal decline.

Meanwhile, studying the newly published Michelin map of Ireland which, in spite of its modest scale, was as big as a spinnaker and as intractable to handle in any sort of breeze, I had what seemed to me a brilliant idea about how to overcome one of the principal factors that made cycling so unpopular with Wanda, namely, hills. (The other was headwinds: she had not forgotten how a freak blast had literally plucked her from her saddle down in County Cork in January.) My idea was to ride westwards from Dublin, not on the N4, which if it was anything like the dreadful N18 was best left to the Irish, but along the banks of the Grand Canal, which begins where the River Liffey meets the Irish Sea in Dublin Bay and eventually comes to an end at Shannon Harbour. I figured this would entail the minimum amount of hill climbing, eighteenth-century canal builders and their financial sponsors being very sensitive to any unnecessary variations in the level of their creations. Another advantage, in theory anyway, was that we would only rarely encounter motor vehicles. And in the unlikely event of the Irish wind choosing to blow from points east instead of west, then that would be in the nature of a bonus.

Which was why, off the boat from Holyhead at Dun Laoghaire (pronounced Dunleary) we found ourselves the following morning astride our bikes, armed with nothing more lethal than a couple of bicycle pumps, in a run-down, spooky, some might say positively dangerous area of Dublin dockland. To be precise, we were down by what were the Grand Canal Docks, otherwise the Outer and Inner Ringsend Basins, until they ceased to be used commercially in 1960. Now the only vessels in this expanse were a couple of small trawlers with no one on board, moored just inside the lock gates. Immediately downstream, the River Dodder enters the Liffey more or less at the point where the Liffey enters the Irish Sea, which is also where Oliver Cromwell landed in 1646 with twelve thousand men and an artillery siege train to begin the subjugation of Ireland.

These Docks are bounded by ruined warehouses, some of them overgrown with ivy and intersected with streets, some of them cobbled, and some, that morning at any rate (just in case the Corporation writes to me inviting me to eat my breakfast off them, in the way corporations do after cleaning up), littered with every kind of imaginable rubbish, including mattresses bursting at the seams and looking as horrible as only mattresses can, enough broken glass to warrant opening a bottle recycling factory on site, and bundles of what had been newspapers but were now gooey masses of papier mâché.

And across the water from where we were standing, beyond Charlotte Quay and what used to be the Dublin Tramway Power House, was the Inner Dock Basin by the Ringsend Bridge, which links Pearse Street with Ringsend Road, which in turn leads into Irishtown Road and Sandymount: streets traversed eighty-two years previously (give or take a few days) by Leopold Bloom, seated uncomfortably on a piece of lemon-scented soap (obtained from Sweeney's the chemist in Lincoln Place), in a funeral carriage that formed part of the modest cortège which accompanied the remains of Paddy Dignam to Prospect Cemetery on Finglas Road, out beyond Mountjoy Prison and the Royal Canal.* There, on 16 June 1904, he was deemed to have been laid to rest in company with, among others, Parnell, O'Connell, Collins and the veteran Fenian, Jeremiah O'Donovan Rossa, who died in New York in

---

*At the time of Paddy Dignam's funeral Pearse Street was still called Brunswick Street. It was not until much later that it was renamed after Patrick Pearse, the devout Catholic schoolmaster turned revolutionary, and one of the leaders of the Easter Rising, who was born at No. 27 in 1879.

1915. Casement's remains were not taken there until 1966, fifty years after his execution in Pentonville Gaol; remains which, some ghouls suggested, were inextricably mixed with those of Crippen the poisoner, which like Casement's had been buried in quicklime in the same patch of unconsecrated ground.

In all this extensive and melancholy landscape on this cool, grey summer's morning the only living things in sight apart from ourselves were a solitary, snooty-looking seagull afloat in the Outer Basin and an over-sized ginger cat which was digging into some ordures in Green Street, off Britain Quay. In spite of this solitude we still had the uneasy feeling that if we stayed around in these parts we might get taken apart, a feeling that comes over one – well, it certainly comes over me – in any derelict, semi-populated urban area, potentially full, as Dublin certainly is, of heroin addicts and muggers. But by the time I had begun to think about saying, 'Let's get outta here!' like the guys in those 1930s B pictures, Wanda was already getting out, head down and pedalling away like mad, up Hanover Quay, along Grand Canal Quay at the foot of Misery Hill, past sundry decrepit gas works and along the Inner Basin,* before she dived under Maquay Bridge where the Grand Canal, Circular Line, begins at Lock No. 1.

Beyond this first lock, lined with noble trees, its grassy banks positively arcadian and in places overlooked by elegant terrace houses, the Canal curved away through unexplored tracts of South Dublin, following the same route as the Circular Road, built around the same time as the Canal in the mid 1790s. Now most of the through traffic follows a more modern route to the north, leaving the inhabitants of the Canal banks and the old road in relative peace. In the first quarter of a mile or so a series of four locks lifted the Canal, and us with it, a dizzy 29.8 feet above sea level without either of us noticing it. If it went on like this we would be laughing all the way to the Atlantic Ocean.

---

*Across the Basin was the site of Boland's Mills, which de Valera made his HQ, as Commandant of the Third Battalion of the Volunteers, on the morning of Easter Monday 1916. Seventeen of these Volunteers, who altogether numbered about 130, occupied a number of houses near Mount Street Bridge; it was here, on the Wednesday following the Easter Monday rising, that these seventeen fought a five-hour action with a British force of battalion strength, causing enormous casualties.

Not a boat to be seen in this section. Hardly surprising. 'It is a good idea to seek the help of the lock keepers passing through the city section and even ask the Inland Waterways Association to provide a shore party,' writes Ruth Delany in her *Guide to the Grand Canal* (1986). Hazards include having one's boat stripped of its contents if left unattended, and being pelted with stones by schoolchildren. The offices of Bord Failte, the Irish Tourist Board, are at the fourth lock, behind expanses of glass that one would have thought would present a much more tempting target for stone-throwing children than a cabin cruiser and its crew, but there is no accounting for juvenile tastes. At this fount of knowledge I stocked up on such free literature as *A Visitor's Guide to Pubs in Dublin*, though I had not much hope of seeing, let alone entering one on this particular trip.

One of the nicest pubs I remembered from time past in Dublin was Doheny and Nesbitt's establishment in Lower Baggot Street, only a short distance from where we were now standing. Full of mahogany, cut and uncut glass, and mysterious partitions of a sort that always made me feel, hiding behind them, that I had come to denounce someone to the Dublin equivalent of the Council of Ten, it had a snug out front and a room at the back for ladies, or was it the other way round? In another half hour it would be open and I would be elsewhere, somewhere up the Circular Line or beyond.

By now the sun was coming out and it was going to be a lovely day. Just beyond this lock, beautifully inscribed on what resembled a headstone, and miraculously unvandalized, was a poem written by Patrick Kavanagh (1905–67), son of a farmer and shoemaker in County Monaghan and himself a farmer – a poem that in the circumstances made appropriate reading, even if it was June not July:

> O commemorate me where there is water,
> Canal water preferably, so stilly
> Greeny at the heart of summer. Brother
> Commemorate me thus beautifully.
> Where by a lock Niagariously roars
> The falls for those who sit in the tremendous silence

Of mid-July. No one will speak in prose
Who finds his way to these Parnassian islands.
A swan goes by head low with many apologies,
Fantastic light looks through the eyes of bridges –
And look! a barge comes bringing from Athy
And other far-flung towns mythologies.
O commemorate me with no hero-courageous
Tomb – just a canal-bank seat for the passer-by.

Just by this stone was the seat for the passer-by, one who in this instance looked more like a permanent fixture: an emaciated Gael –he would probably have described himself, modestly, as being 'on the tin soide' – fortyish, with two mid-front upper incisors missing and wispy hair. He was dressed in a thick, dark, hand-made greatcoat several sizes too large for him, with puke on the lapels and equally over-size boots without laces, as if to emphasize, as the bound feet of Chinese ladies once did, the sedentary position of those who wear such footwear in life's race.

He was not the sort of citizen the Americans call a bum, or the British a down-and-out, but what the Dublin writer Tom Corkery used to say was 'a mouth' to his friends, 'a character' to tourists and 'a non-productive unit' to economists: non-productive, but unlike a real bum or down-and-out, certainly supported by some unfortunate woman, perhaps two unfortunate women and/or other next-of-kin.

'Have a place on Paddy's Seat,' said this non-productive unit graciously, moving sideways a perceptible bit to give me more *lebensraum* if I wanted it.

'Thank you,' I said, 'I won't actually. I'm bicycling and my wife's way on ahead; but before I go, tell me, what do you think of Kavanagh?'

'I tink of him as a toughtful man to give me a seat here by the water, which I can use for the rest of me natural life, God willing, and as a great poet, too. Have you read "The Great Hunger", that's his best in every way, the one that begins "Clay is the word and clay is the flesh"? It's a long poem but I have most of it by heart if you would like to hear it.'

'I'm afraid it will have to be some other time,' I said. 'I've got to get on.' By now I was feeling like the Water Rat when he meets the Seagoing Rat who almost persuades him to go to sea.

'He died of the drink, they say; but he was a good age for a drinking man, sixty-two, or tree. Dere was only one man he couldn't abide, that was Brendan Behan. He was a *comic*, Paddy Kavanagh.'

To the right and left now, 99.9 per cent of it out of sight, was Dublin, inhabited as the spirit and events moved them by Gaels, Norsemen, Normans, Huguenots, Flemings and others: city of Sheridan, Shaw (who hated it), O'Casey, Joyce (who apparently hated it) and so on. Or rather, around us now was what is left of it following the 1916 Rising, the Civil War and the ministrations of vandals, demolishers and improvers in the guise of town planners.

Dublin must be one of the few capital cities in the world which has turned its splendid Parliament House, originally designed by Edward Lovett Pearce, into a bank – the Bank of Ireland – in 1802. Well, they had to turn it into something, not having a parliament any more. The Irish destroy so many of the things they love – or ought to love until they can produce something better to take their place. Instead of simply removing Nelson from his pillar in O'Connell Street, putting him through a crusher and having him re-cycled into some more homely folk hero such as Collins, Casement, or even O'Connell himself, in 1966 they chose to blow the whole thing, pillar and all, to smithereens. Thus, in one mad stroke, was destroyed the last embellishment, apart from the façade of the General Post Office, of what had been one of the more beautiful eighteenth-century streets in Europe.

It is a city in which the inhabitants were, as I remembered, completely indifferent to the march of time (which meant an almost total inability to keep appointments, at least on the right day), to the weather, to what is commonly regarded as edible food, and to their surroundings, but capable of talking the hind legs off the biggest herd of donkeys ever conceived; their folk heroes racehorses (but not the riders), greyhounds and whippets, footballers, hurlers and prisoners, preferably political; impatient of and despising authority; hating what those who were not 'offeecials' referred to as 'offeecials' while longing secretly to be 'offeecials' themselves. A city in which, at this very moment, many of them would be drinking their first pint of the day from a glass without a handle in one of what were, when I was last there, its seven hundred or more pubs; pubs which, ideally for the older drinker, would have an ambiance compounded of brown-painted lincrusta and glittering glass; pubs in which the drinkers used to drink in companies or schools, each one waiting his turn to buy his round of what was called 'the gargle', which ensured that everyone had six drinks instead of three. For this was a city in which few men drank at home unless they were already drunk, or otherwise incapacitated, on the grounds that it didn't taste the same as in a bar: 'Now, Mr O'Leary sir, I tink you've had enough for a bit, sir.' I remembered singing pubs; pubs that looked more like libraries, but with bottles not books on the shelves; theatre pubs; pubs with poetry; one pub reputed to be used only by market women and no men; another a favourite stopping-off place for mourners on their way back from Glasnevin Cemetery. Here, in The Brian Boru House, the wake still flourished and you could drink 'a ball o'malt', Irish whiskey from a wooden cask. Hickey's, on City Quay, had one of the best pints anywhere.

To me the most wonderful of all Dublin pubs was O'Meara's Irish House on the corner of Wood Quay. Its façade was topped by six round towers of the sort but not the size that soar up above Irish monastic settlements and the façade itself was embellished with coloured stucco reliefs of such heroes of Irish nationalism and Catholic emancipation as Henry Grattan (1796–1820), making his last speech to the about-to-be abolished Irish Parliament in 1800, and Daniel O'Connell (1775–1847). But despite these remembrances of things and times past in Dublin's publand, for those of a selective nature or finicky disposition it is worth heeding what Swift wrote in a letter to Charles Ford in August 1725: 'No men in Dublin go to Taverns who are worth sitting with.'

What I remembered most about Dublin was the poverty. The poor lived in what were sometimes large eighteenth-century houses that had once been among the most elegant in the British

Isles, but in Victorian times had become rookeries, teeming with inhabitants; what O'Casey described as 'a long drab gauntlet of houses, some of them fat with filth . . . long kennels of struggling poverty and disordered want . . . the lacerated walls, the windows impudent with dirt'. The poor swarmed in the street markets, filling the air with the adenoidal noises which rose to almost supersonic levels during their violent quarrels, called narks. They were to be found in the food markets high up around Thomas Street, and Meath Street, and Moore Street west of O'Connell Street, and around St Mary's Abbey, and in the junk and antique markets off Cornmarket and down on the quays. The big Christmas market was in Cole's Lane and there were second-hand books behind Bachelor Walk, where a minor massacre of Dubliners by British troops took place in 1914. Second- and third-hand boots and shoes and clothing were on sale in Anglesea Market and Riddles Row – markets more like oriental souks, where some still wore, and you could still buy, the black crotcheted woollen shawls that had been since time immemorial the uniform of the female poor, and were now soon to become collectors' items.

The streets of the poor are almost certainly not now as they were then: there were doorways like the entrances to rock tombs in Chambers Street and in Crompton Court; shrines high on the walls with the lamps burning, just as in Naples; there was the vast cobbled expanse of Smithfield, as big as an airfield; whitewashed cottages with half doors in Camden Row and Sarah Place that looked as if they had been flown in from County Galway. They were beautiful streets, poverty-ridden but full of vibrant life: children swung on ropes from the lamp posts, or skipped with bits of rough cord; washing fluttered everywhere in the breeze; men wearing suits and caps, never without a jacket, sat on the kerb stones waiting for something to happen, watching the horse drays putting the motor traffic into disarray.

And there was Culture, much of it behind glass; and Trinity College, a seat of learning which housed a strange mixture of Northern and Southern Irish, Anglo-Irish, and others, even more exotic, from the third world, and in which, if Donleavy was to be believed, whores were kept in oubliettes under the floors of the lofty Georgian chambers, maturing like port in more conventional establishments.

And food . . . city of the finest roasting beef (to be found in Meath Street) and – as a last resort – coddle-stew of bacon and sausage, or liver and mash *à la* Bloom. But it was to be for me, after thirty years of absence, Bloomsville still unrevisited.

I caught Wanda up, which didn't take long as she was barely making steerage way in a gear about two and a half times too low, and we pedalled on together along the towpath to Charlemont Street Bridge, south of which were the suburbs of Ranelagh, scene of a large-scale massacre of English colonists on Easter Monday, 1209, a day which seems to bring out the worst in Dubliners so far as the English are concerned; and Donnybrook, where an annual fair founded by King John in 1204, and wild even by Irish fair standards, took place every year until it was finally suppressed in 1855.

Then on past Rathmines and Terenure where, at No. 41 Brighton Square, on the borders of these two suburbs, Joyce was born in 1882. Down there too in Ontario Terrace he sited a Bloom residence, the one in which, according to Mrs Bloom, Mary the housemaid padded out her bottom in order to excite Mr Bloom, who appears to have been in a permanent state of excitement anyway, as those explorers who have finally reached page 933 of the unlimited edition would probably agree.

Well, we would not be seeing any of these wonders on this particular trip; nor Synge's birthplace and subsequent residence, both of them not much more than a Jacob's Dublin Water Biscuit's toss from the bank of the River Dodder, down in the undiscovered country on the Rathmines/Rathgar border from whose bourne no English cyclist has ever been known to return. Nor would we visit Mount Jerome, the vast Protestant cemetery which we would soon be raising on the port quarter, which contains the remains of Sheridan Le Fanu; William Lecky, historian; Edward Dowden, Shakespearean scholar; AE, otherwise George William Russell, poet; John Millington Synge, playwright, and a supporting cast of thousands.

At Suir Road Bridge, after a two-mile lockless stretch from Portobello, the Circular Line ended and the Grand Canal, Main Line, began. Originally the commercial terminus of the Canal had been in James' Street Harbour, a mile east of the bridge alongside the Guinness brewery which, at the time of its closure in 1960, was the Canal's principal user. From the brewery, boats used to carry the drink in wooden casks as far as Limerick, which took four days. The boatmen, who were wretchedly paid, were expert in drawing off a number of pints from each barrel on board for their personal consumption. This did not mean that the publican received less than he paid for at the other end, because the men in the brewery who filled the barrels always added a quantity over and above what there should have been, for the benefit of the boatmen. Guinness were only too well aware of this practice but there was really nothing the company could do to prevent it. It was useless to put seals on the bungholes as the boatmen had a far more sophisticated way of extracting the beverage. The company did hope when it introduced metal casks known as iron lungs during the 1950s that these would be impregnable, but the boatmen soon found a way of tapping them too. However, their triumph was short-lived. Soon after this the Canal was closed down altogether.

What a strange sight it must have been to see the crew of a canal boat tapping a barrel, presumably at night and in some remote stretch of the canal, with the tarpaulins thrown back, more than probably in the rain. One man would hold a lantern, another would tap away with a hammer and a cooper's chisel at one of the metal hoops, loosening it so that a small hole that would be invisible when the hoop was replaced could be bored in the barrel with a gimlet. In cold weather two holes might have to be made, and when it was really cold, and the drink became even more turbid, it was sometimes necessary to introduce a red-hot rod into the hole before the liquid would begin to flow. Meanwhile, someone would be waiting to catch the extra pints in one or other of two receptacles: a particular sort of sweet tin for a firkin (a barrel holding 9 imperial gallons) or a certain sort of biscuit tin for a 54-gallon hogshead. These held the precise amount that could be drawn off in each case without diddling the customer.

These canal boatmen were often descendants of those who had worked on the canals since they were first dug, as were the lock keepers, the crews of the dredgers and those whose job it was to keep the canals free of weeds. Unlike canal boatmen in Britain, whose wives and families often accompanied them on their voyages and made up the crew, Irish boatmen had to leave their families at home while working, and lived together in incredible discomfort, often eating from a communal pot. Until 1911, when the Canal Company began to give up horses and equip the boats with Bolinder engines, a crew consisted of six men, including the skipper, who worked six-hour shifts in pairs; one steering for part of the time, the other looking after the horses and operating the lock gates. They had twenty-four hours off a week, from midnight on Saturday until midnight on Sunday, which meant that if they were lucky those who lived near the Canal might be able to spend at least part of that time at home with their families. For the rest of the week they travelled night and day and, except at Dublin, had to handle their own cargoes.

When engines were introduced the crews were reduced to four: the engine-room 'greaser', a boy of about fourteen who also acted as cook and general dogsbody, an engineman, a deckhand and the skipper. During the Famine the boats had to be given a military escort to prevent them being looted, but during the Civil War no guards were provided and the boats were often pillaged.

In 1946, after what the Irish still refer to euphemistically as 'The Armairgancy', and everyone else calls the Second World War, by mutual agreement between employers and employees the crews were reduced to three who worked a sixteen-hour day which sounds terrible but gave them more time at home.

The little, watery world of the Grand Canal ceased to exist in 1960 when Guinness, the last customers to use canal boats, finally gave up doing so. They continued to do what they could to encourage pleasure boating by going into the hire business in 1963, as did Bord Failte, but things were never the same again.

Chapter 13

MAIN LINE TO SHANNON HARBOUR

O Irlande, grand pays du Shillelagh et du bog,
Ou les patriotes vont toujours ce qu'on appelle le
whole hog.
    ANON. '*A l'Irlande*' [par Victor Hugo] in G. W. E. Russell,

Collections and Recollections, 1898

It is wise to make a point of taking Locks 1 to 9 (on the
Main Line) at a dash early in the morning, or during
school hours, to avoid the sometimes boisterous
attentions of children.
                          Guide to the Grand Canal, 1986

Beyond Lock No. 1 on the Main Line, a double lock, which gave both us and the Canal another 14.4-foot boost, the Main Line stretched away uphill to the west into what we hoped would eventually become the Irish equivalent of Wind in the Willows country, but which for the next four miles or so looked more like the twentieth-century equivalent of a landscape dreamed up by Hieronymous Bosch. Taking it at a dash, as the *Guide to the Grand Canal* advised us to do, with the time coming up to twelve o'clock, we pedalled like mad along Davitt Road, named after a famous Fenian who spent seven years in Dartmoor* until we reached what had been the outer suburb of Inchicore and was now rapidly becoming an inner one. Inchicore's streets, as the large-scale street map of Dublin showed, were literally bristling with schools, all full of children many of them no doubt ready for any kind of deviltry, and now only waiting for the noonday bell to toll before concentrating their hellishly boisterous attentions on us.

Five more locks took us up another 80.3 feet without trying, and into a soulless area which until recently, according to the latest ordnance survey map, had been genuine country. Now it was largely covered with housing and industrial estates and overshadowed by pylons. The only non-blot on the landscape was what had been a rather nice old pub on the canal bank, but even

*In Dartmoor Davitt, who had only one arm (having lost the other as a child) and was unable to do the normal work in the granite quarries, was harnessed during working hours to a cart which he was made to drag around behind him. He was lucky to get out after seven years on ticket-of-leave, having been sentenced to fifteen.

this had been recently gutted by fire. The only items of any real interest seemed to be the Guinness Filter Beds on the right bank of the Canal about a mile to the west, beyond Lock No. 8, portrayed on a large-scale street map as an enigmatic octagonal shape outlined in black.

The question was how to get to them. Here there was not a living thing, let alone a boisterous child, in sight. However we eventually located what until recently had been a pretty little lane, flanked by a couple of cottages, high hedges and mature trees. Now the cottages were in ruins, the hedges were filled with wind-driven plastic, the trees looked as if they had been shattered by gunfire and the surface was littered with broken glass, all that was left of various motor cars after the tinkers had finished stripping them, and sundry other macabre junk.

The lane terminated at a locked gate, beyond which a track led away in the direction of some freshly whitewashed huts, from which an extremely savage-looking Alsatian, just released, was now streaking towards us, followed in a rather more leisurely fashion by a comfortably upholstered gentleman of fifty-odd, wearing a pullover and a cap.

'I suppose you've come to see the Watters,' said the comfortable-looking gentleman, and introduced himself through the bars as Christy O'Neill, having perused the letter headed 'To Whom It May Concern' given us by Bord Failte, which by this time was getting a bit frayed around the edges. To our profound relief he ordered back to its lair the awful creature that had been flinging itself against the gate in paroxysms of rage at its inability to knock it down and tear us limb from limb.

'Now, the Watters is very interesting,' Mr O'Neill went on. By now he had unlocked the gate and ushered us into his domain and we were looking at a number of rectangular, brick-lined ponds, some of them roofed in and grass-grown.

Nearby were the huts in which he kept the tools of his trade with signs on them that read, superfluously so far as we were concerned, 'DANGER. DOGS LOOSE IN HUTS', and on the far side of the roofed-over ponds there was a nice little cottage which still had most of its slates on, but now abandoned. Everything was spick and span. If it was a wall it was whitewashed. Here, we seemed to be in the heart of rural Ireland, instead of being within screaming distance of an industrial estate.

'Very interesting they are,' he reiterated, making them sound more like a married couple than some thousands of gallons of fluid, 'although there are some who are disappointed on account of thinking that it is the drink itself they are going to see being filthered. Some people are just *eejits*,' he added pointedly in a way that made me wonder if he included us. To me, a consumer, eejit or not, it was an awe-inspiring thought that the water in these few shallow ponds, when cleared sufficiently by sedimentation to allow it to be pumped to the brewery, four and a half miles away, and there subjected to further, more rigorous purificatory processes, was the liquid ingredient in a drink of which in the fifty-two weeks ending 31 March 1984, 777,689 bulk barrels each holding 36 imperial gallons were exported. This is equivalent to 1,227,257 half pint glasses a day – a sobering thought. Hardly surprising that a couple of Guinness girls could pick up a hotel such as the Cipriani in Venice without batting an eyelid. And it was I who had helped to make it possible for them to do so, and send their sons to Eton and so forth. In fact I had always wanted to shout across to a Guinness or two in the Royal Enclosure, 'But for me, and millions like me with our bottle noses, you wouldn't be here.' They could scarcely say the same to me.

Here, among the filter beds, I experienced similar if slightly less rapturous feelings to those manifested by James Bruce, Laird of Kinnaird, the enormous, red-headed, vain but courageous Scot, when he first set eyes on the source of the Blue Nile in 1768. The source! Looking at all this water it suddenly occurred to me to wonder where it came from. I had always understood that the water from which Guinness is created came from the Liffey. But here we were a good couple of miles from the Liffey and with a considerable amount of higher ground between. Did they pump it over the watershed? If so, why?

'Where does it come from, Mr O'Neill?' I enquired politely.

'Where does it come from?' In spite of his appearance of benign rotundity I had the impression that O'Neill, the Irish Pickwick, didn't suffer fools gladly, let alone eejits.

'The water.'

'The Watter? The Watter comes from the Canal. Where else would it be coming from, the filther beds being where they are, Holy Mother of God?'

'Goodness, does it really?' I said, genuinely surprised; but then, feeling that I couldn't really leave it there, added, 'But where does the Canal water come from?' (I was going to ask how the Canal came to have water in it, but refrained because I thought he might answer, 'Because it is there', like Mallory or Irving of that big hill.)

'It comes from up the country, mostly from the Seven Springs, St James's Well, in the Pollardsdown Fen, under the Curragh, just below the race course. Beautiful soft watter it is, but not bog watter at all. Lots of lime, alkaline – bog watter's acidic.'

'Can we get to these springs on our bicycles?' Wanda asked. She is keen on springs and sources, as I am.

'There's no towpath but if you buy a ticket from Dublin to Kildare you can see them from the train window just before you get into Kildare; but Kildare's not much of a place at all,' said Mr O'Neill, no doubt forgetting that he was maligning what had been the shrine of St Brigid, where the perpetual fire burned until the Dissolution. 'You'se best go on to Cork.'

'What about the Liffey? Does any of that get into the Canal?' I asked Mr O'Neill, courageously risking one of his memorable rebukes.

'Not a drop. It goes under it at the Leinster Aqueduct but not a drop gets into it, or into the Springs either, although it wanders around the hills like a drunken man a mile or two up from them, as if it might be going to contribute a bit. Now, if you'll excuse me, it's coming up for me dinner time.'

Later, we ate what *A Visitor's Guide to Pubs in Dublin* described as 'a variety of hot and cold dishes', all of which were excellent, while sitting in the sunshine outside Healy's Black Lion Inn by the bridge at Clondalkin – 'The in place', the *Guide* went on, 'for the young and sporting fraternity', for which we undoubtedly qualified, if for nothing else, as a couple of elderly sports.

After this we resumed our journey along the Canal, easily resisting the suggestion made in more than one guide book that we ascend the Round Tower of Clondalkin ('approx. 84 ft. Views

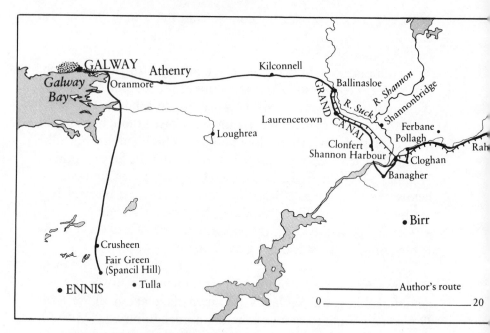

of the Central Plain and the Dublin Mts. To the S.', or words to that effect), preferring to conserve our energies for something we couldn't avoid expending them on, a something which almost immediately made itself manifest.

Although the relevant map in the *Canal Guide* showed quite distinctly that the towpath followed the south bank west of Clondalkin, it also ran a fine, firm, solid line along this section of the north bank, giving the impression that it indicated something superior to a mere towpath. It was this that I very stupidly decided it would be best to follow. Soon, the housing estates which hitherto had flanked the Canal petered out, and we found ourselves in the first real country we had encountered since leaving Dublin. But then, horror of horrors, just beyond Lock No. 11, the fine, firm pathway along which we were happily pedalling under the fine, warm sun suddenly degenerated into a muddy track kept open only by the cows which had somehow managed to crash through the hedges and climb the Canal embankment from the adjacent fields, accompanied by innumerable horseflies, gnats and other insects galvanized into activity by the unnaturally

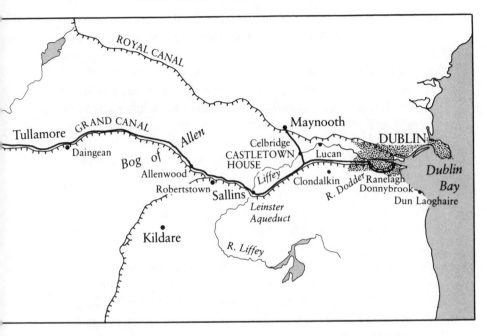

fine weather. This track, which followed a cliff-hanging route along the extreme edge of the Canal, was rendered completely invisible by dense growths of stinging nettles, cow parsley, reeds and other assorted veg, all of it breast-high and all of it loaded with deadly pollen which our passage through it released, reducing me instantly to a sneezing, watery-eyed, hay fever-ridden wreck.

At this point, if either of us had had any sense at all, we should have turned back, but we were now just sufficiently far from Clondalkin Bridge to make the idea unattractive. What followed, with the sun beating down as through a burning glass; with the gnats and the horseflies, all of which seemed to have been weaned on the sort of insect repellent with which we now smeared ourselves; with the nettles into which we fell flat from time to time, stinging ourselves severely; and with the abundance of cows, was a nightmare.

After a few hundred yards it became impossible to ride at all, and we had to push our bikes the rest of the way. This was partly because the Shimano transmissions, in their element hacking down the north face of Fujiyama, rock-hopping along some beach on Shikoku Island or even descending a forest ride in the Quantocks, here got so fouled up with Irish cow parsley that they would barely function; and partly because even if they had, the track was so muddy and full of holes and cow crap that you only had to make one mistake and fall off to the left rather than the right and you would end up in about five feet of water. But the principal obstacles were the cows themselves, out in force enjoying the weather and all refusing to move in any sensible direction.

Twice we came to the boundary of one farmer's land with another's where what in more friendly times had been a stile was now an object so festooned with barbed wire that it looked like something in the Hindenberg Line, and here in both cases the animals turned and prepared to make a last stand, ankle-deep in mud. The only thing to do was to drive them down the Canal embankment using the only weapons we had, our bicycle pumps, unload both bikes completely, then lift them five feet in the air and over the fence, trying to avoid puncturing the tyres on the wire, wishing all the time that we had lightweights instead of mountain bikes weighing in at 38 pounds, and when it was done re-loading everything before setting off to deal with another herd, all fresh and ready for an encounter. We were a bit like one of those competing naval teams at the Royal Tournament which take guns to pieces, sling them across a yawning gulf on a wire rope, and then re-assemble them, except that we had no competition.

However, we did not lack an audience. Apart from the cows, which had been getting a lot of mileage out of us, across the Canal on the real towpath was a meagre line of semi-comatose fishermen, to whom we appeared to be the principal objects of interest. Surrounded by the incredible amount of gear coarse fishermen seemed to need (almost as much as we required to cycle across Ireland), including large green umbrellas to protect their complexions from the pernicious effects of the sun, they watched our exertions with all the animation of a band of fork-tongued lizards about to eat a dinner of flies, although occasionally one would raise himself to a sitting position and shout across to us, 'You'se are on the wrong bank!' What we really needed was a Flymo.

Altogether it took an hour to cover the two miles to the Lucan Road Bridge, by which time we were almost as knocked out, physically and emotionally, as if we had covered forty miles on the N18.

'You've had some pretty crazy ideas in your life, Newby,' Wanda said, rather unfairly I thought, while we were pouring water on our nettle stings, getting the herbage out of our transmissions, scraping cow shit off our trousers, swatting horseflies rendered torpid by over-indulgence in our blood, and generally smartening up, 'but this towpath of yours is the craziest of the lot.'

Beyond this bridge and Lock No. 12 there was no doubt that the towpath continued on the north bank, and here the Canal entered a cutting, burrowing through a huge reef of limestone and passing under a picturesque, ivy-clad bridge that led to the Gollierstown quarries, which supplied most of the stone used in building the Canal. At this point, too, the Canal was completely blocked by a long metal canal boat which was lying waterlogged in the middle, its bows pointing in the direction of the Shannon.

Here, too, we overtook two boys and two girls on bikes who were like us making heavy weather of the abundant vegetation and as we came up beside them one of the girls chose this particular moment to ride off the bank, uttering a despairing shriek as she did so, and fall, still pedalling madly, into what was here quite deep water. For a brief moment she could be seen underwater still sitting on the machine before coming to the surface without it, to be hauled ashore. All of them except the unfortunate Shereen, who now sat shivering on the bank while the two boys wearing nothing but their underpants fished for the 'boike', thought this was wildly funny – 'Just look at the expression on Sher's face! Did you ever see anything loike it?'

Soon after this we abandoned the Canal and set off northwards for St Patrick's College, Maynooth, the great Catholic seminary, where we had been invited to stay the night by its Vice-President, Dr Matthew O'Donnell. En route we stopped at Celbridge, a small but lively place on the banks of the Liffey in order to see

Castletown, the first great Palladian house to be built in Ireland, and the largest. To reach it we rode up a long avenue flanked by enormous limes, through a pair of entrance gates guarded by sphinxes. Inside, a sign read '3-Bed Semi-Detacheds from £25,540', which didn't augur well for the future of the demesne.

More like an Italian urban palazzo than a country house, Castletown's three-storey central block soared 60 feet into the air and, together with a pair of two-storey flanking wings, each linked to the main building by curved Ionic colonnades, made a colossal ensemble 350 feet long of white stone, now shimmering in the afternoon sunshine. These wings performed the function, subsequently much copied in Ireland but unknown in English versions of the Palladian, of being farm buildings in disguise, as they often are in the Palladian villas of the Veneto. Indeed the main building, with its grand staircase leading down to Irish *terra firma*, would have looked more appropriate on the banks of the Brenta Canal.

The house was built for Mr William Conolly who, at his own wish, remained a plain Mr until his death. The son of a publican (others say a blacksmith – though in Ireland he could quite easily have been both), he first became an attorney, in which capacity he soon enriched himself in dealings connected with those Catholic estates confiscated after the Battle of the Boyne. Subsequently he became an MP, first for Donegal, then for Londonderry, a member of the Privy Council and 'ten times a Lord Justice of Ireland during the absence of successive viceroys', according to his biographer, as well as being Chief Commissioner of the Irish revenues, an appointment which, according to Swift, he bought for £3000. But his most famous appointment was that of Speaker of the Irish House of Commons, a post he held from 1715 almost to the day of his death in 1729, which gave him the title by which he was generally known, 'Speaker' Conolly.

The original design for the exterior of Castletown was made by Alessandro Galilei, who amongst other great projects was responsible for redesigning the façade of the basilica of San Giovanni in Laterano in Rome (where Christ is reputed to have appeared to the Emperor Constantine and Pope St Sylvester on the day of its consecration).

The interior, at least in part, was the work of Sir Edward Lovett Pearce, designer of the Irish Parliament House on College Green, Dublin. Another who may have been involved was John Rothery, the master mason, who built that other but much smaller masterpiece, Mount Ievers Court in County Clare, which we had seen the previous December. Inside, the entrance hall, designed by Pearce, rose two storeys high above a black and white marble pavement, a rectangle pierced by tall, pedimented doorways flanked by niches containing busts of helmeted warriors. Above it Ionic columns and half columns supported a pair of galleries guarded by a wrought iron balustrade, from which tapered columns and half columns in turn rose up to support the roof.

One of the most extraordinary rooms in the house is the Print Room, created by the wife of William Conolly's heir, Lady Louisa Lennox, the spirited and intelligent daughter of the Second Duke of Richmond. Her sister, Lady Sarah Napier, who lived close by at Oakly Park, helped her to collect the material, and the two of them stuck the prints on the walls according to a pre-determined plan, a copy of which still exists. This room is now unique in Ireland, although at one time there were others, the most famous of which was at Carton House, Maynooth, another splendid house in the territory of the Fitzgeralds, Earls of Kildare.

From the tall windows of the Long Gallery, embellished with wall paintings in the Pompeian style but decorated in what Lady Louisa described as the wrong shade of blue, a two-mile vista opens up to the north-west across wooded parkland to what is known as the Conolly Folly, and to the north-east to an equally extraordinary brick and stone construction, the Wonderful Barn, both inspired by Mrs Conolly, the Speaker's widow. The Barn, built in 1743, is a multi-storeyed cone composed of four drums one above the other, with a staircase spiralling up the outside to a castellated look-out at the summit. The lowermost drums form a granary into which the grain poured through apertures in the floors of the upper rooms, all of which have domed brick ceilings. It bears a remarkable resemblance to the great Gola, a granary 96 feet high with walls 12½ feet thick which stands on the right bank of the Ganges at New Patna, completed in 1786 at the instigation of Warren Hastings as a safeguard against famine. The Gola's capacity was said to have been 137,000 tons of grain; no one had ever succeeded in filling it, however, because the only way to do so was through a hole in the top, and as the doors at the foot of the building only opened inwards, they could never be opened once the floor was covered with grain.

A couple of miles further along the bungalow-infested road to Maynooth we took a right up a lesser road in search of Conolly's Folly and suddenly there it was, defiled with graffiti, one of the two most splendid obelisks in Ireland (the other is at Stillorgan on the outskirts of Dublin). A hundred and forty feet high, and built of pale grey stone, it is mounted on a double row of deep arches which increase in height towards the centre, the small ones, which look like gazebos, topped with cupolas and pediments crowned by pineapples, the large ones with urns and eagles. Supported by the main arch is what looks like a small temple with a classical pediment which has yet more arches pierced in its sides. Designed probably by the German architect Richard Castle (Cassel or Cassels), assistant to Sir Edward Lovett Pearce at Castletown, it was built in 1740 using local labourers who were each paid a halfpenny a day, with the idea of alleviating the sufferings they had endured in the famine winter of 1739/40.

Mrs Mary Jones, one of Mrs Conolly's sisters, who took a rather deflationary view of her Folly, wrote in March 1740: 'My sister is building an obelix to answer a vistow at the bake of Castletown House; it will cost here three or four hundred pounds at least, but I believe more – I really wonder how she can dow so much, and live as she duse.' But she did. The admirable Mrs Mary Delany *née* Granville, indefatigable observer of the eighteenth-century scene and friend and correspondent of Swift, described how Mrs Conolly spent the so-called evening of her days:

> We have lost our great Mrs. Conolly. She died last Friday, and is a general loss; her table was open to all her friends of all ranks, and her purse to the poor. She was, I think, in her ninetieth year. She had been drooping for some years, but never so ill as to shut out company; she rose constantly at eight, and by eleven was seated in her drawing room, and received visits till three o'clock, at which hour she

punctually dined, and generally had two tables of eight or ten people each ... and if the greatest person in the kingdom dined with her, she never altered her bill of fare. ... She was clever at business, wrote all her own letters, and could read a newspaper by candlelight without spectacles. She was a plain and vulgar woman in her manner, but had very valuable qualities.*

The sun was sinking when we arrived at Maynooth. There, in Cassidy's fine bar, with it pouring in on us, we had a drink with Loughlin J. Sweeney, an ex-banker who specialized in areas of credit policy, corporate finance and the 'harmonization' (splendid word) of banking legislation in the EEC – in a few words the sort of banker people like ourselves never normally correspond with, let alone meet in a pub. He was now Director of Development of Maynooth College and had helped to raise untold sums of money for it. He immediately put us at our ease by saying that he wasn't interested in the sort of money that we could produce, even if we were inclined to do so, since it was much less trouble to go to the founts of the stuff in the heartlands of Irish Catholic America.

The summer term was already at an end and the absence of any students lent an additional scale to the vastness of the College's two great quadrangles: St Joseph's Square, the older part, and St Mary's Square, built during the years of the Great Famine by Pugin.

Later, we dined in the Professors' Dining Room in St Patrick's House, which overlooks both quadrangles and separates one from the other. The others present were the President, the Very Reverend Michael Ledwith, Professor in Dogmatic Theology, Secretary of the Episcopal Committee on Ecumenism and a member of the International Theological Commission in Rome; Dr O'Donnell, Vice-President and Professor of Philosophy, who had kindly invited us to stay the night; and Loughlin J. Sweeney. With this small but extremely potent squad of philosophical and financial talent lined up, it seemed that it might be difficult for the Newbys, with their peanut brains, to find much common ground;

*The Autobiography and Correspondence of Mary Granville, ed. Lady Llanover. 6 vols., 1861–2.

but fortunately the subject of the Spanish Armada came up, on which they were pretty clued up, and this kept everyone on the go for most of the dinner.

At the far end of Pugin's dining room there was a spirited solid silver statue of St George slaying the Dragon which had been presented to the College by the astonishingly beautiful Empress Elizabeth of Austria, who strayed into one of the quadrangles while out with the local staghounds in 1879 during one of her frequent visits to Ireland. Later, hearing that neither faculty nor seminarians were enthusiastic about having an effigy, even a solid silver one, of the patron saint of England (who was also patron of the hunt) on a premises dedicated to St Patrick, she donated a further gift of a magnificent set of cloth-of-gold vestments without asking for the statue back. There is also a portrait of the Empress herself, which one would have thought would have been a good deal more disturbing to professors and seminarians alike.

The original religious college at Maynooth was founded and endowed by Gerald Fitzgerald, ninth Earl of Kildare, in 1521, but in 1538 it was suppressed. The present College was founded and endowed in 1795 by an act of the Irish Parliament, its re-birth greatly assisted by the great Irish-born statesman, Edmund Burke, who died in 1797. It was Burke who corresponded at length about Irish religious toleration with Dr Hussey, afterwards Bishop of Waterford, who became first President of the College. This was at the time when the French Revolution was at its height, the French seminaries had been closed and it was feared that seminarians in other countries might already have become infected with danger-ous heretical ideas. As a result, the majority of the ten professors who attended the first roll call in Stoyte House, the oldest of the College buildings, were refugee members of the *ancien régime*. To the disgust of the forty Irish students who had just been enrolled, they made a point of speaking in French, to which the seminarians retaliated by speaking Irish. Eventually, the *lingua franca* became English.

The College had, in fact, also been a lay College, for men only, from its inception until 1817, when the lay part was suppressed largely, it is said, due to the opposition and intrigue of 'Black Jack' Fitzgibbon, Earl of St Clare and Lord Chancellor of Ireland. In spite of being Irish by birth, he maintained 'an uncompromising resistance to all popular movements and especially to all attempts to improve the position of Roman Catholics', in the words of his biographer, G. P. Macdonnell. 'He died on 28 January 1802,' his biographer continued. 'His funeral was followed by a Public mob, whose curses violently expressed the hate with which a great part of his fellow countrymen regarded him.' In 1826 and again in 1855 the College was the subject of inquiries by Royal Commissions investigating suggestions that it was too Popish, although in 1826 the Vatican itself refused the College the right to confer its own degrees because it suspected that the orthodoxy of its teaching was not all it should have been. After Vatican II, in the late 1960s, although it remained a seminary, the Trustees decided to re-open the College to lay students, but this time students of both sexes.

Later that evening we were taken on an extensive tour of the College, including its completely new campus. Then, after having raced one another up the enormously long, tiled corridor of New House on our bikes, we retired to our respective single rooms, both of us feeling that, although there was no one to stop us, there was something slightly wrong about sharing a bed in a seminary. Lying there in the pale, austere but comfortable room, it was difficult for me, a non-Catholic outsider, to imagine what life had been like in this seminary; however, I did have with me a book that had been given me by Loughlin J. Sweeney, a life of Dr Charles William Russell of Maynooth. It was Dr Russell, scholar and churchman, of whom John Henry Newman wrote in the *Apologia Pro Vita Sua*, an exposition of his spiritual life: 'He had, perhaps, more to do with my conversion (to Catholicism) than anyone else. He called upon me, in passing through Oxford in the summer of 1841, and I think I took him over some of the buildings of the University. He called on me again another summer, on his way from Dublin to London. I do not recollect that he said a word on the subject of religion on either occasion. He sent me at different times several letters; he was always gentle, mild, unobtrusive, uncontroversial. He left me alone.'

Russell went to Maynooth in 1826, at the age of fourteen; he spent his whole life there, first as a seminarian, later as a professor and President, and died there in 1880. At the time when Russell first went there the students numbered 391 and the average age of entry was seventeen or eighteen. The majority had free places and a grant from the British Government which provided for their annual maintenance, which was estimated at about £25 a year. About 110 had to pay their own fees and the remainder received bursaries from their dioceses. All teaching staff and students were required to swear the oath of allegiance to the Sovereign and repudiate any kind of Papal authority, civil or temporal, within the British realm. Russell wrote home to his mother in his first term that 'we have a great deal of praying to do here', and that he had bought a bed and furniture for £5 10s and engaged a washerwoman to do his laundry at 7s 6d a quarter.

At Maynooth, as indeed at almost any other great seminary, the everyday life of the students in many ways resembled that which Islamic students had to put up with in a *medersa*, a college of Koranic theology in a city such as Fez in Morocco. First, the long years of study: the full course lasted seven years (in Fez anything from three to ten years), the first four being the equivalent of a Bachelor of Arts course at a lay university and the last three devoted to theology. As at Fez, a great deal of time seems to have been spent learning accepted texts and studying lecture notes. Second, the long hours: in summer the students' day began at 5 a.m. (6 a.m. in winter), and continued until 9 p.m. Wednesday and Saturday afternoons were free. Sunday was a pretty full day of religious exercise, with the celebration of Solemn Mass and Divine Office, the daily service of the Roman breviary, both of which it was obligatory to attend. Even out of term time it was rare for seminarians, or for that matter the professors, to be allowed home. It very much depended on the attitude adopted by the bishop in whose diocese they resided. Some, such as the Bishop of Down and Connor, preferred them to remain in College during the vacations. One professor recalled that in the course of six years, he was only allowed home on three occasions, and he thought this was about average.

A third similarity was the coarse and monotonous food. Russell recalled Lenten repasts consisting of 'ling, oil, vinegar, mustard, etc., all jumbled together'. But on St Patrick's Day 1827 he wrote that for dinner they had 'fresh fish, which is a most uncommon thing here, two eggs each person, and an apple pie' followed by wine, three bottles to each table of eight students.

Contrary to what was widely believed in the outside world the majority of seminarians, especially in the early days, came not from peasant communities but from comfortable, sometimes very comfortable backgrounds. Generally speaking they were strongly nationalistic. Some took part in the Rebellion of 1798, and were subsequently for O'Connell and for the Young Irelanders movement, which split with him in 1847 to found the Irish Confederation and helped to inspire the bloodless revolution in Paris the following year. They supported the Fenians in the 1860s and the Easter Rising in 1916, in the course of which the President had the utmost difficulty in preventing the students, who saw the sky bright with flames over Dublin, marching on the city and taking part in the insurrection. At one point he considered sending them all home.

It was at Maynooth, too, that Eamon de Valera, who had been a part-time lecturer in mathematics there, was hidden when he was being hunted by British troops. And it was from Maynooth that the bishops (not the faculty as such) issued their manifesto sanctioning resistance to conscription in April 1918 and in June 1919, a statement which described the British regime as being 'the rule of the sword, utterly unsuited to a civilized nation, and extremely provocative of disorder and chronic rebellion. The acts of violence which we have to deplore,' they went on, 'and they are few, spring from this cause and this cause alone.'

To me, lying in my seminarian bed, it was an awe-inspiring thought that from this strange, architectural hodge-podge of buildings, which somehow managed to be an entity, something like ten thousand seminarists become priests have gone out, some of them to proselytize in the most inhospitable regions on earth – although I'm forced to admit that even martyrdom or the cannibals' pot must have lost some of their terrors after seven winters passed in an establishment in which for more than a century the only heating was in the lecture room.

The following morning was grey, with a cold wind from the north-east (which from our point of view was better than any sort of wind from the west or south-west), and after a final bike ride

down the corridor to the ablutions, a breakfast in the Professors·
Dining Room which would have given many a seminarist second
thoughts about emigrating after ordainment if they had been
served up with it a century or so ago, and a visit to the Library
with the President in order to see the Hibernian Bible Society's
recent lavish bequest, we left this hospitable place and took to the
road again. Our last act there was to sign the visitor's book on the
page following that on which the Italian President had written his
name, and preceding that on which the King and Queen of Spain
were due to sign theirs in the course of the next week or so.

'Fame at last,' Wanda said, as she took up the pen.

We eventually rejoined the Grand Canal near Sallins, just east
of the Leinster Aqueduct which carries the Canal over the valley
of the Liffey, the one that Mr O'Neill, Overlord of the Guinness
waters, had told us about, which has seven arches, is 400 feet long
and rises 30 feet above the river. Hereabouts, frozen, we had a pot
of tea in a pub and heard on the radio news of yet another attack
on the ill-fated Virgin of Ballinspittle. Three miles beyond the
Aqueduct at Lock No. 18, the last rising lock going west, we
reached the summit level of the Canal, at 279.1 feet, a level it was
to maintain for five and a half miles before starting to descend
towards the Shannon and the Atlantic, just beyond Robertstown,
over the border in County Offaly.

Now the sun came out and for the next two days we rode
westwards along the line of the Canal with a warm wind
breathing down our necks. Beyond Allenwood, a small village in
County Offaly, the enormous concrete cooling towers of a peat-
fired electricity generating station loomed above a countryside
that now looked a bit like parts of Siberia as seen from the Trans-
Siberian Railway. Here the Canal began to cross a part of what
was said to be, give or take a few thousand acres (I wondered who
added them up), the 240,000 acre expanse of the Bog of Allen, a
part of what was Ireland's 2,830,000 acres of bogland before
some of it got reclaimed.

Here in the central plain the bog, which is up to twenty feet
thick – mountain bog is shallower – displayed a remarkable range
of colours, according to the weather, the time of day and also,
apparently, the time of year: whitish brown, reddish brown,

purple, burnt sienna and brownish black (in autumn it was said to become a fiery red). Where it had been cut for fuel it looked like slices of very rich Christmas cake, much of it now covered with white bog cotton, waving in the breeze. Through this spongy wilderness, some of it reclaimed as pasture and woodland, some of it covered with heather in which grew silver birches and blazing yellow gorse, the Canal stretched away apparently to infinity, its banks now alive with yellow irises and marshmallows. The only man-made objects in sight for much of the way were the complex machines that are now used to cut the peat, the miles of light railway that transport it to the factories that turn it into briquettes and to the power stations, and small white farmhouses, though occasionally we saw a ruined castle or church, a lock keeper's cottage or a pub, and the little rectangular wooden boats used by the farmers to cross the Canal to the far side. We saw very few people: once we saw some tinkers, camped with their carts and hobbled ponies near an aqueduct, who were cooking something in a big black pot over a fire; and we saw lock keepers and fishermen, their hooks baited, according to what they were after, with red worms, ordinary worms, maggots, bread flake, dead fish, spoons or plugs, sweet corn, sausage or meat, dreaming of record catches of bream, rudd, roach, perch, tench, carp or pike. We saw herons, swans, some coot, swifts towards evening, but surprisingly few other sorts of birds; and a couple of water rats but no toads.

Sometimes the towpath was almost impassable with mud and grass, and cycling along it was like trying to force one's way through a sea of porridge, or it simply disappeared. This meant making detours along other tracks and lanes in the course of which we sometimes lost the Canal altogether. From time to time there were more of the awful stiles which meant unloading the bikes completely. During those days the outside world receded, as did memories of the internal combustion engine, except when we passed through Tullamore, where we spent the night in a B and B whose owner was very glad to see us as a wedding party had failed to turn up, giving no reason.

In the course of the entire journey from Dublin to the Shannon we only saw two pleasure boats actually on the move. Stretched out on the bank, enjoying the sun, and looking out over this treeless and hedgeless bog, it was difficult to believe that it had once been a huge forest of oaks. In it had been found the skeletons of humans and animals (in some pre-glacial parts of it giant deer had been unearthed); the arctic willow; dug-out canoes and other artefacts of bone and wood; hoards of gold and silver; oak, now of an ebony colour and often used to make hideous objects for sale to tourists; and huge, pale fir roots which are highly inflammable. In these fastnesses the early Christians took refuge, building themselves retreats in which they produced wonders of Irish religious art, and where they survived by cultivating the fertile meadows known as *cluains* which they reclaimed from the bog. These Fir Cell, Men of the Churches, built seven monasteries around Tullamore alone. Even the Normans failed to make any real impression on the bog country. They conquered it, but they soon found themselves assimilated.

One day we ate a picnic lunch of soda bread and Irish spam in a pub which was also an undertakers, the only other occupant of which was an elderly man dressed in the traditional garb of the Irish countryside: black suit and black cap, as black as the bogs themselves. He had spent most of his life since the age of fourteen cutting peat in the bog by hand, and was only too happy to tell us about it.

Neither of us caught his name, as what emerged was extremely heavily accented; he was also rather impatient – 'Will you listen to me now, for Pete's sake!' he would say if I interjected a query when he got to some, to me, otherwise unintelligible portion of his narrative.

'What we use is the slane* and the slane needs to be made by a smith, not a factory one, and it needs to be good and loight, the spade-tree [the handle], elm or larch. A good slane always has a cow horn for the grip.

'There are two ways of cutting but here in the deep bog you're breastin', that means cutting horizontally with the wing set well back. But first of all you take off the top foot or so, using an

---

*A slane is what I know as a turf spade; a turf spade has a narrow, straight-edged steel blade with what is known as a wing set at right angles to it. Its purpose is to detach a turf at a single stroke of the blade. The proportions of the blade and the wing vary according to the size of turf required and the type of bog.

ordinary spade [an ordinary Irish spade has a narrower blade than its English equivalent] and these parings are put between the cuttings so that the man who wheels the turf away in his barrow has a dry footing. Then we leave the turfs spread on the ground for a week or so – this is in April or May, the driest toime. Then we put them up in little poiles in the shape of a roof to catch the wind. Then on through summer we turn them and stack in bigger and bigger poiles, either by the bog road, or against the gable of the house. And we call them, according to soize, turfurts, astles, aamps, ickuls and eeks' – or that was what it sounded like.

'Would you mind saying them again so that I can write them down, Mr Er —?' I said.

'Will you listen to me now, for Pete's sake!' said Mr Er — who when dealing with interrupters and other eejits bore a strong resemblance to Mr O'Neill, now some twenty-five miles away down the Main Line. 'Oime not yet finished about the turf, not by a good bit. Now what we ·call underfootin', cuttin' in the mountain bogs, that's a different business altogether. Now what you do is . . .'

So I never did write them down. And what I did find out from a book over the water in the London Library weeks later may not be right: turfurts were turnfoots; astles, castles; aamps, clamps; ickuls were rickles, and eeks, reeks.

On the way west we passed Daingean, which used to be called Philipstown, of which someone wrote:

> Great Bog of Allen, swallow down
> That odious heap call'd Philipstown
> And if thy maw can swallow more,
> Pray take – and welcome – Tullamore.

We had a second memorable pub contact on another day, at Gallagher's Pull Inn in a very rural situation by the Canal at a hamlet called Pollagh. Mrs Gallagher, the innkeeper's wife, who was thirty-nine and very handsome, had been married for thirteen years and the pub swarmed with her eight children, all good-looking and in rude health, the older ones taking good care of the small ones. In answer to our request for a sandwich she cut such an enormous quantity that what we left would have provided a square meal for her entire family. This Irish Catholic equivalent of a Heroine of Socialist Labour in the USSR first met her husband-to-be while working in a pub in Galway, although she neither smoked nor drank. Like almost every other married woman we had met on our travels in Ireland she was strongly anti-divorce. And now for our benefit she prophecied, quite correctly as it turned out, the result of the Irish government's national referendum on divorce which was to take place a few days later, and in which the voters were to reject a proposed constitutional change allowing divorce by a majority of 63.5 to 36.5 per cent, thereby confounding the government.

Finally, after a four-mile detour, because the towpath was impassable, to a place called Cloghan where Wanda wanted to buy a marble bust of Aesculapius (which fortunately turned out to be plaster-of-Paris), we rode the last couple of miles down to Shannon Harbour, which turned out to be on this fine Saturday in June a sort of rocking marina, with a fair in full blast, people cooking their evening meals on board their motor cruisers, and others sitting drinking on the grass outside the pubs. All this against an incongruous, dilapidated, early nineteenth-century background – the Grand Canal Hotel of 1806 (out of action), a police barracks and some old warehouses (out of action too), and what had once been the agent's house, all strung out along the bank below Lock No. 25.

A quarter of a mile further on, 81 miles, 7 furlongs and 44 locks from the Ringsend Sea Lock, we reached the Shannon, beautiful as it always was, now glittering in the evening sun, with what looked liked an Edwardian pleasure steamer aground in it and some thoroughly wild-looking horses zooming about in a nearby field. It was nearly six-thirty. It wasn't much of a journey to write home about, or even write about, but it had been fun and we had made it, with a total of four thorn punctures en route.

Chapter 14

TO THE FAIR AT SPANCIL HILL

At the big ass-fair in County Clare,
In a place called Spancel Hill,
My brother-in-law James hit me a belt of a hames,
Poor Paddy he nearly killed.

We laid him out in a blue trap-car
While over him Kate did stand
And I heard her say 'Bad cess to the day
That I joined the tinkers' band!'

Irish ballad

We spent the night in Banagher, a small town a couple of miles downstream from Shannon Harbour, in a nice B and B on the main street. Here, Trollope started work for the Post Office as a surveyor in 1841 and wrote his first two novels, both with Irish settings: *The Kellys and the O'Kellys* and *The MacDermot of Ballycloran*. It poured all night and the next morning, while Wanda attended Mass, I spent some time studying the most remarkable shop window I have ever seen, before or since, in Ireland, that of Messrs Hunts in the main street. It displayed the following, each in their own individual showcases, embellished with mosaic glass: a rubber instrument for unstopping blocked sinks, a bricklayer's trowel, a rat trap, three wooden handles with nothing on the end of them, two bath plugs, and a used golf ball.

By now it was a beautiful, rain-washed morning, one on which you could see for ever, and we took the road to Ballinasloe, fourteen miles to the west as the crow flies, but considerably more by road, leaving County Offaly for County Galway. The idea was to catch a train from Ballinasloe to Galway, which some local case had told us would leave at 13.13. And in spite of stopping off to see the great Romanesque doorway of the Protestant Cathedral at Clonfert, and the Bishops' Palace behind it, an enviable building now in ruins whose last tenant had been Sir Oswald Mosley, not to mention a fine, fourteenth-century wooden statue of the Virgin and Child, said to have been found in a tree and now housed in the Catholic church, we still managed to arrive twenty minutes before the time of departure, only to find that our man in Banagher – 'May the Lamb of God stick his hoof through the floor of heaven and kick you up the arse below in hell!' as the old Irish curse picturesquely puts it – had forgotten that it was a Sunday and the train had left hours ago. Oh, dear! We had already had as awful a row as one can possibly have while pedalling heavily laden bicycles, on account of me trying to make Wanda go faster up the hills than she could possibly manage, and now the next train was at 20.15, arriving Galway 21.30. There were no buses either. In a word we were stumped. We could have stayed on but who wants to stay on in Ballinasloe on a Sunday? Every second emigrant to the United States from Ballinasloe has gone there precisely to avoid doing this. And we were about fourteen weeks too early for the Ballinasloe Fair, still with the Old Lammas Fair in Ballycastle, Co. Antrim, the greatest fair in Ireland and at one time the greatest horse fair in Europe. It was founded 1722 by Frederick Le Poer Trench, Earl of Clancarty, whose family seat, Garbally Court, now a Catholic school for boys, is on the west side of the town. In 1790, 73,300 sheep and 8,600 horned cattle changed hands on the fair days and these numbers continued to increase until the peak year, 1856, when 99,680 sheep and 20,000 cattle were sold. Throughout this period, and further into the nineteenth century, it had the reputation of providing the best draught horses and the finest cavalry horses for the armies of Europe. 'I know nothing of England or Ireland,' General Platov, a Russian commander, told a member of the Clancarty family whom he happened to meet in 1815 at the Congress of Vienna, 'apart from the Fair at Ballinasloe.' By which time, together with the fair at Nijni Novgorod, which was attended by 130,000 people from all over Europe and Asia, Ballinasloe had become the greatest fair in Europe.

The Fair, which still in 1912 'presented a scene to English eyes of rare confusion', in the words of one who saw it, was customarily held on the first Tuesday in October and the four following days, partly in the Clancarty demesne and partly in Fair Green below the church on the hill. It was a wonderful spectacle: all the roads converging on the town for miles around on the evening preceding the Fair were jam-packed with sheep. The crush on the first day was intense and the fatigue endured by men and animals very great. But by 1912 the sale of sheep had fallen to about 30,000 (most of them were taken direct to Dublin by rail), although cattle were still selling at around 12,000 head and good horses were still in great demand.

Reading about all this convinced us that if we happened to be in Ireland at the time of the fair we would make every effort to attend it. But the Curse of Ballinasloe, which had just so effectively fouled up our train ride to Galway, was to be in operation once more on our next journey, when we tried to travel from Sligo to Ballinasloe on the morning of the first Tuesday in October, and discovered that it would have been easier for General Platov to get there from Vienna on horseback in 1815, one way and another.

It is thirty-five miles to Galway by rail, if you are fortunate enough to be able to make use of this service; and the shortest route by road is 39½ miles, 'mainly through bleak, exposed bog country with some distant mountain views', as our guidebook put it. Still barely on speaking terms, although our shared misfortune had brought us slightly closer, we rode a boring eleven miles to Kilconnell, which has the remains of a very beautiful friary, with a wealth of extravagant tombs within it and a tablet recording the unfortunate Baron Trimlestone, 'whoe, being transplanted into Conaght with others by orders of the Vsvrper Cromwell, dyed at Monivae, 1667'.

Here, at Kilconnell, in one of Ireland's ever-open grocery halls, we bought yet more soda bread and worked-over ham that was, if anything, even less attractive than the spam, of both of which we were rapidly beginning to tire. And for the next three quarters of an hour we sat in the extraordinarily ruined back parlour of one of the pubs, on plastic-covered seats that had either been saved or looted from a cinema, munching our tenderized ham sandwiches and watching a video of scenes of hideous violence in the company of three chain-smoking, very pimply but friendly boys. All three were dressed identically in big, black leather-type jackets, greasy black trousers and winkle-picker shoes which could have done with a coat or two of Tuxan renovating polish before being donated to a museum. The boys really loved the film: whenever any of the protagonists, of whom there were inexhaustible supplies, got what was coming to them, either by being *flammenwerfered*, hanged from cranes or in lift shafts, or simply by being kneed between the legs, the foetid parlour rang with cries of 'Dat's roight! Give it 'um! Give it 'um eggen!' which made us glad that we were, as it were, 'on the same soide'.

It would be tedious to describe the rest of the journey through bog and limestone country, in which the fields, instead of being hedged as they had been in Offaly, were enclosed with stone walls and were full of eskers – known more economically as 'os' – rather dreary ridges of stone deposited by the streams that ran under the melting glaciers, at the end of the Ice Age.

Eventually, at eight-thirty, having spent half an hour asleep on the roadside and having consumed a pot of tea in a pub which was still going full blast at four-fifteen, we arrived in Galway by an interminable and extremely ugly main road and there, in the birthplace of Nora Barnacle, indomitable companion of James Joyce, by luck rather than judgment we put up at the premises of Mrs J. Robinson and her husband at Frenchville House, Gratton Road, the most economical, remarkable and the best bed and breakfast we ever stayed in while biking round Ireland. We were given cake, whiskey and wine in abundance on arrival, followed by a cooked meal.

The Robinsons' house was on what had been the Claddagh (the Beach) before it was reclaimed, westwards of the mouth of the Galway river which here enters Galway Bay, and the old site of the fish markets. It was a labyrinthine fishing village of low, thatched cottages, inhabited by a community of Irish-speaking people of Irish descent, unlike the great bulk of the population who were of Anglo-Norman ancestry. At one time back in the 1840s they numbered between five and six thousand. They were very moral, very religious, and never fished on Sundays or other holidays or festivals. And if the day was regarded as 'unlucky', too, nothing would make them take to their boats (called *pucans* and *gleotags*) in search of the herrings, sunfish and turbot with which the bay abounded. On the eve of the Nativity of St John, which falls on 24 June, the entire community went in procession through the town, and the election of a mayor or 'king' and other officials took place. Fires were lit and Claddagh boys and girls danced round them, armed with long-handled brooms made from dock stems.

The King, who seems to have borne a certain resemblance to some twentieth-century union leader, ran the community according to its own rather peculiar laws and settled internal disputes without recourse to the laws of the land. At sea, where he acted as Admiral, the King's vessel was distinguished by a white sail and colours flown from the masthead.

The women wore a blue mantle, a red gown and petticoat, a scarf bound round the head and went barefoot, winter and summer. Once ashore, the fishermen gave over to them the responsibility of selling the fish, before setting off to drink in the *shebeens*. At sea, however, they only drank water and lived on oatcakes and potatoes which they cooked themselves over a fire in the boat. In 1937 the whole of the Claddagh, with the exception of its austere Catholic church, was razed to the ground and replaced by concrete houses, and with it this way of life passed away also.

The next day, Monday, was the day of the Fair at Spancil Hill which we had first heard about from Mr O'Hagerty while drinking at his establishment at the Crusheen crossroads in County Clare the previous December. As it turned out, it was extremely difficult to find out anything more. Although almost every Irish man, woman and child knows at least some words of the immortal song 'Spancil Hill' – The cock crew in the morning, he crew both loud and shrill / And I woke in California, many miles from Spancil Hill – far fewer have any idea of where Spancil Hill actually is; the most precise directions we heard were 'somewhere up or down Limerick way, or thereabouts'. It doesn't appear on the half-inch Ordnance Survey map of the appropriate area; that otherwise trustworthy compendium of fairs and cattle marts, *The Genuine Irish Old Moore's Almanack, 1986*, has not a word about it, and all the other guides I had read were silent on the subject.

Eventually one of Bord Failte's spies in County Clare came up with the information that it was held at a 'crass' somewhere between Ennis and Tulla, and that 'if the parties concerned were still in Galway city they'd best get a move on as the fair had been going all night, and the latest news was that there had already been a bit of fighting, but not with sticks, so far'. So after a mammoth breakfast – eggs, tomatoes, rashers laid out like a sheaf of banknotes, sausages, four kinds of bread and toast (white, brown, soda, and soda with currants) not to mention several sorts of jam and marmalade (coarse and less coarse cut) and goodness knows how many sauces and gallons of tea ('or would you rather have coffee – there's plenty of everything') – we managed by a whisker to catch the Expressway Service to Ennis, 43 miles away. During this journey, while Wanda snoozed, recharging her batteries for whatever horrors lay ahead, I took the opportunity to bone up on The Divorce Question, as dealt with in a couple of reject newspapers I had found on board that had been used for packaging sandwiches. I soon got bogged down in the letter pages, most of whose correspondents were respectfully suggesting to their opponents that they should read the Gospel according to Mark, chapter 10, verse 10; while their opponents retaliated with Matthew 19, verse 9, in which Our Lord appeared to give a conflicting judgment on the subject to the wretched Pharisees. Various Irish ecclesiastics also used these columns to tell the laity that they should do what they had been told to do, and not to push their luck. All of which soon put me in a coma, too.

The bus deposited us at Ennis railway station which, like so many Irish railway stations and most Indian ones, was sited more for the convenience of the builders of railways than for the inhabitants of the towns the names of which they so misleadingly appropriated. And if you don't believe me, try doing a four- minute mile from Ennis to Ennis station, or for that matter from Ballinasloe station to Ballinasloe *centre ville*. From here we telephoned for a taxi, which arrived like lightning, driven by a female who thought she knew everything, including the whereabouts of the Fair at Spancil Hill but, as became painfully clear, didn't. When we found ourselves well on the way to Magh Adhair, the Inauguration place of the Kings of Thomond on the banks of the Hell River, a site we had 'done' back in December, I shouted 'Whoa' and asked her to reconsider her position vis-à-vis our proposed destination.

'It's not much of a thing at all, I'm told,' she said airily, when she finally deposited us at a 'crass' which, if not the right one, was somewhere pretty near it, if the vans, horse boxes, lorries, cars, jeeps and trailers, all parked with fine abandon, were anything to go by. To which I would have replied if I had had my Irish curse book handy, '*Ualach se' chapall de chrè na h-ùir ort!*' or 'Six horse-loads of graveyard clay on top of you!', for being such a pain-in-the-neck. At the same time I handed her the £5 Irish she asked for, which seemed little enough considering the miles we'd travelled together, albeit many of them in the wrong direction. The only soul in sight to ask the way of was a middle-aged, horsey-looking individual with a pair of very bright brown eyes and a beaky nose, who was wearing the remains of what must once have been a gabardine raincoat with huge, padded shoulders which made him look a bit like an over-size, moulted bird of prey.

'It's way down from de odder crass, way up dere, past Duggan's Place,' he said, pointing with a switch he had just cut in a hedgerow.

This in answer to my absurd English, 'I say, excuse me, could you possibly tell me the way to Spancil Hill, the Fair I mean', which, judging from the facial contortions he had to indulge in to stop himself literally falling about with mirth, must have sounded as extraordinary to him as his 'crass, way up dere' did to me. One of the few major pleasures of travelling is that of hearing what others do to one's own native tongue, a pleasure equalled by the amusement they get from listening to your version of theirs.

We had a drink at Duggan's, which was full of smoke, debris, and human beings in various stages of decay. I asked one of the barmen if it had been quiet, remembering to keep a low profile and not to call him 'old fruit' and he said, yes, it had been pretty 'quoyat', on account of their having closed at 2 a.m. and only opened again when the customers could see their hands in front of their faces without the aid of lights.

Just up the road an official sign read 'Cross of Spancil Hill', and here the air began to be full of the sort of murmuring noises flocks of starlings make when talking to one another, in this case emanating from the punters at the Fair.

There's no hill at the Cross of Spancil Hill, just a farm building, and nearby, according to the map, the remains of a castle invisible from the road. From it a lane leads off to a hamlet marked on the map as Fair Green, the principal ingredients of which consist of Brohan's pub, an outbuilding or two and Kelly's which, on this grand morning, was serving cooked breakfasts and, from 11.30 on, dinners as well. After this momentary flirtation with city lights it leads out into what the Germans, who, with Americans, still make up the largest number of visitors to Ireland, call the *ewigkeit* – in this case the eternity of rural Ireland.

The actual scene of the action was the lane outside the pub, and a field on the other side of it edged with trees, and entered through newly whitewashed gateposts which acted as a navigational aid for those leaving the pub with a skinful. The ground around it was now a sea of glutinous mud. Beyond this more fields extended away gently upwards to something you might conceivably describe as a hill if you'd never seen a real one. It was a beautiful day. In a sky of indigo blue a warm wind was ushering towering masses of cumulus in across the Atlantic from the New World, as if it was moving day.

The lane itself was more or less choked with fish and chip vans, burger stalls, stalls at which quoits could be pitched and tossed, tables with roulette wheels ready to roll, tinkers finding-the-lady or playing heads-or-tails surrounded by little circles of men and boys, the players, all looking skywards when the coin went up as if expecting the Second Coming. And there were junk sellers, and little tinker boys with bleached hair, riding sixteen-hand hunters bareback up and down it, showing them off to the customers, and there was all sorts of music. And further down the lane, beyond Brohan's and Kelly's, there were some barrel-shaped tinkers' carts, most of them now occupied by very self-conscious *Stonehengevolk* masquerading as tinkers, with their ladies ostentatiously suckling their offspring on the steps, some of whom looked big enough to be clamouring for second helpings of muesli. Any real tinkers living on this hard hat site would have been in sumptuous motorized caravans, their interiors ablaze with polished brass. Meanwhile, out in the field, there were any amount of stallions, geldings, mares and their foals, Connemara ponies, donkeys and mules, all waiting to change hands, either tethered, or hobbled, or being made to show their paces or display their teeth or their hocks. There were even a few goats. And there were any number of two-wheeled flat carts pulled by donkeys, and pony carts, all running around loaded with the fancy. And there were people selling tea, and sausages and saddlery, and other tack.

And there was every sort of horse-fancying man, woman and child for miles around, and further. If no mishaps had befallen them there would be Josie Kerrin from Ballyla, and Thomas Conroy and Thomas Ford from Tubber, and Paddy Lynch from Newmarket-on-Fergus, and all the Cashes, and Harold Lusk from up north, and Patrick O'Connor from Kanturk, and Michael O'Looney from Ennis, and Mick Moloney and Michael McKenna from Ogonneloe, and Mick Sheehan from Kilbane, and Michael Scanlan from Carranboy and John Ryan from Boher, and Frank

Casey from Ennis and a power of others. And somewhere out there, though we never found him, must have been our old friend Mr O'Hagerty from Crusheen.

And the air was full of neighings and whinneyings and breakings of wind and the ghastly noises donkeys make when they think themselves unloved, and such remarks as:

'Sure, and hasn't he got a foine chest on him, loike ther Greatwallerchoina!'

'Looks a bit narrer to me. Put a bitta weight on him and he'll knock his legs about somethin' terrible.'

'He's not narrer at all! Look at his great chest, willya! Loike a barrel a porter!'

'Looks a bit shaller to me. Shouldn't wonder if he wasn't short-winded.' At the same time pinching the animal's wind-pipe and when that failed to provoke a reaction, pinching it again – 'See what I mean, short-winded.'

'And what a noice oye he's got!'

'Looks like a pig's oye to me.'

Occasionally, but you had to wait a long time to see it happen, like waiting for the cameras to roll on location, a sale would be made and the third party presiding over the deal would make sure buyer and seller both spat on their hands before the handshake that clinched it. Meanwhile, across the lane, in Brohan's, which was a bit like a parish hall in urgent need of restoration, the clientèle were ten and fifteen deep at the bar, all intent on ordering enough of the nourishment in one go to make it unnecessary to put in another requisition until evening. What Brohan's did for customers for the other 363 days and nights of the year when there was no Fair was unclear. They probably made enough to see them through to the following one. When it closed, at 4 a.m. on Tuesday morning, the Fair would be finally over.

Altogether it was a great day, more lively than ever, the experts said, with moderate prices ranging from £1700 for a chestnut likely to make a hunter, to £3000 in the heavy hunter class, and equivalents in the pony, donkey and mule departments. Hours later, back on our bus to Galway, we passed a solitary figure leading a horse he had bought, or failed to sell, a good seven miles from Spancil Hill.

Chapter 15

TO THE ARAN ISLANDS

The Islands of Aran (Ir. Ara-Naoimh, Ara of the Saints) are still believed by many of the peasantry to be the nearest land to the far-famed island of O'Brazil or Hy Brasail, the blessed paradise of the pagan Irish. It is supposed even to be visible from the cliffs on particular and rare occasions.

Murray's Handbook For Travellers in Ireland, 1912

As we worked out into the sound we began to meet another class of waves, that could be seen for some distance towering above the rest. When one of these came in sight, the first effort was to get beyond its reach. The steersman began crying out in Gaelic '*Siubhal, siubhal*' ('Run, run'), and sometimes, when the mass was gliding towards us with horrible speed, his voice rose to a shriek. Then the rowers themselves took up the cry, and the curragh seemed to leap and quiver with the frantic terror of a beast till the wave passed behind it or fell with a crash behind the stern.

J. M. SYNGE. *The Aran Islands*

By the time we got back to Galway it was pouring with rain and the streets were almost deserted. We were ravenous. By a miracle we not only found a wine merchant's that was still open but also a shop in which the assistant sold us half a pound of delicious smoked salmon, soda bread, and butter, throwing in a lemon for luck, and allowed us to sit down and eat the lot on the premises, something that would be unthinkable in England.

Because of all this we felt a bit silly when we got back to Frenchville House to find that Mrs Robinson – whom may the Saints preserve – had prepared a substantial and delicious repast.

This we ate in the company of two mature and highly entertaining students from Dublin who had just returned from a long day's excursion to the shores of Lough Corrib on a couple of hired bikes and the air fairly rang with the 'I tinks' and 'I tought' of these hopes for the future of Ireland.

'I was doin' philosophy, den I heard that if I did Welsh it would be easier to get a good pass, so now I'm doin' Welsh,' said one.

'Oim workin' to be a ship's radio operator, loike they had on the *Titanic*,' said the other, 'but by the toime I get me pass with luck there won't be any ships to operate in.'

That evening some extra-sensory information was fed into Wanda's brain box informing her that the strawberries were ripe for picking back in the beds in Dorset and a telephone call to a friendly neighbour confirmed that this was so. We had agreed before setting out that in what seemed the unlikely event of them ever ripening, Wanda should return and set in train the manufacture of a year's supply of strawberry jam.

So on Tuesday morning, after bidding a melancholy farewell to Wanda (melancholy because I am of a gregarious nature), I set off alone in good time to catch the steamer to the Aran Islands. But nobody had bothered to tell me that the boat only sailed on Tuesdays to one island, Inishmore, so what followed was another *dies non*, the high point of which was putting my feet up that evening back at Mrs Robinson's and watching someone else's death throes in *Dynasty*.

On Wednesday I tried again. I got to the dock so early that there wasn't anyone in the ticket office to welcome me, take my money or clip my ticket, so I went aboard and waited. I must say I hadn't expected luxury, having travelled this way twenty years before, but it did seem pretty sparse accommodation; there was no seating of any kind and a hellish wind blew through the whole boat, which on this dark, grey morning was more like a marine version of a house of horror than a passenger vessel. By around 08.45, with the boat due to sail at 09.00 and with no one else in sight, I began to experience sensations of unease. At 08.50 I went down into the deep-frozen bowels of the vessel where I eventually met an enormous ginger-headed man encased in bright orange plastic who informed me I was aboard not a passenger ship, but a deep-sea trawler which was about to leave for the Porcupine Bank, 180 miles out in the Atlantic, or thereabouts, where they would be fishing for prawns for an indefinite period. He went on to explain that the Aran steamer at this time of year left from quite another part of the docks, some 700 yards away round the opposite side of an eight-sided basin. As the gangway was so narrow that I had had to unload the bike completely to get it aboard, he very kindly helped me carry the bags ashore. I caught the boat, the *Naomh Eanna*, after the bow and stern lines had already been cast off.

There are three main Aran Islands, Inisheer, Inishmaan and Inishmore, and the boat called at all three. There were few other passengers and because the weather was still beastly most of us sat below in the austere bar/tea room, looking out through the portholes at the Burren, grey and ghostly away to port. I sat opposite a rather lugubrious islander who watched me with unblinking gaze while I put a shine on my camera lens, and finally asked me to take a picture of him. His reason for wanting me to do so was unusual. Some time previously he had picked up a bottle that had been thrown up on the foreshore of his island, which was Inishmaan, the middle island of the three. The bottle contained a message written by the barman of the Midships Bar on the QE2, which he had thrown overboard in mid-Atlantic. The islander now wanted to send him a likeness of himself that would, presumably, encourage him and other members of the crew and passengers to write more messages, seal them in bottles and throw them overboard in the hope that they, too, would be washed up on a beach at Inishmaan.

At this point the ship sailed out of the gloom that enveloped the Burren and the greater part of Galway Bay. The wind, instead of being easterly, was now warm and blew softly from the west-south-west and the sun shone down from a cloudless sky of the deepest imaginable blue. Summer had come. It was a day in a million. Another twenty minutes and the *Naomh Eanna* was lying off Inisheer. Apart from the lack of trees we might have been off Tahiti.

I had been here before, with Wanda, in the autumn of 1966. We had even travelled there in the same ship, or one that looked remarkably like it, which sailed to the islands twice a week, 'weather and circumstances permitting' as the timetable stated, returning to Galway the same evening, just as it would today.

Of the islands, Inishmore was then the most developed for tourists and the most self-conscious; it was said that its people had never recovered from the pride of taking part in O'Flaherty's film, *Man of Aran*, filmed there in 1934. At Kilronan, the principal town on Inishmore, passengers disembarked from the ship at a jetty, while on Inisheer and Inishmaan landings were made in *currachs*. On Inisheer the landing took place on a sandy beach and the chances of being weather-bound were less than on Inishmaan, the least visited of the group, where the landing place was a stone slip on the east side. On the ship we saw island people for the first time, returning after a few days on the mainland. Their shore-going clothes were unremarkable, although the women still wore the shawls which by then were a comparative rarity on the mainland. The men were mostly tall, and they gave the impression of being quiet people, speaking mostly in undertones.

We had planned to stay a week. There were no hotels and only the largest island, Inishmore, had guest houses; otherwise the only accommodation was in private houses and in the summer months these were always very booked up. At that time, at the end of September twenty years ago, we had been told that we would find rooms but that we would have to be prepared to stay on one island only: in October the inhabitants began to lift the potato crop and were reluctant to cross the sounds to the other islands because they were too busy, and there were often dangerous shifts of wind. We had no idea on which island we wanted to stay, but the first stop was at Inisheer and when the ship lay off the shore and the *currachs* came racing out to her, as they did now, twenty years later, we found the place irresistible.

There was a storm beach with some vestiges of pale grass among the dunes and a settlement of low houses, most of them roofed with slate, some still thatched and others, roofless ruins. Behind the houses rose tiers of dry-stone walls which enclosed the 'gardens' and the fields, and to the left, on a rock, was a fifteenth-century castle of the O'Briens, ruined by Cromwell's soldiers. There was a cemetery on a huge dune which concealed a prehistoric midden full of limpet shells and bones that had been broken for their marrow; and a long house from which donkeys were carrying quantities of *laminaria*, the long, sjambok-like sea-rods, down to the shore in sacks. They were ferried to the ship in *currachs*, and sold to iodine extraction factories on the mainland at £10 a ton.

The *currachs* are between 19 and 20 feet long. The hulls consist of a light framework of laths covered with tarred canvas; long ago they were made of cowhide. They have square counters and prows which turn up sharply, which are good in the surf. The oars are tapered, their laths almost bladeless, and they fit over a single thole pin, which enables them to be left unshipped in the water while the crew are fishing. Most of them have three oarsmen. They are very deep and can carry almost anything in good weather: up to twelve persons; more than a ton of potatoes; pigs, sheep, beds, mattresses, even tombstones. Larger livestock such as cows still have to swim to the ship when being embarked for the market at Galway, and very few actually drown. If one does inadvertently swallow a lot of water and looks about to sink, it is winched up by the hind legs and given the kiss of life on board. If that fails, its throat is cut and it is sold unofficially on the mainland, for meat. When fully loaded there is not much more than an inch of freeboard in the stern of a *currach*. Empty, they float like corks and are very volatile – too hard a pull on one oar is enough to send them spinning round and in inexpert hands they can be extremely dangerous.

Almost all the men in the boats at that time, young and old, wore the costume of the islands: very thick tweed trousers, split up the side seams so that they could be rolled up when the boats were launched through the surf, finger-braided woollen belts in colours made from natural dyes which ended in tassels, called *criosanna*, large tweed caps, thick indigo blue flannel shirts with stand-up collars and leg-of-mutton sleeves, and waistcoats made from a hairy, grey-blue tweed in which the ribbed pattern became more pronounced as the nap wore off. Some wore heelless shoes of raw cowhide with the hair on the outside, which are very pliable when wet. Until recently all the wool for the flannel and the tweed had been woven at a mill in Galway, but the mill had been burned down and in 1966 the costume seemed doomed to die out in a few years, when any stocks of material on the islands had been exhausted.

When the pandemonium of the disembarkation through the surf had abated, the various goods and chattels had been carried away, and the *currachs* had been carried up the beach, upside down over the heads of rowers so that they looked like strange six-legged monsters, a peace descended on Inisheer that was to remain unbroken until the boat returned five days later.

The following day was Sunday. The people were all Irish-speaking and the Mass was in Irish. The men wore their uniform and sat or stood at the back of the church, the women and children were in the front. The older women wore deep, full red flannel skirts which they had dyed a shade of madder and which positively glowed in the pale autumn light. Some had shawls to match, or had rare brown ones from the Galway mainland that were beyond price. It was a wonderful sight to see, the costumes. When the Mass was over the young men and boys left first, the old men and women last. Then the priest was rowed a couple of miles across An Sunda Salach, otherwise Foul Sound, for the service on Inishmaan.

Inisheer, only 1400 acres in area, is a table-land of bare sheets of limestone slanting from north to south and dropping away completely into the sea where the lighthouse stands. From it the herculean labour of successive generations had removed millions of stones, which had been piled up to form great cairns and labyrinths of high dry-stone walls. In the thousands of stone enclosures so formed, which acted as windbreaks, here and on the other islands, the soil had been man-made too, by laying down alternate levels of sand and seaweed ferried in panniers on the backs of donkeys. The principal crop was potatoes (a boiled Aran potato is one of the most delicious culinary treats), but oats, cabbages and carrots were also grown. The grass was excellent, which is why cattle fattened so well, and in October giant daisies appeared in the fields. There were hardly any trees except a few osiers, growing in sheltered places, which were used to make baskets and panniers for the donkeys. There were no gates: the walls were knocked down to let the animals in and out, after which they were rebuilt. On the two smaller islands everything was carried down the *boreens*, the little lanes that on the two smaller islands run parallel to one another the length of them from north to south. Everywhere were the remains of the kilns in which seaweed was burned to make kelp, the rock-hard substance from which iodine is extracted, and the circular seaweed stands and lengths of wall for drying the sea-rods.

Down at the south-western end of Inisheer near the lighthouse, towards sunset, alone in this world of stone, 1650 miles from St John's, Newfoundland, give or take a few miles, we really felt that we had come to the end of the road so far as Europe was concerned – at that time we had not ventured as far west as the Great Blasket. For five days we stayed in a house in Baile an Lurgain, one of the five villages on Inisheer and of the twenty-six villages on the three islands, all of which have the most intricate boundaries which were already in danger of being forgotten. During this time I managed to wangle myself into a *currach* as a third member of the crew, having satisfactorily demonstrated that

I was a fairly skilled oarsman, and went lobster-potting with them around the west side of the island. They had some good catches. The weather was calm so I shall never know now how good I would have been as one of the crew in bad weather. To prove what the sea can do in these parts was the wreck of the freighter *Plassy*, which went on the Carraig na Finnise reef in March 1960 and was later thrown high up on the shore, well above normal high tide level, where she remains to this day. What we both remember most about Inisheer was the intense cold in our bedroom. The only dishes we can recall were the amazing potatoes and the endless dollops of Birds custard.

Our host was an archetypal islander, very tall, with a large, long nose and grizzled straight hair, and he spoke *veery* slowly in beautiful English for our benefit, as if it was caviar not words he was dealing in. Every night we were there – there was no such thing as television on the island – he grilled me about New York, having heard that I had been there on several occasions, questioning me *veery, veery* slowly in his beautiful English, and *veery, veery* thoroughly. On the day we left he let us know that he had been janitor of a building on Lexington Avenue for something like fifteen years. I could gladly have murdered him.

In summer the islanders did well out of lobster fishing and tourism. In winter, even then, many of them were on the dole; but they had strong links with the United States (as I now well knew), to which many of them emigrated, and they had rent-free houses and a grant for speaking Irish, for this part of the world is regarded as one of the founts of the language. In fact it is thought they may be descended from an English garrison that was maintained there in the seventeenth century, but, nevertheless, must also have links with people who inhabited the islands much further back in time. Perhaps their lineage stretches back to when the Duns, the great stone forts of Aran, were built, the oldest in the Iron Age: Dun Aengus, Dun Oghil, Dun Onact and Dubh Cathair (the Black Fort) on Inishmore; Dun An Mothar and Dun Conor on Inishmaán; and Dun Forma on Inisheer. Or to the time when the churches, chapels and oratories of early Christian anchorites flourished, some of which are buried in the sand, and the holy wells, saints' beds of stone, caves, pillar stones, *clochans*, altars, cross slabs and monastic settlements. Notable among early Christians was St Eanna, otherwise Enda, the first to introduce monasticism in the severest sense of the word into Ireland. Here he lived and worked, giving St Brendan his blessing before he set off on his perilous voyage. And here he was buried in about 530, surrounded, it is said, by the 127 saints whom he had taught. Eanna's Household, Tighlagheany, is the holiest place in Aran, its great church surviving until it was destroyed by the Cromwellians.

Whatever their antecedents, the Islanders, at least the male ones, can be almost breathtakingly venal. On the day in October 1966 that we left Inisheer for the mainland it turned out that the only *currach* at that moment available to take us out to the ship was the one in which I had gone out fishing on several occasions with the two-man crew, with whom I had struck up what seemed a pleasant relationship. I had also treated them with considerable generosity in the pub each time we came ashore without, as I recall, ever being given a drink in return. In spite of this they now demanded something in the region of £5, which was at that time an outrageous sum, to take us 100 yards to the ship, which they did with the air of men who had never set eyes on either of us before. Not only this but our host, the ex-janitor from Lexington Avenue, who was down on the beach to see us off, did nothing whatever to dissuade them. There was nothing to do but pay up.

Altogether, at that time, the islanders were the envy of many people on the mainland who did not enjoy the same subsidies. They themselves, however, did not think themselves particularly lucky: 'Ach', they used to say, in voices as soft as the wind, 'that's how it goes.'

Now, in 1986, things were different; but not all that different. The skyline was the same, although there were now tractors down on the beach and souvenir shops and craft shops, and a craft kitchen, whatever that was, and a restaurant and two pubs with shops attached, and a camping gas shop, and a public convenience and a camp site and an air strip with daily flights from Galway city, and a co-operative weaving venture; and television ruled the waves. A *currach* now cost £500; many of them were fitted with out-boards and you were still grossly overcharged to ride in one. No one wore the costume anymore, as far as I could see, with the exception of the caps. I didn't see a single donkey but I expect they were there all right, working away up in the *boreens*. I got my biggest shock as soon as I embarked in Galway, on seeing the entire upper deck space of the ship forward taken up with plastic sacks filled with Dutch potatoes, bound for Inishmore.

This was the week in which fishermen in eight *currachs* off Inishmaan, wearing balaclavas and carrying sacks of stones, confronted three Irish fishery protection vessels which were forced to withdraw from the scene after their crews had been pelted with stones 'as there was a serious threat to life and limb'. The islanders were protesting against the confiscation of their illegal, small mesh monofilament drift nets with which nearly 90 per cent of all salmon reaching the Irish coast were being caught and which the Western Regional Fisheries Manager described as 'a threat to salmon angling and spawning'. One islander was said to be earning £17,000 a year fishing from his *currach* with these nets. Their right to fish was defended by the local curate, Father Liam MacNally, who said that it was a question of survival for the Inishmaan men, who needed the summer salmon and lobster season to put food in their children's mouths and were entitled to use the best nets available. It was unfair, he said, that large trawlers could put down three and four miles of drift netting, while smaller, local boats were being interfered with. When I left the dispute was still continuing.

Off Inishmaan we went through the whole paraphernalia of putting passengers and freight ashore by *currach* and then loading up again – one *currach* put off for the shore with all the window frames for a house on board. Then we sailed on past what must be one of the most beautiful white sand beaches, the water turquoise in the shallows under a blazing sun. At 2.45 we berthed alongside the jetty at Kilronan on Inishmore, and really it looked just as attractive as it had all that time ago. There were still the horse-drawn carts to take you about the island and now a brisk business was being done in bike hire; but I had my own bike.

The Captain told me he was sailing at 4.45, even if I wasn't back, and I set off at a terrific rate to visit the greatest of the duns of Aran, Dun Aengus, using the Shimano oval chainwheels to some effect and glad, really, that Wanda wasn't there to be told that she was in the seventies gearwise when she urgently needed to be in the thirties. For the last part of the way you cannot ride even a mountain bike, so I left mine in a ditch and continued on foot. I'd decided I wasn't mad about mountain bikes. When you get to an Irish version of Kilimanjaro you have to carry them anyway.

To attempt to write about Dun Aengus and bring some sort of freshness to it is rather like trying to perform a similar service for Stonehenge: so many people have attempted it before that one is tempted to give up. What one is looking at is not only one of the wonders of Ireland, but of the entire western world. It is the greatest of the Irish stone forts; George Petrie, the nineteenth-century Irish landscape painter and antiquary, thought it 'the most magnificent barbaric monument now extant in Europe' when he visited it in 1821.

It stands on the edge of a sheer 270-foot cliff which overhangs the sea, on a sheet of the bare limestone of which the islands are composed. Approaching it along the one road that spans the entire length of Inishmore it loomed on the skyline to the west, a sombre cyclopean mass with a single cyclopean eye, an entrance gateway through which the light of day was shining.

The walls are dry-stone, built of unworked blocks laid in courses, some of them up to 7 feet long. I went through the now ruined outer walls into an enormous enclosure, the first of three, all roughly concentric, the innermost of which is the citadel. In this first enclosure one is faced with what looks like a dense forest of fossilized tree stumps up to 3 feet high which seem to grow from the living rock or else sprout from the wall in which they have been immovably planted. This abbatis, or *cheval-de-frise* (although the use of cavalry at such a time and in such a situation can scarcely have been envisaged) extends outwards from the wall for a distance of 80 feet in some places and beyond this are the remains of other walls, which formed outworks. Through these defences a sloping pathway leads into the second, middle enclosure through a gateway surmounted by a huge lintel stone.

Beyond this middle enclosure is the citadel, an astonishing construction with walls 18 feet high in places and nearly 13 feet thick. All the walls have terraces, reached by steep flights of steps. A low gateway leads into the heart of Dun Aengus, which one would expect to be a claustrophobic enclosure, hemmed in as it is on all sides, with perhaps an Irish version of the Minotaur roaming in it. In fact there is nothing. Just the enclosure, with the walls terminating at the edge of the great cliff, and below and beyond it the Atlantic, stretching away to what the islanders believed was Hy Brasil, the enchanted island of the west.

Back on board, everyone sunbathed on deck until Black Head on the coast of County Clare was abeam and there we once more entered the realms of rain and suicidal darkness. Fortunately, it was only necessary to look astern to see the islands still swimming in a glittering sea to remember that the day had not been simply some extravagant dream.

Chapter 16

STORMY WEATHER

And this I dare avow, there are more rivers, lakes, brooks, strands, quagmires, bogs and marshes in this country than in all Christendom besides; for travelling there in the winter all my daily solace was sink-down comfort. . . . I was never before reduced to such a floating labyrinth, considering that in five months' space I quite spoiled six horses, and myself as tired as the worst of them.

WILLIAM LITHGOW. *Rare Adventures and Painfull Peregrinations,* 1614–32

Thunderstorms are without doubt the most dramatic weather phenomenon experienced in Ireland. They occur in the unstable atmospheric conditions favourable for the development of heavy showers, but their unique and spectacular features are of course thunder and lightning.

Monthly Weather Bulletin, June 1986, published by the Meteorological Service, Dublin

The following morning – the day of the Great Irish Divorce Referendum – was warm and hazy, and I went to the bank to draw some money to pay Mrs Robinson for the accommodation. As it turned out, I drew much too much. The bill for four nights' B and B – two nights for two of us, two for myself alone – plus various delicious meals and snacks, drinks and cups of tea at odd hours of the day and night, came to an unbelievable £42. I said goodbye to them with genuine regret. They were a splendid pair. Mrs Robinson was a woman of demonic energy and invincible goodwill and spirits. Her husband, John, had been badly wounded by a German stick grenade while serving with the British Army at the crossing of the Rhine in 1945. After the war he had become a staff photographer on a local paper, specializing in wedding groups, but had eventually been forced by bad health to give up, although he sometimes did some work for his son, who had a flourishing agricultural machinery repair business and a nice, modern house up the coast a bit. They also had three grown-up daughters, one of whom had just arrived from Canada with her husband and their newly born baby.

Then I took the road out of Galway for Headford, the wind now dead ahead from the north. It looked all right, this road, on a map that had last been revised in 1957, but it was filled with lorries loaded with unsecured crap bound for the City of Galway municipal dump. As a result I was showered with plastic bags, ashes and, even worse, planks studded with four-inch nails that had once added up to a garden shed, which fell from one lorry into the road at approximately 100-yard intervals. Most impressive was something called a Portaloo, a sort of mass lavatory which had been wrenched from its foundations and was being carried on a flat car to the same destination, a Galway *Côte d'Ordures*, with its plumbing still dripping.

After this disappointing beginning, the road, now dead straight for seven miles, entered an expanse of bog full of bog cotton, irises and flaming gorse – all the usual bog ingredients, plus a grassy tumulus or two – that stretched away towards invisible Lough Corrib and the distant hills beyond. This was to the left of the road. To the right what until recently had been the same bog was invisible behind what had become a ribbon development including the Municipal Dump, a car wreckers' establishment, a trucking depôt, and a large antiques emporium.

After some miles I stopped at a pub at Cloonboo (what a name) where a very pretty girl served me with a pint and, as it was Referendum Day, with the whole Irish nation agog, gave me a free run-down on the situation as she saw it.

'Sure, and I'm all for it,' she said, and when I asked her what she was all for: 'The divorce, I mean, fellers being what they are. But I'm in a minority,' she went on. 'Most of the girls and boys round here, what I call the "teenagers", them's against it.'

Beyond Cloonboo, I entered a region where it was sheep-shearing day and from time to time the road was choked with sheep that had either been newly shorn and had had new number plates stencilled on them, or else had just been dipped in antiseptic and smelled foul. The road beyond this village became even more boring; how I envied Wanda quietly harvesting a bumper crop of strawberries. To effect my escape from it, and to get away from the north wind, I made an enormous detour eastwards to see Finnbheara's Castle, a splendid walled cairn, part ancient, part Georgian folly, with a genuine prehistoric cairn nearby.

Finnbheara's Castle is on top of Knockmaa, a whacking great hill miles from anywhere, in the demesne of eighteenth-century Castle Hacket, burnt 1923, rebuilt 1929. I rose slowly and majestically to the summit, along a path hemmed in by dense woods and rhododendron groves, passing an earlier castle with trees growing inside it, and from the top I could see for miles in almost every direction. The insect life was prodigious. This hill is the legendary otherworld seat of Finnbheara, ruler of the fairies of

Connacht, who fought a battle here against those of Munster. Who won? It isn't important. They were fighting for the fun of it, like all good Irish fairies.

Towards evening I arrived at Cong, a pretty village in County Mayo on an isthmus which separates Lough Corrib from Lough Mask. Rather like Dingle and its peninsula, Cong and its environs have almost too great an abundance of relics of the past. I booked in at the White House, Prop. Mrs Connolly, who was uncertain about divorce and hadn't voted (only 40 per cent of eligible voters had), and spilled the contents of my pannier bags over the fitted carpet in the huge room I had commanded for £8. Then I washed some intimate garments, which an anti-British goose tried to prevent me from hanging on a line in the back yard, before setting off for the area in the north known as the Plain of Southern Moytura.

This plain, a strange and haunted place, was the site of one of the great battles of Irish myth between the Tuatha De Danaan, a tall race with magical propensities, and the small, dark Firbolgs, or Men of The Bag, known as such because they were forced to carry bags of earth while enslaved in Greece. The battle lasted four days and the Firbolgs were defeated;[*] their King, Eochy (otherwise Eochai), was killed and interred beneath the cairn which bears his name, a mighty heap of pale stone concealing within it a passage grave, the entrance to which is as well concealed as the route leading to it. Even the official directions in the *Guide to the National Monuments*, 'Access: half a mile up a laneway [which laneway?] then left down another laneway, and then 300 yards across six fields and stone walls. Not signposted', gives only a bare idea of how difficult it is to reach this haunting monstrosity which stands, for those of faint heart, forever unattainable in a labyrinth of sub-standard *boreens*. But it is worth the effort, if only for the view.

---

[*]After the Firbolgs' defeat, they retreated to the Aran Islands and other islands off the coasts of Ireland and Scotland. On Inishmore, according to legend, they built the nearly circular fort of Dun Onact, otherwise Dun Eoghanachta, which stands on a knoll west of Kilmurvy. There, having finished the job and being fed up with such arduous labour, they buried their tools in a nearby mound, which is still to be seen.

There is another large cairn, 60 feet high, at Ballymacgibbon North, east of Cong. According to Sir William Wilde, surgeon, Irish antiquary and father of Oscar Wilde, who lived at Moytura House nearby, on the shores of Lough Corrib, it was raised by the Firbolgs, who each threw down a stone for each member of the Tuatha De Danaan they had slain on the first day of the battle, when they were still winning – a romantic theory subsequently discredited, no doubt correctly but drearily, by modern savants.

Then back to Cong for tea and scones in The Ladies' Buttery, after which I cycled through what looked like a chasm, but was in fact man-made – the Lough Mask–Corrib Canal. In the late 1840s and early 1850s hundreds of workers, some paid as little as 3d a day, took five years to cut it for a distance of three miles through the limestone, only to find that when the water was finally admitted, it simply seeped away. It must be the only canal anywhere with a hand ball court in it. Meanwhile, in what was now the rapidly growing gloaming, anglers were unsuccessfully flogging the beautiful waters of the river Corrib for salmon and Cong, with its almost too neatly tended abbey ruins and its gigantic fortress, Ashford Castle, built by a Guinness, now a luxurious hotel, became like India in the gloaming, intolerably melancholy. I rang Wanda. The news was terrible. Within the space of twenty-four hours from the time she set off to gather them, squirrels had not only cleared the kitchen garden of every ripe strawberry but every white unripe one too, though they had spared the raspberries. Sometimes it is difficult to remain a lover of wildlife.

At six the following morning my alarm went off. I woke to find that although it was only a week after the longest day, when sunrise or at least a lightening of the eastern sky can be more or less confidently expected in these parts around a quarter to four, it was still so dark that the birds were carrying on roosting, apart from the owls around the abbey ruins, which could be heard complaining to one another at the excessive length of their working night. Then the heavens opened to the accompaniment of violent thunder and lightning, with Cong village its apparent target, which sent the birds shrieking into the air and made the White House shudder. Unlike most storms, this one went on and on. So, having eaten a very good breakfast and packed my still sodden underwear in my stuff sac, and having said goodbye to the goose by hissing at it through clenched teeth, I delayed no longer and set off northwards, bound for Ballinrobe and Westport, thinking it must end soon.

I hadn't gone very far when I realized that it was getting worse. By now I was on a stretch of road on which the only shelter was provided by trees on which were descending enormous, distorted prongs of lightning produced by the discharge of anything up to 1000 million volts every twenty seconds – the equivalent of ten nuclear bombs of the sort dropped on Hiroshima. I was frightened. In fact I was so frightened that when I came to the next stretch of dry-stone wall I abandoned my bike, distanced myself from its lethal steel, and cowered down with my back to it waiting for the trees above me to catch fire and shrivel. No sooner had I assumed this foetal position than whoever was responsible moved the storm away eastwards into Galway and Roscommon, although the rain still continued to fall in torrents.

Altogether, it was a great storm in a country in large areas of which violent explosions are part of the way of life. It continued to blast its way round Ireland throughout Saturday and part of Sunday morning, making a total of two thousand lightning strikes on the Electricity Board's installations, and cutting thousands of telephone, telex and cable television lines, although how anyone could detect any difference in the telephone service before or after it is something only the Irish can decide. It left twenty thousand houses without electricity, the Malin Head weather station with a total of fifty-seven power cuts during Saturday night, and produced hailstones as big as golf balls in County Wexford. At Gibbon's pub in Neale, a hamlet, south of Ballinrobe, where I stopped for a drink, the landlady had been so frightened that she had taken to her bed and buried her head under the clothes, a position she was still in when I arrived and shouted up the stairs to tell her that it was all over.

From Ballinrobe I set off on a horribly long detour to Castlecarra, on the shores of Lough Carra, the last part down a lane so muddy, so teeming with insects that I felt like a moose in the north of Canada.

Castlecarra was a truly enchanting place. The castle, a tower in a walled enclosure, stood on a tree-clad promontory overlooking the Lough. In the woods around it were the ruins of houses and outbuildings, all moss- and ivy-grown under the trees. Down on the beach a little band of boys who had also arrived here by bike were bathing – those who could swim at all energetically dog-paddling. It was a wonderful afternoon now, with the wind in the east rustling the trees. Offshore to the west was the island on which the novelist George Moore is buried. I had been to his house, Moore Hall, on the way to Castlecarra. Square and grey and austere, it was a shell, burnt out in 1923. Now it was hidden in a hideous Forestry Department conifer plantation which blocked what had once been a splendid view from it over the Lough.

Now the sky became jet-black and it poured for the next sixteen miles all the way to Westport where by 5 p.m. in June it was as dark and wet as it would have been in December. That evening I put up at P. Dunning's pub which stands on one of the eight sides of the Octagon, part of a large-scale eighteenth-century piece of town planning initiated by Peter Browne, second Earl of Altamont, and carried out by James Wyatt, in the course of which the town of Westport was rebuilt more or less as an appendage (or servants' quarters) to Westport House, the seat of the Brownes, later Marquises of Sligo as well as Earls of Altamont, near the shores of Clew Bay. Their great wealth had come from the marriage of the second Earl to the heiress to vast sugar plantations in Jamaica. In the middle of this Octagon was what remained of a memoral to George Glendinning, banker and son of the Rector of Westport, who did everything he could to alleviate the sufferings of the local peasantry during the Famine. The only thanks he got was to have his statue pulled down in 1922 during the Civil War, and the inscription on it defaced. He was a friend to Ireland, albeit British, which makes what the Irish do on occasion to their enemies scarcely surprising.

Here, I was treated to a fine technical discourse from the barman on the subject of comparative Irish and English whisky prices: 'And wat you get over dere, two English nips, at 75p English a nip, each nip's a sixth of a gill, dat's a third of a gill at £1.50, and wat's more it comes outta litre bartle sploiced wid watter so dat de feller workin' de tap and fillin it up is gettin' 68 nips fram a bartle. Whereas, over here in Westport you're gettin' two Oirish tots, dat's quarter a gill each, at £1 Oirish a tot, dat's £2 Oirish half a gill, but we're not sploicing it.'

Like the morning's storm this rumbled on and on until I was thoroughly mixed up with English nips and Oirish tots and gills and Oirish pounds, and like the storm it, too, gave me a headache.

The next day was beautiful, everything rain-washed and crystal clear, and having ascertained from the proprietress after a good breakfast that it was four miles to Murrisk at the foot of Croagh Patrick, the Holy Mountain; from the waitress that it was eight miles; and from a man cleaning up in the bar that it was between seven and nine miles, I measured it and found that it was six. Westport was nice, a very civilized place with an almost continental air to it. A little river enclosed by low walls, and shaded by lime trees, runs down the middle of the Mall and from it through the demesne of Westport House.

Down at Westport Quay was a port that reached the height of its importance in the transatlantic trade, and was killed off by the Famine and the introduction of the railways. Even on such a morning as this its tall, deserted warehouses and quays contrived to have an air of almost unbearable Irish melancholy, which the arcadian demesne of the great house behind it, with its groves and waterfalls and pretty church, did their best to dispel. Built by Richard Castle with additions by James Wyatt, it will become yet another Irish ruin if the present heirs fail in their valiant attempt to keep it going.

Chapter 17

AN ASCENT OF CROAGH PATRICK

Every pilgrim who ascends the mountain on St
Patrick's Day, or within the octave, or any time during
the months of June, July, August and September, and
PRAYS IN OR NEAR THE CHAPEL for the intentions of
our Holy Father the Pope may gain a plenary In-
dulgence on condition of going to Confession and
Holy Communion on the Summit or within the week.

From the Notice to Pilgrims
at the foot of Croagh Patrick

At Murrisk, on the coast road from Westport to Louisburg, I left my bike behind Campbell's pub, above which, at present invisible in mist, the quartzite cone of Ireland's most holy mountain, otherwise known as 'The Reek', rises from sea level in Clew Bay to 2150 feet in a horizontal mile and three-quarters. Here, I bought a supply of fruit and nut chocolate, filled one of the bottles off the bike with water and bought a pamphlet from old Mrs Campbell, entitled *Croagh Patrick, The Mount Sinai of Ireland*, by F. P. Carey, an irresistible title if ever there was one, which cost 20p Irish. Published by the *Irish Messenger*, it contained powerful endorsements: A *Nihil Obstat*, (No Objection) from Gulielmus Dargan, S. J. Censor Theol. Deput., and an *Imprimi Potest* (You Can Print It) from Joannes Carolus, Archiep. Dublinem, Hiberniae Primas, which put the book on pretty sound ground, theologically speaking.

The last time I had climbed Croagh Patrick had been in 1966, the year we had gone to the Aran Islands. Then, two of us had done it in an hour; but to do this meant reaching the saddle at the foot of the summit cone in thirty minutes. For it is at the far western end of this saddle, at the foot of the cone, that the pilgrim's troubles really begin.

I was by now in fairly good condition after all this biking and I decided to try for the top in an hour again, something Wanda would have forbidden, had she been present.

I left at eleven in brilliant sunshine under a cloudless sky. Only the summit had a wig of white vapour firmly clamped on it, against which the gleaming white statue of St Patrick, where the climb begins, loomed dramatically. From here to the saddle the track through the heather was channelled and eroded by rain and the feet of innumerable pilgrims, and full of stones. To the right was the deep, dark combe known as Log na nDeamhan which runs up to the precipitous north-east face of the mountain, into which a horde of demons who were bothering the Saint were cast by divine intervention. Soon after I set off I overtook a very fragile, elderly man who looked as if he was taking his first steps after a long illness, accompanied by what appeared to be his wife and daughter. Supporting himself with two sticks, he was climbing the mountain barefoot with infinite slowness; he had obviously spurned the help of his companions.

On this section, the last part of which is pretty steep, I passed six more people, including a woman with two children of about six and eight. All of us, with the exception of the barefooted man, whom the Almighty appeared to spare this further discomfort, were assailed by a sort of yellowish green horsefly which flourished here in large numbers.

I got to the eastern end of the saddle five minutes late, at 11.35. This is the place where Tochar Phadraig, Patrick's Causeway, the original route to the summit, joins the modern route from Murrisk. It was this causeway that the Saint used when he climbed the mountain on Quinquagesima Sunday 441, the Sunday preceding Ash Wednesday, to begin his forty days of fasting.[*] He started from The Church of Aghagower, which he himself founded, some five miles to the east of the mountain. In fact the Causeway is much longer; it has been traced at least as far as the Abbey of Ballintober, north of Lough Mask some fourteen miles from the mountain, which, together with Aghagower formed the last link in a chain of religious houses which catered for pilgrims from distant parts of Ireland in the same way as eastern caravanserais.

From the saddle the mountain fell away northwards, the

---

[*]The traditional day for performing the pilgrimage is Domhnach Crom Dubh, the last Sunday in July or the beginning of the harvest season, and the day on which the first of the year's food crop was eaten, all of which appear to indicate that the pilgrimage to the mountaintop has pagan antecedents going back far beyond the lifetime of the Saint, who has no connection with this day. In fact some people still believe that the Friday of Crom Dubh is the day on which the pilgrimage should be celebrated, and do so.

direction from which I had climbed it, to the innermost part of Clew Bay which is filled with innumerable grassy islets. To the south it fell away to a lonely lough beyond which what looked like a rough sea of hills and mountains – an area called The Murrisk – extended as far as the eye could see, down towards the border of Counties Mayo and Galway. Westwards now the track stretched away up the length of the saddle for just over a mile, an easy walk, to the foot of the summit cone, before climbing steeply towards the top around its south face. The mist had now dispersed completely. This part of the route had a number of small, roofless shelters along it, occupied on the nights and days of pilgrimage by sellers of refreshments, and I remembered on my first visit the track glittering in the sunshine with the glass of innumerable broken bottles, rather as the open spaces in Russian cities used to shine, but more dully, with the metal caps of equally innumerable vodka bottles. Now, there was very little glass to be seen at all.

Then, after passing a couple of sets of official loos, I reached the first of the penitential stations: Leacht Mhionnain, the Memorial of St Benignus, a heap of stones on the track near the head of Log na nDeamhan, into which the demons were consigned. Benignus, otherwise Benen, Patrick's very youthful companion on his missionary travels, acted as his driver and servant. Later he became his psalm singer in charge of music for religious services, was ordained and eventually became Second Bishop of Armagh. Of him, the most impetuous of Patrick's native born bishops, it was said, 'Restrain him not, that youth shall yet be heir to my kingdom.' There is a legend that Benen remained at this spot, being too tired to continue to the summit, and that when Patrick came down from it he found that Benen had been killed by the retreating demons; it was Patrick who caused the monument to be raised in his memory. Here, the pilgrims making their *tura*, or journey, recite seven 'Paternosters', seven 'Ave Marias' and make seven circuits of the station, and the ground had been worn smooth by their constant passage. At one time these rounds, and the rounds at all the other stations on the mountain, were performed on the knees, often bare knees.

The next part up from the monument to the summit on what is called Casan Phadraig, Patrick's Path, over steep, loose scree

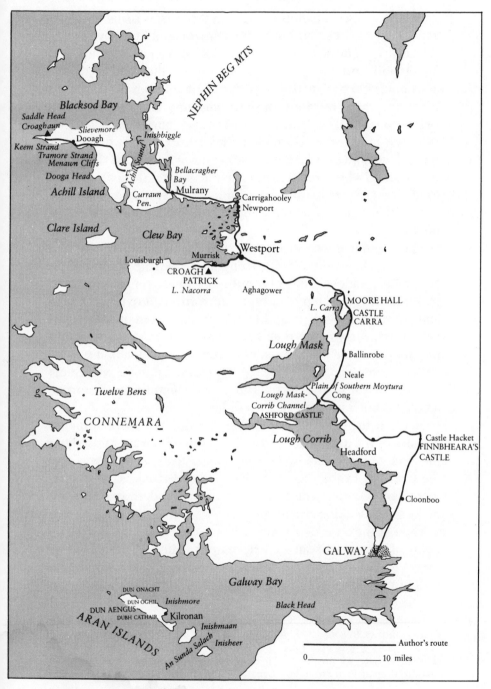

NEPHIN BEG MTS

Blacksod Bay

Saddle Head
Croaghaun
Slievemore
Dooagh
Inishbiggle

Keem Strand
Tramore Strand
Menawn Cliffs
Dooga Head

Achill Sound

Bellacragher
Bay
Mulrany

Carrigahooley
Newport

Achill Island

Curraun
Pen.

Clare Island

Clew Bay

Murrisk

Westport

Louisburgh

CROAGH ▲
PATRICK
L. Nacorra

Aghagower

MOORE HALL
CASTLE
CARRA

L. Carra

Lough Mask

Ballinrobe

Neale
Plain of Southern Moytura
Cong

Twelve Bens

Lough Mask-
Corrib Channel
ASHFORD CASTLE

CONNEMARA

Lough Corrib

Headford

Castle Hacket
FINNBHEARA'S
CASTLE

Cloonboo

GALWAY

Galway Bay

DUN ONACHT
DUN OGHIL   Inishmore
DUN AENGUS
DUBH CATHAIR   Kilronan

Black Head

ARAN ISLANDS

Inishmaan

An Sunda Salach   Inisheer

Author's route

0 ——————— 10 miles

which here pours down the slopes in torrents, is really tough for almost anyone. It is certainly difficult to imagine how anyone who is in any way infirm, and some of the pilgrims who make the climb are literally on their last legs, can reach the top, even with assistance. On this final section the terrible flies were still out in force and there were a few sheep chewing away at the sparse vegetation. Here, I caught up with a young Dutch couple who had left a few minutes earlier than I had. Inspired by this competition the girl went away with a very strong finish to beat me to the top. It was 12.10 when I reached it; I was ten minutes slower than I had been twenty years before. I was unlikely to be doing it in 2006, even with the aid of sticks. As a prize I gave her one of my fruit and nut bars.

The summit is not in fact the point of a cone. The cone is truncated; the summit a flat, stony area covering about half an acre. On it stands an oratory, built in 1905 to replace an earlier building with the help of subscriptions from all over the world, and constructed with great difficulty in such a remote place. The first Mass, on 30 July that year, was attended by a thousand pilgrims (the figure is now around sixty thousand) and it was the Archbishop of Tuam, Dr Healy, who served it, who was chiefly responsible for saving the pilgrimage from extinction. Unfortunately, it is not a very attractive building.

Here on the summit, kneeling pilgrims, having overcome the agonies of the ascent in darkness and often pouring rain, saying the rosary on the way, say seven more 'Paters', seven 'Aves' and the Creed at Leaba Phadraig, The Bed of Patrick, a bit like the mouth of a well to the north-east of the modern oratory, and make seven walking circuits of it.*

Then at the altar of Teampall Phadraig, Patrick's Church, the vestigial remains of an earlier oratory, fifteen 'Paters', fifteen 'Aves' and the Creed are said, also kneeling, and the pilgrims make fifteen circuits of the entire summit, praying all the while.

---

*Until some time in the early nineteenth century, according to the Rev. James Page, author of *Ireland: Its Evils Traced to Their Source* (1836), the station at Leaba Phadraig was performed only by those pilgrims who wanted to have children but had been unsuccessful in doing so. They usually spent the night on the summit, sleeping in or around the Bed.

After this, back to Leaba Phadraig for seven more 'Paters', seven 'Aves' and the Creed, and seven rounds before repairing to An Garrai Mor, The Great Garden or Enclosure, some way down the side of the mountain in which there are three mounds of stones. There, they recite a final seven 'Paters' seven 'Aves' and the Creed, and walk seven times round each of the three mounds and seven times round the perimeter of the Enclosure. This brings to an end this remarkable pilgrimage and penance, although some conclude by making further rounds at a holy well at Kilgeever, on a hill at the foot of the mountain to the west.

On a day such as this, from the top of Croagh Patrick you could see almost for ever: north-west across Clew Bay to Achill Island and out across the wastes of County Mayo to Slieve League, the high cliffs on the north side of Donegal Bay; westwards to Clare Island and south-west to the Twelve Bens in Connemara. Looking out across the screes seawards it was not difficult to believe that it was supposed to be possible from a certain point to see the streets of New York.

St Patrick spent forty days and forty nights on the mountain, fasting, and keeping the discipline of Moses and Elias and Christ. The first account of his sojourn was in the *Breviarium* of Tirechan, who lived in the second half of the seventh century. The account was subsequently enlarged upon in the *Vita Tripartita*, the Tripartite Life, written at the end of the ninth century. During his sojourn the Saint was visited by demons in the guise of hideous black birds who subjected him to awful temptations and who were so numerous that they blacked out the sky and rendered the sea invisible as they swooped around him, attempting to savage him with their beaks and beat him with their wings. Meanwhile, the Saint-to-be chanted psalms, prayed to the Lord for assistance, and rang a bell given to him by St Brigid, all without success, until finally his prayers were answered and he threw the bell after the demons, breaking a piece off it as they fled down Log na nDeamhan, to sink into the sea beyond Achill Island. There they remained for seven years, seven months and seven days and nights, after which they surfaced once more on the north-west coast to make life a misery for its inhabitants, until they were finally driven out by St Colmcille. Patrick was then visited by an angel who arrived with a flock of white birds, representing in material form the souls he was to save in the future.

Local folklore, not the *Tripartite Life*, goes on to say that after sending the demons helter-skelter down the combe he had to face an even more formidable enemy in the shape of the Devil's mother, the Corra. He succeeded in driving her down into the lonely lough below the saddle on the south side, now known as Lough na Corra, from which she subsequently escaped to perish later in Lough Derg.

There is a much less arduous route to the summit from the saddle near the station of St Benignus, as I discovered when I came to make the descent. It runs along the edge of the precipice above the demons' combe and is mostly over heather. It was at this moment being used by a band of, like me, *nicht so jung* Germans who were plodding doggedly upwards. A further mockery of human effort was made by the arrival overhead of a helicopter with a sack suspended below it loaded with a ton of sand and cement and planks for the repair of the Oratory. During my descent, which if anything is more tiresome than going up, it made several journeys at a cost to the Church of £3000. By the time I got to the eastern end of the saddle the barefooted man with the two sticks had just reached it. The two women with him looked completely exhausted by the emotion of watching him. I always wonder if he made the summit.

Later that afternoon, sitting in brilliant sunshine outside P. Dunning's pub in the Octagon surrounded by boys and girls in T-shirts, drinking Harp under the gay pub umbrellas provided by You Know Who, what I had seen and felt on the Mountain seemed like yet another dream.

Reluctantly quitting my ringside seat in the Octagon from which I was enjoying watching the procession of the human comedy, I took my bike and baggage across the way to the Grand Central Hotel, which was nice-looking rather than grand, and took my place in a queue for the 16.05 bus bound for Newport, Mulrany, Achill Sound, and finally Dooagh. It looked as if it was going to be pretty heavily ballasted, not only with locals going home for the weekend but also with what used to be known back in the 1930s as *Wandervogeln*, now loaded with those enormously tall back packs which make those who carry them look as if they are transporting menhirs on their backs.

Among the back packers was a very serious young Protestant couple from Ulster who comported themselves rather like early Christians in a lions' den, which may well be what it feels like for an Ulster Protestant holidaying in the Catholic South. And there was a rather awful Swiss-German boy who spent part of the trip explaining with heavy jocularity to Mrs Monaghan the meaning of *Jungfrau* and *Liebfraumilch*, something she didn't grasp at all.

We travelled first through boggy, undulating country that I was glad I wasn't cycling through, catching an occasional view of some of the hundred islands swimming in Clew Bay. Beyond Newport, which was once a stop on the railway line from Westport to Achill Sound, with a viaduct to prove it, we turned westwards. To the right now parts of the Nephin Beg Range rose, at first gently, then more steeply into the air. From here you could walk northwards, crossing it and the Bog of Erris for twenty miles until you reached the north coast of Mayo, through some of the loneliest parts of Ireland, without seeing any human habitation, apart perhaps from a shooting lodge or the remains of one or, for that matter, any human being.

To the left now somewhere down by the shore was Carriga-hooley, one of the strongholds of Grace O'Malley (Graine Ui Maille in Irish), Queen of Clew Bay. The daughter of a family of sea-rovers, she married first the chieftain of Ballinahinch, and secondly Richard, chief of the Burkes of Mayo and master of Carrigahooley. She had her own fleet and her own army, and her greatest enemy was Sir Richard Bingham, English Governor of Connaught, who captured her, built a gallows to hang her for plundering the Aran Islands, and only let her go on a pledge of good behaviour given by her son-in-law, known by the English as 'The Devil's Hook' and by the Irish as 'The Fiend of the Sickle'. Bingham himself described her as 'a notable traitress and nurse of all rebellions in the province for forty years'. She went to London, after a serious defeat by Bingham, and is there said to have met Queen Elizabeth and asked for her protection. She died in poverty around 1600, and is thought to have been buried on Clare Island at the mouth of Clew Bay.

It was on the rocks of Clare Island, twelve years previously, that the great Armada vessel *El Gran Grin* went down. The survivors, who numbered a hundred and included Don Pedro de Mendoza, her captain, were all massacred on the orders of the chief of the island, also an Ui Maille, who hoped to ingratiate himself with the English by doing so.

It was a fine sight, Clew Bay, with the islands in full view now, Croagh Patrick rising above it like some dormant Irish Vesuvius and Clare Island apparently swimming across the mouth of it. Meanwhile, eccentric very ancient Achill Islanders of picturesque appearance, no doubt commissioned to do so by Bord Failte, perambulated up and down the bus welcoming monoglot foreign back packers to Ireland and their island and driving the more timid locals, who no doubt have to put up with them every Saturday in summertime, to distraction.

At Mulrany there were green meadows down by the sandy shore, in which cattle and horses grazed, and above them woods filled with flowering rhododendrons, fuchsia hedges and *erica mediterranea*, a sort of flowering heather. Beyond it the road crossed a narrow isthmus onto the Curraun Peninsula, following what was once the railway line. To the right was Bellacragher Bay, with lines of lobster pots and a scattering of houses, some roofless, down by the shore. Here, whole families were out together in the bog below the bare, steep Curraun Hills, cutting turf and stacking it and making the most of the fine weather. Here, around five in the afternoon in the last days of June, the world looked good, even from the windows of a bus at boiling point.

We crossed the sound which separates Achill Island from the mainland by a swing bridge, and there everyone seemed to be cutting and stacking turf too, or else raking hay by hand and piling it up into cocks, something unknown in England for goodness knows how many years. We were now in a sort of undulating rocky plain, with mountains above it dark against the evening sun and huge cliffs, a landscape full of white, slate-roofed houses, fields with dry-stone walls and what had been until recently thatched cabins, now roofed with corrugated iron and used as barns or tool sheds. It was a man-made landscape filled with rusting reject motor cars, tractors and other agricultural instruments, a more or less treeless land in which their place was taken by the telephone poles that marched across it in every direction, supporting endless cat's cradles of wires. They made me feel in some places that there was a net separating me from the sky, just like the squirrels in Wanda's strawberry bed back home must have felt.

By the time we got to Dooagh, the end of the road for the bus, it was almost empty, the locals having melted away at request stops and the visitors having descended en masse at Tramore Strand. At this hour, with no one making the *passegiata* at Dooagh or giving poteen-making demonstrations, it seemed slightly uninspiring, so I pedalled back the way we had come towards Tramore, stopping off en route for a pot of tea at Higgins' Fast Food Eatery.

At Tramore the golden sands were extensive enough to absorb the few tents and caravans that stood on the edge of them. There, the boy and girl from the North were in process of pitching a tent so small that it seemed impossible that any couple could sleep in it without adopting the missionary position. Perhaps they were missionaries, sent by the Rev. Paisley. Beyond the Strand, across the Bay, were the Menawn Cliffs, plummeting eight or nine hundred feet sheer to the sea at their southern end – seen from the sea among the most fantastic cliffs in the British Isles.

That evening I put up in a B and B of incredible cleanliness and rectitude. I was the only guest. The pub was entirely populated by locals with whom it was difficult to have any social intercourse, on account of them all having long-term contracts to listen to one another; after a while I would have welcomed the interruption of one of the characters on the bus. After this I had a temporary increase in good spirits eating at the Late Date Restaurant, which was also a butcher's shop, though again I was the only customer, apart from a couple from the beach who conversed in unnerving whispers. My lamb chops were accompanied by wine from a bottle labelled 'Vieux Ceps' (Old Stocks), which was just what it tasted like. Then I rang Wanda to tell her I wished I wasn't here, as it were, but I didn't get much sympathy as some deer had just made a meal of her Peace roses.

By now it was ten o'clock on a cloudless night with the sun still in the heavens and in the twilight I took to the road and cycled towards the foot of Slievemore, like Croagh Patrick another cone of quartz, this one shot with mica and more than 2200 feet high. At the foot of Slievemore there is a very old cemetery, its graves outlined in pebbles from the shore, and a walled holy well, dedicated to St Colman of Kilmacduagh. To the left, a muddy track leads through the ruins of Slievemore village, extending away to the westward into the sunset for nearly a mile. Abandoned as a village in the late nineteenth century, it continued to be used as a *buaile*, a milking or pasturing place, to which the men of the nearby and by then much more considerable village of Dooagh used to go at certain seasons, living in the 'booley houses'. This form of transhumance, already rare in other parts of Europe, continued into the early 1960s. Standing now, in the last of the twilight, among its roofless houses and bothies, it was difficult to believe that this village had only been disused for twenty-five years or so.

Mrs S. C. Hall, who travelled extensively in Ireland during the 1840s, described the houses as they were at that time:

> The habitations of the islanders are very singular. Their houses are heaps of rude stones moulded by the tide, procured from the beach uncemented; they are rounded at the gables, and roofed with fern, heath and shingles, fastened on by straw bands. In the village of Dooagh, consisting of about forty cabins, there is not a single chimney. Some of the wealthier graziers, however, have an odd custom of residing in such houses, or in houses of a still more simple construction, only during the summer months, when the fishing season is 'on', and their cattle are brought down towards the coast to feed on the young herbage. These houses they call 'Builly Houses'.

Achill, Mrs Hall wrote elsewhere in her book, had some of the most wretched cabins anywhere.

> A few months ago we examined one, of which an artist by whom we were accompanied made a sketch. Seven persons

were housed there. We measured it; it was exactly ten feet long by seven feet broad, and five feet high, built on the edge of a turf bog; within, a raised embankment of dried turf formed a bed, and besides the clothing of the more than half-naked children, a solitary ragged blanket was the only covering it contained. The family had lived here for two years; some work recently undertaken in the neighbourhood had given the man employment, and he was on the eve of building himself a better house. Close to this hovel were two others scarcely superior; and, indeed, nearly every cottage in the district was almost as miserable and destitute of anything approaching to comfort. . . . Much of this evil is no doubt attributable to the exceeding and unaccountable apathy of the peasant; for in this very locality, huts were pointed out to us inhabited by men substantial enough 'to give a marriage portion of a hundred pounds with a daughter' – a common way in Ireland of estimating the possession of wealth. This evil [she concluded] will vanish before an improved order of things. It had grown out of long suspicion – a belief that the acquisition of money was sure to bring an increase in rent, a belief not ill-founded in old times. We have ourselves known instances where the purchase of a single piece of furniture, or the bare indication of thrift and decent habits, was a certain notice to the landlord that it was his time to distrain for arrears due; arrears being *always* due under the ancient system.

The sky to the west was now a Schiaparelli Shocking Pink and two eccentric rainbows tinged the same colour spanned the entire sky from north to south as I pedalled back from this haunting, haunted place to the pub.

The following morning everything was shrouded in cold, wet mist. In it I rode about four miles to a place called Keem Strand below Achill Head, which really is the end of the road. There I locked the bike to a fence behind a derelict hotel, and began the treat which I had so long promised myself, the ascent of Croaghaun, up through boggy sheep country filled with wild irises. It took about an hour in the mist.

Standing on the edge of Croaghaun, it was difficult to believe that I was now on the edge of the highest sea cliffs in the British Isles, where the mountain suddenly comes to an end and falls 1950 feet to the sea in a series of vast, rocky, partly grass-grown slopes. It was difficult to believe because beyond twenty feet in any direction, up, down or sideways, it was impossible to see anything at all. All I could hear was the sea sighing far below, and the dismal crying of the gulls.

The next day, Sunday, it poured all day. There was no bus until Monday, so I knew I had to either ride it out or see it out. By a miracle I managed to buy four English Sunday papers, which would see me through until evening, and after watching the World Cup on TV in company with a very drunken fellow who kept mumbling, 'Goo' Ol' Arshentina! Barshtard British!' (who weren't playing anyway), I went to bed. I had already decided to get out of Achill, and out of Ireland, too, until things improved. Monday was the day when the summer bus service came into operation and the first bus was at 07.05. No sooner had I set out to catch it, having paid my bill, than I found that a huge nail from a donkey's shoe had punctured the rear tyre and I had to strip the bike before turning it upside down in the rain and repairing it, almost weeping with vexation. I missed the bus, but by riding seventeen miles or so in the rain to Mulrany on the mainland, assisted by the strong westerly blast, I managed to catch the train to Westport, and get to Dublin, and thence to Dun Laoghaire for the night ferry. The next day I was in Dorset, enjoying a strawberryless lunch with Wanda.

PART 4

OCTOBER

Chapter 18

LAST DAYS IN IRELAND

North of the district we are describing [Newport,
Achill, etc.], are the baronies of Erris and Tyrawley;
savage districts, but full of interest and character. . . .
Into this wild region civilisation has scarcely yet
entered; even now the roads are few, and impassable
for ordinary carriages; and probably there are hundreds of the inhabitants, at this moment, who do not
even know that a queen reigns over Great Britain.
Achill, and its vicinity are primitive places; but . . .
they are refined in comparison with Erris and
Tyrawley.

MR AND MRS S. C. HALL. *Ireland: Its Scenery,*
*Character &c.,*1846

Few but sportsmen and poor-law officials know much
about Erris.

HARRIET MARTINEAU. *Letters from Ireland,* 1852

At the beginning of October we resumed our travels. This time we made some dramatic changes in what we took with us. Out went all the guide books except *Murray's Guide* 1912, the resulting spaces in the pannier bags being more than filled up with sleeping bags, bivouac bags, ground sheets, inflatable mattresses, gas stove, frying pan, cooking pots etc. By now neither of us could face any more bed and breakfasts, however welcoming, or for that matter evening meals in them or in cafés or restaurants, and we were both determined to sleep in sheds or barns or caravans if it rained, or else in the open. This was not as heroic as it sounded. The whole of Ireland had enjoyed an exceptional September, after almost the worst summer in living memory, and according to an archetypal figure who dwelt on Glasnevin Hill, Dublin, in the temple of the Irish Meteorological Service, the fine weather was likely to continue.

We decided to start from Belmullet in north-west Mayo. One of the more remote places in Ireland, it stands on an isthmus only about 400 yards wide which joins the mainland of Mayo to the Mullet Peninsula, which is itself separated from the rest of the country by two enormous anchorages capable of accommodating whole fleets of ships: Broadhaven to the north and to the south, Blacksod Bay.

The problem was how to get there. The nearest railhead (173 miles from Dublin Heuston) is at Ballina on the River Moy to the east, from which Belmullet is separated by forty miles of almost uninhabited mountains in the Nephin Beg range, and by the Bog of Erris. A bus service runs from Ballina to Belmullet on weekdays, passing en route the Musical Bridge at Bellacorick, and it was on this providentially provided bus – May all the Blessed Saints bless the Provincial and Expressway Bus Services Division – that we made our way there.

The Musical Bridge at Bellacorick was built of limestone in the eighteenth century to span the Abhann Mhor. Here, at our special request, the bus stopped long enough to enable us to produce musical sounds by running stones along the northern parapet, which is somewhat worn as a result of this practice. The southern parapet is more or less non-musical, possibly because the limestone was set in cement when the bridge was repaired during the Troubles. In the middle of the seventeenth century Brian Rua O'Carrabine, the 'Erris Prophet', foretold that when the bridge was built it would never be completed, and it never was. It is said that anyone who tries to complete it will come to a sudden end and, indeed, when some years ago an official of Mayo County Council did put the last coping stone in place he died almost immediately after – he was, however, a sufferer from chronic asthma. An Assistant County Engineer also had it placed in position but the following morning it was no longer there, and it lacks a final coping stone to this day.

Belmullet is not much more than a main street which, if one cycles westwards down it, lands you in the waters of Blacksod Bay, that is if the tide is in, otherwise in mud. Thirty-five varieties of fish (including blue shark, cuckoo ray and larger spotted dogfish) have been caught in these waters and those of Broadhaven to the west and north, with which it is linked by a canal.

Long before the First World War great plans had been afoot to build a port for transatlantic liners at the southern end of the Mullet Peninsula, which would have been linked with Ballina and the rest of Ireland by rail, but nothing came of what was to be known as 'The All Red Route to Canada'. Just as nothing ever really came of the deep sea fishing for herring and mackerel, which existed in extraordinary quantities, simply for lack of any method of onward transportation. Most guide books referred rather disparagingly to the Peninsula, which in fact has both on it and off it, on some now uninhabited islands, some pretty strange things and, indeed, one or two pretty strange people.

Out to the west at Termoncarragh, which is or was the last Irish nesting place of the phalarope, down near the shore among the sand dunes there is a cemetery, very overgrown, full of old tomb enclosures and some official gravestones recording British merchant seamen whose bodies were washed ashore from ships torpedoed or wrecked off the coast here during the last war. There is also a weird family vault, through a hole in the side of which skulls and skeletons are visible. Nearby, at Doonamo, a high and lonely headland bare of vegetation because of the big seas that break over it, there is a prehistoric fort like Dun Aengus with a cheval de frise, but much smaller. Further south, about a mile and

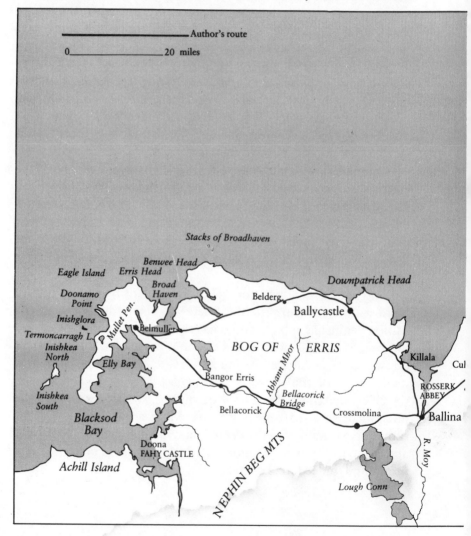

a half offshore to the west are two low-lying islands, Inishglora and Inishkeera. On Inishglora, where there are the ruins of a monastery founded by St Brendan, the nails and hair of the dead were said to grow as vigorously as they had done in life: 'On Inis Gluair in Irrus Downan,' wrote the author of the *Book of Ballymote*, which dates from about 1400, 'the bodies thither brought do not Rot, but their nails and hair grow and everyone there recognises his father and grandfather for a long time after death; and no meat will putrefy on it even without being salted.'

Here, the Children of Lir (himself one of the Tuatha De Danaan), who had been changed into swans by their jealous

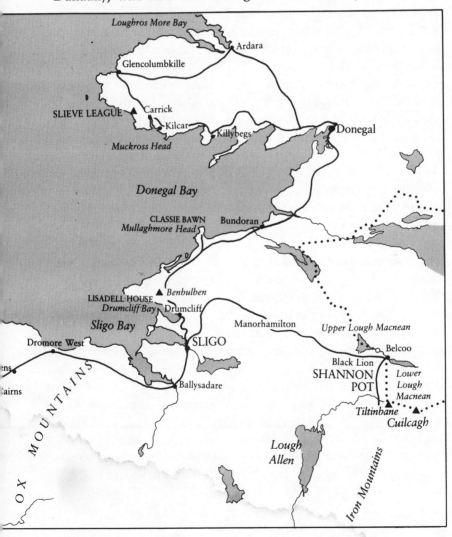

stepmother, Aoife, swam in the Atlantic for the last three hundred years of their nine-hundred-year enchantment. The first third of their sentence had been spent in Lough Derravaragh in County Westmeath; the second in the often inhospitable waters of the Sea of Moyle, near Fair Head in County Antrim, and in the mouth of the nearby Margy River at Ballycastle. Their fate was especially cruel because they retained their human memories of what had befallen them through the centuries. Even in the guise of swans they had beautiful singing voices which brought joy to all who heard them. As swans, they were looked after by St Mochaomhog until Lairgen, King of Connacht, tried to steal them, at which point they turned back into human beings, albeit rather old ones. Fortunately, the Saint had time to baptize them before they died. As punishment for causing all this trouble Aoife was turned into an airborne witch.

Further south are two more islands, Inishkea North and South, separated by a narrow channel. On Inishkea North there is a mysterious mound 500 feet wide and 60 feet high, a shell-mound and prehistoric dye factory in which purple dye was produced from shellfish. In the 1900s, when the population of the two islands was 212, the Norwegians established a whale factory on it, where they converted the blubber into oil, the meat into cattle feed and the bones into fertilizer. Each island had its own king, and both were evacuated in 1931.

To the east was Blacksod Bay where, on 6 or 7 September 1588, yet another Armada galleon, *La Rata Encoronada*, with Don Alonso de Leyva and a band of young noblemen on board, anchored westwards of Doona Castle. The *Rata* dragged her anchors, stranded, and had to be abandoned. De Leyva and his men landed and immured themselves in the Castle of Doona, together with any treasure and armour they could salvage before burning the wreck. Two other ships, one of them the *Duquesa Santa Ana*, the other perhaps the *Nuestra Senhora de Begona*, also came in to the bay seeking shelter, and the *Santa Ana* anchored in Elly Bay, on the shores of which the hated Sir Richard Bingham, Governor of Connaught, had a castle. His first act on returning to Ireland from the Netherlands in September to re-assume his office as Governor had been to issue orders that all

Spanish refugees cast ashore on the coast of his province should be brought to Galway and put to death. However, de Leyva and his men, having abandoned the Castle of Doona, joined forces with the crew of the *Santa Ana* and managed to sail away.

The other ship which had come in, the *Begona*, had no long boat to make contact with the land and put to sea again after a week; it was this ship which brought the news of the loss of the *Rata* to the crew of the *Zuniga* after she left her anchorage in Liscannor Bay to sail back to Spain.

What subsequently happened to de Leyva, the young noblemen and the combined crews of the two ships now aboard the *Santa Ana* is like something from an heroic work of fiction. On 15 September the wind once more backed to the south and, with another gale building up, the *Santa Ana* was forced to sail northwards. She went ashore in Loughros More Bay, north-west of Ardara in County Donegal, and was wrecked, apparently without loss of life. There, for nine days, the crews remained entrenched near the wreck, after which they marched south through wild, potentially hostile country to Killybegs, now a small but important fishing port on the north shore of Donegal Bay. There they found the *Gerona*, lying with a broken rudder and other damage, together with her crew of five hundred men: one of three Armada galleasses which fetched up here at Killybegs, and the only one not irreparably damaged.

On 16 October, having repaired the *Gerona*'s rudder, they again set sail with a total of thirteen hundred on board, with the intention of going east about round the north of Ireland and then south through the Irish Sea. They succeeded in rounding Malin Head, the most northerly point of Ireland, but then the rudder again gave way and the ship was driven at midnight on to a rock westwards of the Giant's Causeway in County Antrim, a wreck in which all but nine of the men on board were drowned. The survivors were conveyed to the Castle of Dunluce, the residence of the MacDonnells, later Earls of Antrim, which stands on the edge of precipitous rocks detached from the mainland, east of Portrush. There they were kindly treated by the chieftain, Sorley Boy MacDonnell, Lord of the Route and Constable of Dunluce, who took the opportunity to salvage some of the guns from the wreck, 'three fair pieces of brass among the rocks of Bunboyes, where Don Alonso was drowned', which he used to reinforce the defences of his castle.

Of the people on the Mullet, the least attractive to me was one who, while we were plugging down the length of it on our bikes into a strong south-westerly, allowed his horrible anti-British sheepdog to bite my ankle to the bone and having witnessed it happen (he could scarcely say he hadn't with the damn thing continuing to hang on to it like a vampire taking nourishment) said nothing and simply went on loading dung on to a trailer. In fact, apart from Wanda, the only sympathy I received was from the girls in Casualty at the Belmullet Hospital – 'And what sort of man, and what sort of dog is that, if you please?' – who gave me a free tetanus injection. They also gave me a document which attested that I had suffered 'one small dog bite'. How big do they have to be to rate as 'big' on the Mullet Peninsula? After which, having found the custodian of a now empty-for-the-winter caravan we slept in some comfort after dining magnificently on great big steaks.

The following day, in brilliant weather, we did our best ever ride together, more than fifty miles from Belmullet to Ballina by the coast road, which for the first twenty miles passes through the wild and almost uninhabited country of the Bog of Erris. To the north were the great cliffs which extend all the way eastwards from Benwee Head, the northernmost point of Mayo, almost as far as Ballycastle. Again we slept in a caravan, this time at Ballina, and dined on lamb chops preceded by hot rum, a bottle of which Wanda had thoughtfully bought on the ferry crossing over. We didn't see much of Ballina – we were whacked.

The next day we set off on the main road to Sligo, which runs along the feet of the lonely Ox Mountains. About nine miles from Ballina we came to a crossroads bearing a large sign to the effect that 'Our Lady of Carns. Site of Apparitions' was away to the right. This was what we had come to see – a Site of Apparitions, not a boring stretch of road along the south side of Sligo Bay.

The shrine, which had only recently been completed, was built of stone and stood on a platform reached by three steps. It was in the form of a Gothic archway, the arch itself however being faced with glass, rather like a shop window. Behind it stood a statue of the Virgin: Our Lady of Carns, as she was now known to countless thousands. Four girls, aged between fourteen and sixteen, witnessed the original apparition at ten on the night of 2 September 1985, in what was then a grazing field belonging to Kathleen Conmy. They had been accompanying another girl back to Bolan's, a shop which we had passed down the road, and after buying some chocolate they began walking home together. It was a dark, moonless night but when they reached the field all four of them were confronted by an apparition of Our Lady overhead. She appeared to be about 12 feet high, and wore a white veil which concealed her hands. Her face was pale and sad, and a star shone to the right of her head. At her side was another figure, whom two of the girls recognized from pictures they had seen of her as St Bernadette. The two figures followed the girls, who were by now frightened, to the house of the eldest, Mary Hanley, though her mother did not herself see them when she opened the door.

The Virgin appeared to them the following night and to some thirty local people who had gathered in the field; this time her face was seen in the moon and she mimed the words 'faith' and 'hope'. To her right was a headless blue statue. The farmer who rented his field from Kathleen Conmy, fed up with having his hedges trampled and walls knocked down by the growing numbers of people who flocked to the site, refused to let a gathering take place the night after that, but he was prevailed upon to relent, and as the apparitions continued the crowds grew nightly. On the seventh night, with three thousand people present, the majority saw an orange ball shooting across the sky, and some saw drops of blood coming from what they identified as the Sacred Heart. The skies then opened to reveal a dazzling, revolving light. Some saw a cross among the clouds; others, the Virgin walking towards them, leaving behind her the scent of roses. By this time the ecclesiastical authorities began to display their customary unease when confronted by the supernatural; what the farmer said may have been recorded but is not available. It was decided that thenceforth the girls should gather at the 'Apparitions Site' on every feast day connected with the Blessed Virgin.

Now, as if in a play, three of the girls appeared in the lane, on the way, as they had been when the whole extraordinary chain of events began, to stock up with chocolate at Bolan's. They were comely, un-trendy, un-selfconscious, un-pious, completely typical Irish country girls. 'No,' they said, 'we don't mind having our pictures taken', and 'No, we never saw them again, the apparitions, after a certain point.'

About twenty people were present at the shrine, talking in whispers, about four carloads. The price of petrol in Ireland does not encourage joy riding. Among them was Mr Martin James McDonnell, one of the masons who built the shrine. He had what he had seen off by heart: 'At eleven-fifteen on the ninth of September my daughter and myself stayed until midnight, and we both saw the Sacred Heart light in a long-distance view. It had a sort of background of a round golden ring – in a reddish heart shape with a light in the middle of it, like it might have been a candle light. It moved to three different places, each about thirty feet apart, each time vanishing before appearing again.

'At about a quarter after midnight we were about to go home when we saw a large statue appear on the piece of wood where the small statue was. (This was the statue which was brought to the field when the apparitions began and which is now displayed on the side of the shrine.) It was about five feet high. . . . On Saturday the fourteenth I saw a halo in the sky, about four times – a good few others saw it as well. On Sunday the fifteenth I saw the sun dance before sunset – a good few saw that, too. I wasn't there again until the twenty-fourth of September, with my daughter, Teresa – we both saw the moon breaking through the clouds – very bright and egg-shaped. And a good few people saw that as well. Then on the eleventh of October I saw the Blessed Virgin once more – this time just like a statue, her hands joined. I could even see her eyes, her eyelids, eyebrows and nose. She was small, about twenty inches high. A lot of other people saw her too, and one girl saw her disappear and a cross stand there in her place – but I didn't see that happen.'

Since then Mr McDonnell had seen further apparitions, the last only a couple of weeks before our arrival. It is forbidden by the hierarchy for Mass to be celebrated there, a prohibition which will almost certainly continue.

EPILOGUE

With 54,000 occupants Cavan is not thickly populated, but it is magnificently served by roadways,
which are traffic-free.

A. J. O'RIORDAN. *The Cavan Guide*

'Any questions?' said Wanda, as one or other of us always did when confronted, as we were now, with a water source. It was an old family joke, originally uttered by our son, aged twelve or so, when after infinite difficulty I succeeded in locating one of the places in the Belgrade Forest outside Istanbul from which derives the bottled water to which so many of its citizens are addicted. It turned out to be in a field of churned-up mud, its only occupant an old Turk who was squatting in a sea of bottles, filling them from a tap. Now, thirty-five miles from Sligo, from where we had set out that morning, at the foot of the boulder-strewn Cuilcagh Mountains, on the border of the Republic with Ulster, we found ourselves in yet another muddy field, this time looking down into a hole in the ground surrounded by trees and bushes, into which water was bubbling up from somewhere below. To get to it we had had to break through a cordon of cattle, determined to defend to the last their right to foul it up.

What we were looking into here, 256 feet above sea-level and 224 miles from its mouth at Loop Head, was Shannon Pot, the source of the Shannon, known to Irish speakers as Log na Sionna and to Irish English speakers as 'Ther Part'. The half-inch map is excessively vague about its location, and finding it had been diabolically difficult. It was, in fact, reminiscent of the experience of the lively Chevalier de la Tocnaye, a young French Royalist and ex-cavalry officer who escaped the Revolution to walk the length and breadth of Ireland in 1796–7, and wrote a very amusing book about it.[*] He legged it round the country with his belongings

[*] *A Frenchman's Walk Through Ireland*, 1796–7, reprinted 1984, Blackstaffe Press, Belfast.

on the end of a swordstick, onto the other end of which he had fixed an umbrella. ('It made the girls laugh. I can't think why,' he said.)

'As with all great personages,' he wrote, referring to the infant Shannon, 'the approach to this one was very difficult. As with them, too, access did not reveal anything very remarkable. However,' he went on,

> there are few rivers which, having such a beginning – a stream of four or five feet wide by two or three deep, flowing out of a round basin about twenty feet in diameter and, they say, without a bottom – can show such result in such short space. Within a mile ... the Shannon forms Lough Clean, three miles long by one mile wide, and then ... expands into an infinite number, of which the principal are Lough Allen, Lough Bofin, Lough Ree and Lough Derg.

Indeed, the Shannon ends up by draining one fifth of the entire area of Ireland.

The only guide book which I now had with me was what was left of *Murray's Guide*, 1912. Opening it at the appropriate page to read to Wanda, I immediately wished I hadn't. ' ... the traditional source,' wrote John Cooke, quoting a maddening but no doubt perfectly correct pedant named Hull,

> is a tributary stream which takes its rise in a limestone cauldron ('The Shannon Pot') from which the water rises in a copious fountain. *The real source of the water* [my italics] is, however, not at this spot, but at a little lough, situated about a mile from the Shannon Pot, which receives considerable drainage from the ground surrounding it at the base of Tiltinbane [the second summit of Cuilcagh], but has no visible outlet. The waters from the little lough flow in a subterranean channel till they issue forth at the so-called 'Source of the Shannon'. Mr W. S. Wilkinson has proved by experiments the truth of this, having thrown hay or straw into the little lough, which on disappearing, has come up in the waters of the Shannon Pot.

'Do you mean to say,' said Wanda after digesting this

information with much the same relish as one would a fishbone, 'that after five and a half hours' cycling here from Sligo and another half hour going up and down and round and round looking for it, this isn't the source of the Shannon?'

'Well,' I said, 'not strictly speaking. That is, if Cooke, Hull and Wilkinson are anything to go by.'

'In that case,' she said, 'Cooke, Hull, Wilkinson and you, too, should all be bloody well shot.'

'You don't want to try and find the other little lough, the one into which Wilkinson threw his hay, or whatever?' I said. 'It must be quite close.'

'You must be joking,' she said.

Altogether we had seen a lot of things since we had first taken to coming to Ireland, and met a whole lot of people we would not otherwise have met; but however interested one is in the world about one there is a moment when one has to say, This is enough – something the reader may have said long ago.

It was a mild, grey afternoon in mid-October. Although we were only a few miles from the border, we turned our backs on it and began the long ride back to Sligo. Our bike rides round Ireland were over. We had seen a lot more of Ireland than there is space to write about, penetrating far into northern Donegal, to the cliffs of Sheve League and the magical valley of Glencolumbkille. The weather had been wonderful, and much of the time we had slept under the stars, sometimes waking up in the morning covered in windblown sand like prospectors in their graves. Ulster would have to wait until another year. On 16 October satellite pictures still showed clear skies over Ireland, but a thick bank of cloud was moving in eastwards from the Atlantic, to disperse the anti-cyclone that had made September and October months to remember. It was the last day of summer.

Now that the whole thing was more or less over I realized that we hadn't really needed mountain bikes at all: there had been no point at which we had required those enormous great tyres, and two chainwheels and twelve gears would have been quite sufficient.

'Next time . . .' I was about to say to Wanda, but I just managed to stop myself.

BIBLIOGRAPHY

Attwater, Donald. *The Penguin Dictionary of Saints*. London, 1965.

Bartlett, W. H. *The Scenery and Antiquities of Ireland*. Text: J. Stirling Coyne. London, 1842.

Bence-Jones, Mark. *Burke's Guide to Country Houses*. Vol. 1: Ireland. London, 1978.

Blue Guide to Ireland (ed. Ian Robertson). 4th edn, London, 1979.

Bulfin, William. *Rambles in Eirinn*. Dublin, 1909.

Coghlan, Ronan. *Pocket Dictionary of Irish Myth and Legend*. Belfast, 1985.

Corkery, Tom. *Tom Corkery's Dublin*. Dublin, 1983.

Cyclists' Touring Club Irish Road Book, Part 1 (South) (comp. and ed. R. T. Lang). London, 1899.

D'Arcy, Mary Ryan. *The Saints of Ireland*. Cork and Dublin, 1974.

de la Tocnaye, Chevalier. *A Frenchman's Walk Through Ireland, 1796–7*, Trs. John Stevenson. Belfast, 1917. Facsimile edn, Blackstaffe Press, Belfast, 1984.

Delany, Ruth. *A Celebration of 250 Years of Ireland's Inland Waterways*. Belfast, 1986.

Delany, Ruth and Addis, Jeremy. *Guide to the Grand Canal of Ireland*. New edn, Dublin, 1986.

Dictionary of National Biography.

Dorris, Paul. *Pocket Irish Phrase Book*. Belfast, 1983.

Drabble, Margaret (ed.). *The Oxford Companion to English Literature*, new edn, Oxford, 1985.

Facts About Ireland. Dept of Foreign Affairs. 6th edn, Dublin, 1985.

Spotswood Green, William. 'The Wrecks of the Spanish Armada on the Coast of Ireland'. Paper read at the Royal Geographical Society, London, and published in the *Geographical Journal*, No. 5, Vol. XXVII, May 1906.

Guinness, Desmond and Ryan, William. *Irish Houses and Castles.* London, 1971.

Hall, Mr and Mrs S. C. *Ireland. Its Scenery, Character &c.* 3 vols. London, 1846.

Harbison, Peter. *Guide to the National Monuments of Ireland.* Dublin, 1970.

Illustrated Ireland Guide. Bord Failte, Dublin, 1967.

Illustrated Road Book of Ireland. Automobile Association, Dublin, 1966.

Ireland Guide. Bord Failte, Dublin, 1982.

Ireland of the Welcomes Magazine. Nov/Dec 1978 (The Brendan Voyage); May/June 1986 (The Dingle Peninsula; St Brendan).

Irish Coast Pilot. Ministry of Defence. 12th edn, Taunton, 1985.

Jones, Barbara. *Follies and Grottoes.* London, 1974.

Kee, Robert. *The Green Flag. A History of Irish Nationalism.* London, 1972.

Kee, Robert. *Ireland: A History.* London, 1980.

Kenmare Journal, Kenmare Literary and Historical Society, 1982.

Killanin, Lord and Duignan, Michael. *The Shell Guide to Ireland.* 2nd edn, London, 1967.

Lehane, Brendan. *The Companion Guide to Ireland.* Revised edn, London, 1985.

Macardle, Dorothy. *The Irish Republic.* London, 1968.

Macaulay, Ambrose. *Dr Russell of Maynooth.* London, 1983.

MacDonagh, Steve. *A Visitor's Guide to the Dingle Peninsula.* Dingle, 1985.

MacNeill, Maire. *The Festival of Lughnasa.* Irish Folklore Commission, Oxford, 1962.

Maxwell, Constantia. *County and Town in Ireland Under the Georges.* London, 1940.

Murphy, Dervla. *Ireland*. Photographs Klaus Francke. London, 1985.

Murray's Handbook for Travellers in Ireland. Last edn, revised and ed. John Cooke, London, 1912.

Nicholson's Guide to Ireland. London, 1983.

Oram, Hugh. *Where to Go in the West of Ireland*. Belfast, 1984.

Power, Patrick. *The Book of Irish Curses*. Dublin, 1984.

Severin, Tim. *The Brendan Voyage*. London, 1978.

Sheehy, Maurice. Discovering the Dingle Area Using Your Feet. 1981.

Sheehy, Terence. *Ireland and Her People*. London, 1983.

Somerville-Large, Peter. *Cappaghglass*. London, 1985.

The Genuine Irish Old Moore's Almanac. Dublin, 1986.

The Official Irish Tourist Board Guides (one for each County). Bord Failte, Dublin, various dates.

The Traveller's Guides. Ireland: Munster (ed. Sean Jennett). London, 1966.

Tiobin, Colm (ed.). *Seeing is Believing*: Moving Statues in Ireland. Laois, 1985.

Woodham-Smith, Cecil. *The Great Hunger, Ireland 1845–9*. London, 1962.

Yapp, Peter (ed.). *The Traveller's Dictionary of Quotation*. London, 1983.

Books on the Islands

Flower, Robin. *Western Island, or The Great Blasket*. Oxford, 1978.

O'Crohan, Tomas. *The Islandman*. Trs. Robin Flower, Oxford, 1985.

O'Crohan, Tomas. *Island Cross-talk. Pages From a Diary*. Trs. Tim Enright, Oxford, 1986.

O'Sullivan, Maurice. *Twenty Years A-Growing*. Oxford, 1984.

O'Sullivan, Paul and Godwin, Nora. *A World of Stone: The Aran Islands*. Dublin, 1985.

O'Sullivan, Paul and Godwin, Nora. *Field and Shore: Daily Life and Tradition: Aran Islands, 1900*. Dublin, 1985.

Robinson, Tim. *The Aran Islands. A Map and Guide*. Cuill
Ronain, 1980.
Sayers, Peig. *Peig: The Autobiography of Peig Sayers
of the Great Blasket Island*. Trs. Bryan MacMahon,
Dublin, 1983.
Synge, J. M. *The Aran Islands*. Oxford, 1984.

INDEX